Prayer and worship are our greatest works as believers, and Dick Eastman has powerfully related them to the mission of the Church. Read this exciting book and see how the Great Commission is being fulfilled in our lifetime.

DR. NEIL T. ANDERSON
Founder, Freedom in Christ, Franklin, Tennessee

Dick Eastman shows us how to ignite God's passion in our lives and on behalf of the world. We always thought that worship and prayer were important. Dick Eastman tells us why, and he goes on to show us how to weave the two together to lead the Church toward the great endtime harvest.

MIKE BICKLE
Director, International House of Prayer, Kansas City, Missouri

Worship is a subject that is difficult, sometimes painful, for many believers today. Dick Eastman, a beloved and godly brother, shows us how worship is not only infinitely pleasing to God and vital to our spiritual growth but is absolutely necessary to bring the nations to a saving knowledge of our Lord and Savior Jesus Christ.

DR. BILL BRIGHT (1921–2003)
Founder, Campus Crusade for Christ

The emergence of biblically focused worship is a fountainhead where the life within the Church and within the individual moves from flow to overflow. As we exalt Jesus Christ, Dick challenges us to call on God's authority to eliminate the adversary's position as nations are brought to their knees in front of joy. The culmination of the Great Commission will b[...] on the foundation of anticipatory, prayerful wors[...] destiny God intended for each of His [...]

TOM PHILLIPS
Vice President of Crusades, Billy Graham Eva[...]

This work is not only a thorough, insightful explanation of a fascinating subject but also a description of a radical biblical practice being reborn in our day—something long prophesied but never before attained.

JOHN DAWSON
Founder, International Reconciliation Coalition
International President Emeritus, Youth with a Mission

The best leaders are God's worshiping servants. Dick Eastman has spent decades humbly leading us deeper into worship and prayer. In a whirlwind worldwide tour, Dick invites us to join with others who are experiencing God and to put some "fight" into our intercession.

FRANCIS FRANGIPANE
Founder, River of Life Ministries, Cedar Rapids, Iowa

Dick Eastman's gift of an intercessor's passion for—and power in—partnership with God is multiplied over and over to us all by means of the understandable, practical, "believe-I-can-do-this" guidance. Under Jesus' touch, he teaches us to pray.

JACK W. HAYFORD
Chancellor, The King's Seminary, Van Nuys, California

Dick Eastman's writing style is honest and enjoyable and will bring you into a deeper relationship with the Lord. The linking of worship and evangelism is one of the major keys to releasing a massive end-time harvest into the nations.

CINDY JACOBS
Co-founder, Generals International, Ovilla, Texas

This book takes us into the heart of what it means to war and to worship. Dick Eastman explains how the specific worship pathways King David followed are the same pathways that are central to God's plan to fulfill the Great Commission. This is an exciting time to be alive! Church, let's cooperate with God's plan—in the way we worship and in the way we intercede—to bring people to Himself from every tribe, tongue and nation.

DUTCH SHEETS
Founder, Dutch Sheets Ministries, Hamilton, Alabama

INTERCESSORY
WORSHIP

COMBINING
WORSHIP &
PRAYER
TO TOUCH THE HEART
OF GOD

DICK EASTMAN

Regal

From Gospel Light
Ventura, California, U.S.A.

Published by Regal
From Gospel Light
Ventura, California, U.S.A.
www.regalbooks.com
Printed in the U.S.A.

Library of Congress Cataloging-in-Publication Data
Eastman, Dick.
Intercessory worship : combining worship and prayer to
touch the heart of God / Dick Eastman.
p. cm.
Includes bibliographical references.
ISBN 978-0-8307-6057-2 (trade pbk.)
1. Worship. 2. Intercessory prayer—Christianity. I. Title.
BV10.3.E273 2011
248.3—dc23
2011028577

Rights for publishing this book outside the U.S.A. or in non-English languages are
administered by Gospel Light Worldwide, an international not-for-profit ministry.
For additional information, please visit www.glww.org, email info@glww.org, or write
to Gospel Light Worldwide, 1957 Eastman Avenue, Ventura, CA 93003, U.S.A.

To order copies of this book and other Regal products in bulk quantities,
please contact us at 1-800-446-7735.

DEDICATION

To Bill: My friend in the desert!
Thanks for launching me
on this incredible journey!

Contents

First Thoughts

The Richest of Foods

My journey began with a strong inner urging to set aside 40 days for fasting and prayer. (Don't be alarmed—this is not a book about fasting and prayer. I didn't mean to scare you! That's just where my story happens to begin.) It was late February 2000. This was the second prolonged fasting experience in my life. Inspired by a dear friend and mentor, the late Dr. Bill Bright of Campus Crusade for Christ, I fasted for 40 days in the fall of 1996. That was a truly life changing experience; it was also rather grueling. I have often jokingly said that I promised God on the tenth or eleventh day of that first fast that if He would just keep me alive for all 40 days, "I will never do this again as long as I live!" But with the dawning of a new decade *and century* (and, indeed, a new millennium), I strongly sensed that God was leading me into a second 40-day season of this challenging discipline.

I soon learned this fast would be significantly different from the first. In fact, it would open my understanding to extraordinary vistas of the transformational power of what I have come to know as "intercessory worship" (an expression I will carefully define later).

My introduction to intercessory worship began on the very first day of that second prolonged fast. At the outset, I was uncertain as to any specific focus for this fast. But the ministry I was leading at the time (and still direct), Every Home for Christ, was about to begin a large building project called The Jericho Center, and I felt we needed much more focused prayer to see this project properly launched. I determined that my fast would begin on March 8 (Ash Wednesday) and continue 40 days until April 16 (Palm Sunday).

On the first day of the fast, at noon, I joined with hundreds of other worshipers at the World Prayer Center in Colorado Springs. At the time, they conducted a noon-hour of open worship for the entire community every Wednesday.

Frankly, as I entered into that time of worship, I had difficulty getting my mind off myself—more specifically, off the fact that this was but day 1 of 40 days of physical denial. My stomach was grumbling and growling, already complaining in anticipation of the 39 days to follow. I thought more than once of Martin Luther's description of one of his prolonged times of fasting: "My flesh was wont to grumble dreadfully."

Yet, I felt it would be appropriate to begin my season of fasting and prayer in just such a worship atmosphere. Little could I have known how significant that decision would turn out to be. So there I was, trying my best to engage in a meaningful time of worship while thinking of the many days of the fast yet ahead. More than once, I gazed longingly at the large loaf of bread on the communion table that worshipers visited spontaneously throughout these times of worship. Communion bread was the one food I partook of during such a prolonged fast. I couldn't help imagining how big a piece I would allow myself to take from the loaf! The warfare with my flesh had clearly begun!

It took at least 15 or 20 minutes before I affirmed inwardly that I was really there for one purpose—to focus my attention fully on the Lord.

Suddenly, the worship leader, who normally said very little during these times, spoke a single Scripture, even as worshipful music continued. That lone verse launched me into one of the most extraordinary seasons of seeking after God in my life.

"As we worship," the leader declared, "let's think on these words of King David." He then boldly read verse 5 of Psalm 63: "You satisfy me more than the richest of foods. I will praise you with songs of joy" (*NLT*).

I immediately found myself weeping. I knew the Lord was speaking; it was that familiar gentle whisper in my heart: "I'm not calling you to a season of fasting and prayer as you thought!" For a split second I felt relief, imagining God was "un-calling" me from what I was just beginning. But before I could voice a grateful "thank you very much," the whisper of God's voice continued: "No, I'm calling you to 40 days of fasting and worship!"

The thought was new to me. I really could not remember hearing the terms "fasting" and "worship" linked before. It had always been "fasting and prayer."

The impression continued. "Did I not commission my apostles, Paul and Barnabas, through fasting and worship?"

The Lord brought my mind back to Acts 13:2, where we read, "While [the Early Church leaders] *were worshiping the Lord and fasting*, the Holy Spirit said, 'Set apart for me Barnabas and Saul for the work to which I have called them'" (emphasis added).

I was later reminded of the powerful impact Paul and Barnabas had as they began a ministry that literally transformed cities and regions throughout Asia and Europe with the gospel. Consider these statements: "Almost the whole city gathered to hear the word of the Lord" (Acts 13:44) and "The word of the Lord spread through the whole region" (v. 49). There was also great power in Paul's and Barnabas's preaching: "They spoke so effectively that a great number of Jews and Gentiles believed" (Acts 14:1). Of their ministry in Derbe we read: "They preached the good news in that city and won a large number of disciples" (v. 21).

DELIGHTS AND DESIRES

Fasting and worship, it seemed, produced powerful results when linked to proclaiming the gospel. *Could worship-saturated prayer be a powerful key to transforming cities and nations today? And what would this kind of praying look like?* These thoughts flooded my mind as I entered those early moments of that first day of my prolonged "worship fast." But I still didn't know how my times of prayer during those 40 days might differ from my first such season of fasting and prayer.

As I continued worshiping that Wednesday, my heart was flooded with additional passages of Scripture—all providing direction for the coming 40 days.

First, there was a verse I had memorized years earlier as a teenager: "Delight yourself in the LORD and he will give you the desires of your heart" (Ps. 37:4). I felt the Lord asking me, "Isn't it your desire to see every nation on earth touched with My love, home by home and family by family?"

My response, through tears, was an obvious yes. The ministry I lead, Every Home for Christ, has this vision. Today, our global staff of 4,000 supported workers, along with some 30,000 monthly volunteers, visit more than 200,000 homes daily with the gospel. Still, the challenge for accomplishing the goal of reaching every home on earth remains formidable, especially in restricted areas like the Middle East and various regions of Asia.

The Lord continued speaking. "Doesn't My Word say that if you delight in Me, I will give you the desires of your heart?" The answer to that question was equally obvious.

My heart then heard what was to be the key to the remarkable worship encounters that lay ahead for me: "I'm calling you to new heights of delight in Me during these 40 days!"

But I still didn't know what it meant in practical terms to "fast and worship." So I inquired of the Lord, and an immediate impression followed: "For the next 40 days, I want you to *sing* all your praise and prayers to Me, not merely speak them."

This was certainly unlike anything I had ever done over such a sustained period. True, I had spent times in spontaneous singing to the Lord, once even for almost an entire day, but that was with a roomful of other worshipers. This would be alone—and for 40 days.

As worship continued during that Wednesday encounter, I opened my Bible to meditate momentarily on Psalm 37:4, where we read about delighting in the Lord. Immediately my eyes caught a glimpse of a passage in the previous chapter. It further confirmed that God was leading me to new dimensions of delight in Him. I read, "All humanity finds shelter in the shadow of your wings. You feed them from the abundance of your own house, letting them drink from your rivers of delight" (Ps. 36:7-8, *NLT*). I pictured myself at the edge of a glorious river of God's delight, drinking from it freely for the next 40 days! (I share more about the significance of this in part three of this book.)

My journey of joy was about to begin. It would take me to those new heights of delight God had promised me during that worship experience on day one of my fast. It would also confirm in me the profound significance of the role of intercessory worship—not only in evangelizing the world, quite literally, but also in transforming individuals, families, nations and entire people groups in the process. As you'll soon see, the results have been astonishing!

THE KEY TO TRANSFORMATION

The pages that follow describe what I believe will be the key to this transformation movement. In the three major sections of this book, we will examine "realities of worship," "reforms of worship" and "rivers of worship." Worship, unlike anything the Church has ever experienced, along with resulting intercession at levels of authority and passion few could have conceived of even a few years ago, will be that key. I believe this will bring about unified strategies of alliances and partnerships throughout Christ's Body that will be unparalleled in Church history—not just in evangelizing people and nations, but also in truly discipling and transforming them. A glorious awakening marked with worship-saturated prayer is on the global horizon and it's heading your way! It's closer than you think.

PART ONE

REALITIES

Intercessory Worship

A Vision of Africa: Holy Smoke

I had a vision of Africa.

It flashed with such clarity that it has stayed on the front burner of my consciousness for years now, and I see the same picture again and again. As often happens with such experiences, this vision-encounter, rather than fading with time, seems to grow in intensity each time I contemplate it.

It happened in Colorado Springs, where our ministry is headquartered. It was mid-March, and I was 10 days into my 40-day worship fast. Our staff had gathered to pray over a team of intercessors and strategists preparing to go to Zimbabwe in southern Africa.

The team planned to visit the famed Victoria Falls, discovered by British missionary-explorer David Livingstone in 1855, and then trek into interior regions to visit villages only now hearing the gospel. They would approach the work systematically—going from home to home and hut to hut, ensuring that everyone had an opportunity to hear the message. In addition to delivering gospel booklets in the language of these villagers, the missionaries would use creative ways to witness to nonreaders. They were to carry large picture charts vividly depicting how Christ comes into a person's heart and drives away the dark, evil forces that these superstitious villagers feared and worshiped.

Suddenly, as we placed our hands on the shoulders of these worship warriors, I was transported mentally to the very region they would be visiting. I was in Africa, gazing from an elevated ridge far into the interior of the Zambezi River basin. Later I would be told I was looking out over the vast Gwembe Valley of Southern Zambia. I could see smoke rising from villages in almost every direction, thousands of them, perhaps tens of thousands.

Instantly, my mind reflected back to one of missions' most memorable statements of passion, voiced by Robert Moffat. It was 1839, and Moffat had returned home after an exhaustive missionary tenure in southern Africa. At a meeting of the London Missionary Society, he pleaded for would-be missionaries to pick up the mantle of missions and come to "the dark continent." Painting a word picture of the vastness of un-evangelized Africa, Moffat declared:

> I have sometimes seen, in the morning sun, the smoke of a thousand villages where no missionary has ever been.[1]

Sitting in that gathering was a 26-year-old medical student named David Livingstone. Almost immediately, Livingstone picked up Moffat's mantle and within 24 months had settled in Kuruman, southern Africa, where Moffat had been laboring. Three years later Livingstone would marry Robert Moffat's daughter, Mary, and the rest of the story is remarkable missions history.

There it was, a century and a half later, and I was mentally seeing a picture similar—or so it seemed—to the one Moffat saw in 1839.

But I was looking at the smoke of *many thousands* of villages, not Moffat's "thousand."

"Lord," I said with concern, "are there yet that many villages where the gospel has not gone?"

"No," came the instant impression on my heart, "that's not what you are seeing. You are seeing the smoke of the incense of worship rising from thousands and thousands of villages now transformed by My glory. You are seeing villages that have become worship centers of My presence."[2]

The team with which I was praying would soon discover that entire villages were indeed turning to Jesus in this present extraordinary season of global harvest. They would verify the research reports that Africa is truly experiencing spiritual awakening in spite of its obvious troubles. A report I read at the time indicated that the number of Christians in Africa had increased 2,000 percent, from 9.9 million to 203 million, in the past century. Each year since then, the continent has gained 6 million new Christians each year. "The rate of growth seems only to be increasing. In 1970, about 12 percent of Africans were Christians. Now, nearly half are," wrote Don Melvin in the *Min-*

neapolis Star Tribune. "In 1970 one-tenth of all Christians in the world were Africans. Now the continent is home to more than a fifth of the world's Christians."[3] The Lord was confirming in my heart that the already-expanding global harvest of people coming to Christ was soon to increase even more dramatically.

As I pondered my vision, I became convinced that the smoke I was seeing rise from these thousands of villages represented intercessory worship—a theme that presently is spreading across Christ's Body globally like a wildfire, as you'll discover in the pages that follow. As I'll also describe, what has happened in the very region of Africa pictured in my vision of 2000 is nothing short of remarkable!

INTERCESSORY WORSHIP: THE HARP AND BOWL SYMBOLISM

What is intercessory worship?[4] The term "intercessory worship," I believe, refers to concentrated, passionate "worship-saturated prayer" that rises with the fragrance of incense before God's throne. In response, God releases His power to accomplish His purposes for the harvest (see Rev. 5:8-10; 8:1-6).

A unique picture of intercessory worship can be seen in the harp and bowl symbols described in Revelation 5:8-10. Here we read:

> And when [the Lamb] had taken [the scroll], the four living creatures and the twenty-four elders fell down before the Lamb. Each one had a harp and they were holding golden bowls full of incense, which are the prayers of the saints (v. 8).

Interestingly, the worshipers coming before the Lamb with harps (symbols of worship) in one hand and bowls (symbols of prayer and intercession) in the other seem to combine these two symbols in a song never sung before. It is a song of global harvest. The text continues:

> And they sang a new song: "You are worthy to take the scroll and to open its seals, because you were slain, and with your blood you purchased men for God from every tribe and language and people and nation" (v. 9).

It is not without significance that the harp and bowl picture here is linked to the redeemed coming from every tribe, language, people and nation. This clearly is a harvest song.

In Revelation 8:1-6, we see "the prayers of all the saints" (a picture of intercession) being released with "much incense" (a picture of worship) at the throne (v. 3). Eugene Peterson's paraphrase of this passage describes smoke rising up before God's throne saturated with the "incense-laced prayers of the holy ones" (Rev. 8:4, *THE MESSAGE*). This release results in the final unfolding of God's plan through the sounding of seven trumpets, the last of which sends forth a blast that accompanies a great shout in heaven:

> The kingdom of the world has become the kingdom of our Lord and of his Christ, and he will reign for ever and ever (Rev. 11:15).

However we might interpret all of this, we can be certain that worship-saturated intercession will be a key to the last great harvest on earth. To me, the harp and bowl intercessory worship movement may well become the greatest prayer movement in the history of the Church. It certainly seems to be spreading significantly through prayer ministries and movements across the planet.

Helping me understand the role of worship in fulfilling the Great Commission was John Piper's timely book, *Let the Nations Be Glad!* Piper writes:

> Missions is not the ultimate goal of the church. Worship is. Missions exists because worship doesn't. Worship is ultimate, not missions, because God is ultimate, not man. When this age is over, and the countless millions of redeemed fall on their faces before the throne of God, missions will be no more. It is a temporary necessity. But worship abides forever.[5]

In my unfolding journey to new heights of delight in God, I quickly discovered the link between worship and intercession, the harp and the bowl, in God's plan for transforming nations. But at the outset (especially immediately following my 40-day worship fast), it seemed the Lord especially wanted to highlight the harp side of the equation.

THE WORTH OF WORSHIP

A review of the general topic of worship will prove worthwhile in laying a foundation for the insights that follow. My purpose in sharing these pages is not merely to provide one more book on worship to our already well-stocked devotional libraries. My objective is to describe how I believe the glory of God, released through worship-saturated intercession, will *transform* entire nations and people groups, including our families and neighbors. Let me begin with a personal definition of worship. To me, in a sentence:

> Worship is any act, thought or expression of willful adoration that exalts and enthrones God, thereby defeating and dethroning Satan.

When intercession—that is, prayerful intervention in the needs of others—is added, we have intercessory worship. As you will see before we finish, there are very practical ways to see this happen, both personally and corporately. But first, we need to take a closer look at the matter of worship itself.

Our word "worship" is derived from the Old English word *weorthscipe*, which means "to ascribe worth, to pay homage, to reverence or to venerate."[6] Worship focuses on the issue of worth or worthiness.

Let's establish at the outset that worship is not merely some activity engaged in during a typical Sunday morning worship service; it is a lifestyle. It is the reason we live. A. W. Tozer said it succinctly: "We are called to an everlasting preoccupation with God."[7]

Recall the words of the apostle Peter: "But you are a chosen people, a royal priesthood, a holy nation, a people belonging to God, that you may declare the praises of him who called you out of darkness into his wonderful light" (1 Pet. 2:9).

As chosen people, we are to "declare the praises" of God. The *King James Version* translates this phrase, "[show] forth the praises of Him."

Worship, then, is both how we live and why we live. Tozer explains, "Worship of the loving God is man's whole reason for existence. That is why we were born and that is why we are born again from above. That is why we were created and that is why we have been recreated." This wise worshiper concludes, "That is also why there is a church. The Christian church exists to worship God first of all. Everything else must come second or third or fourth or fifth."[8]

STYLES AND STEREOTYPES

Worship, of course, means different things to different people. There are certainly a variety of styles of worship that various streams in the Church have developed. There are also a number of stereotypes that have arisen around these styles. Amplifying this thought, I recently had one of the strangest dreams in my life, and I've had my share of unusual ones. Of course, I've learned over the years that not all dreams are messages from the Lord. Some are messages from the stomach regarding what we ate earlier that night.

Still, since I began this chapter with an unusual personal vision, which occurred more than a decade ago, of the smoke of incense rising as a symbol of worship from a multitude of African villages, I suppose it wouldn't hurt to share a dream that happened only a few days ago. After all, we're told that in the last days "young men will see visions . . . [and] old men will dream dreams" (Acts 2:17). Being ten years older now, I'm afraid I may have entered the "dream stage" of life.

In this recent dream, I was invited to join a journalist (who disappeared in the middle of the dream) in visiting a hugely popular church that was growing significantly. The journalist informed me that the church was unique, and he would like me to see their rather unusual style of worship. When we arrived at the front of the church, it looked much like any typical church in suburban America. But as the journalist opened the door, I could see at once that this experience was going to be strikingly different.

For starters, we had to climb down a rather long wooden stepladder to get into the main sanctuary. Then, what I saw of the worshipers startled me. The entire room was completely dark, except for candles that seemed to hover like tiny spaceships in front of each worshiper—waist high. In addition, every person had his or her arms stretched as high as possible. *Amazing!* I thought. I asked the journalist what the name of the church was, and he informed me it was "The Church of the Litten Candles and Upraised Hands"!

I responded, "Don't you mean 'lit' candles?"

He said, "No, litten! They insist on using the word 'litten'."

As we moved toward the packed pews to get a seat, an usher stopped us and asked if we intended to join the worship that day. We responded in the affirmative. He told us, "Then you'll need some arms."

I explained that we both had arms, but he informed us that the services were very lengthy, and because everyone had to keep both arms held high for the entire service, the church provided wooden arms for each worshiper. These, he added, weighed not much more than balsa wood and were attached to small pulleys so they could be held high for hours with minimal effort. The arms, he advised us, were conveniently available from a number of arm racks in the foyer. (You probably think this is the weird part of the dream, but it gets even stranger—trust me!)

We went to the arm racks and both selected right and left arms from separate racks. Then the usher showed us how to strap them on. There were indeed little pulleys attached to each arm that allowed the worshiper to raise both arms while exerting little effort.

We were ready to head back into the sanctuary when an usherette stopped us to inform us we each needed a candle. She held something like a large communion tray laden with numerous burning candles. She showed us how we could hold our candles comfortably in front of us with one hand while using the other hand to hold the straps attached to the arm pulleys in order to keep our arms raised for the entire service. I now understood why, when we first climbed down the ladder, it looked like candles were hovering, mid-air, in front of people in the darkened sanctuary. Worshipers were actually holding them. It was an optical illusion.

Suddenly, we were in the midst of the crowd, trying to figure out the song they were singing (it was an odd one, to say the least), when I noticed people around me looking at me strangely. When I looked up I could see why. One of my wooden arms was significantly shorter than the other. I had different-sized wooden arms! I hadn't realized, back in the foyer, that there were short- as well as long-arm racks.

Fortunately, a man behind me, a church regular, took pity on me and offered to take the short arm back to the foyer and bring me another longer one. (Bear with me.) When he returned and snapped the long arm on, others around me began laughing, out loud. The would-be "Good Samaritan" had taken the new long arm off a "thin long arm rack" rather than the "regular long-arm rack." Now I had one thicker long arm and a thin one, though each was of the same length. I essentially had deformed wooden arms! A guy in front of me stared in disbelief, not at me but at the man who had just brought me the thin long arm. He whispered to his wife, loudly enough for the "Good Samaritan" and all others around us to hear, "What a dufus!"

My panic subsided when someone came to usher me out. But I quickly learned he was not ushering me out of the building but to the platform. I had been selected to preach that day's sermon. This stunned me because I hadn't been informed by anyone that I was to be that day's preacher.

Not being adequately prepared, I stammered as I began. The content of my very short sermon is rather vague in my memory, but I believe it had something to do with the fact that there are many different styles and ways to praise the Lord and included an admonition to respect others no matter their manner of worship. I think I also mentioned the passage in Revelation that describes a vast crowd of worshipers that no one could number, hailing from all tribes, tongues, peoples and nations (see Rev. 7:9-10), and all worshiping in harmony, though likely through a diversity of worship styles and sounds. Although I can't recall my exact words, my message ended with something like, "We must always remember—no single denomination or ministry has a corner on worship. Christ's Body is simply too diverse."

No matter the specific content or how my sermon ended, what I do vividly recall is that whatever I said drew immediate negative reactions. This no doubt accounts for why my sermon was so short. Members of the congregation literally chased me out of the building, wooden arms still raised and flailing about. That's when things became really weird (as if what happened up to this point was anything close to normal!).

As I rushed up the ladder to flee the church (I'm not sure what happened to the journalist), the crowd started throwing snowballs at me (yes, snowballs!). I'm not sure how they did it with their wooden arms flopping about, but it was certainly a sight to behold.

I arrived at the cab of the semi-trailer truck we had arrived in (I hadn't noticed we initially arrived in such a vehicle) and found that the window of the cab was open. I turned and shouted to the angry mob, "You picked the wrong preacher to attack," and reached in through the open window of the huge truck. Without actually seeing what I was reaching for, I instinctively sensed there was a large cardboard box on the front seat of the cab filled with exactly what I needed to repel the attack. So, I reached blindly through the open window and into the box, which, believe it or not, was filled with frozen ice balls. I began pelting my attackers with these rock-hard objects, and the mob quickly dispersed as people fled, wooden arms still raised and flapping in the breeze.

Since having this dream, I've shared it publicly a few times and already have received some interesting interpretations. I'll let you draw your own inferences. It did, of course, make me think. Now, I suppose it's only fair that I mention what I had for dinner that night, just to keep things in perspective. My dinner included four pieces (all wings) of Kentucky Fried Chicken (original recipe) with mashed potatoes and gravy, coleslaw and two ears of corn. (I'm not sure I needed that second ear.) I also probably shouldn't have topped it all off with that late-night bag of Cheetos, and I almost certainly shouldn't have partaken of the divinity candy with walnuts on top that I bought the day before at a Stuckey's convenience store.

Still, I'll never forget that dream as long as I live! I do know God doesn't want phony, contrived worship. Fake never earns God's favor. He longs for those who worship Him "in spirit and in truth" (John 4:24). This is critical for us to remember as we pursue this subject of worship-saturated prayer.

Also critical to remember as we cultivate this new worship awareness is that worship not only is, as the old Westminster Catechism describes it, "the chief end of man," but it also becomes the chief means toward that end. Worship, indeed, is ultimate. It is certainly much more than a mere musical style; it is a lifestyle. Worship must be a way of life. When linked with intercession to the extent that such intercession *is a part of* and *flows directly from* that worship, it becomes what we are referring to as intercessory worship. Out of intercessory worship there appears to develop a climate for the transformation of whole cities, peoples and nations.

The purpose of these pages is to show this relationship between intercessory worship and the global harvest. My desire is that the insights that follow will not only inspire you in this regard, but also serve as a manual to guide you in the process of practical involvement. Seven worship realities will get us started. Let's take a look.

FIRST REALITY

WORSHIP ENTHRONES GOD
A BIG CHAIR FOR GOD

During my 40-day worship fast, I felt the Lord calling me not only to new delights in His presence, but also to a clearer understanding of what we are describing as intercessory worship. As we learn to hold out our harps of worship together, along with our bowls of intercessory prayer, we will make possible the completion of the Great Commission so all the world might experience God's glory, in Christ! Toward this end, the Lord showed me seven worship realities that I have come to describe as intercessory-worship principles.

Simply stated, a principle is a truth that is foundational to other truths. I believe an examination of these worship realities and related principles provides a meaningful platform for understanding the role of worship, particularly intercessory worship, as it relates to the coming great ingathering of the last days' harvest.

Essential from the outset of our study is the recognition of what I feel is the first fundamental worship reality: *Worship enthrones God.* Stated more fully as an intercessory-worship principle:

Worship provides a place for God to dwell on earth in all His fullness.

A HEAVENLY CLIMATE

In a uniquely profound way, the praises of God's people literally bring them into alignment with His throne and, thus, His full purposes and power. Said another way, God establishes His very throne in the physical place and among those people who are praising Him. This first worship reality is essential to our understanding of how and why worship (and, in particular, worship-saturated prayer) is so vital to fulfilling God's purposes throughout the world. Worship creates a heavenly climate for the fulfillment of the Great Commission.

The psalmist declared, "Sing praises to the LORD, enthroned in Zion; proclaim among the nations what he has done" (Ps. 9:11). Here we note how the spirit of the Great Commission ("proclaim among the nations") is linked in this text with enthroning God—"Sing praises . . . enthroned . . . among the nations." It is not without significance that within this admonition to sing praises to our Lord we see reference to proclaiming what the Lord has done among the nations.

Elsewhere, King David sang to the Lord, "But You are holy, enthroned in the praises of Israel" (Ps. 22:3, *NKJV*). The *King James Version* translates this verse, "Thou art holy, O thou that inhabitest the praises of Israel." The Hebrew word translated "inhabitest," *yawshab*, comes from a root word meaning "to sit." Of course, the place God sits is His throne, thus leading to the accurate use of the expression "enthroned."

The thought here is that God dwells—reveals Himself—where His people praise Him. He inhabits that very place. One Japanese translation of this verse reads, "When God's people praise Him, He brings a big chair and sits there."[1]

What a wonderful thought—and one that is clearly compatible with the original Hebrew expression. Our praises become God's throne—they literally *enthrone* Him.

Jack Hayford, discussing this same verse of Scripture, wrote:

> This oft-quoted statement from Psalm 22:3 deserves our greatest understanding, since the implications of the verb *yawshab* [inhabitest, *KJV*] are dramatic. Though the basic idea of the word is to sit down, when the King of the universe is the subject it is appropriately translated "en-throned." This great truth resounds to every generation: *Praise creates a dwelling place for God in man's present situation!*[2]

All of this is profoundly significant in our understanding of intercessory worship and its resulting enthronement of God, whether in our daily personal lives or in participating in the establishing of God's plan for the nations.

Worship enthrones God! This first worship reality suggests that when we begin declaring God's praises over our needs or distant nations, we are literally establishing His throne amid those needs or nations.

THE CASE OF CASEROS

This reality was dramatically illustrated in an event that involved the ministry I lead, Every Home for Christ (EHC).[3] A team of worshiping intercessors prayer-walked through the neighborhoods of their city (the town of Caseros) in Argentina, declaring God's praises over each home in every neighborhood as they walked. They asked God to prepare the hearts of their neighbors to receive the good news.

Caseros, with a population of 390,000 at the time, had been targeted for an Every Home campaign. But Caseros was not an easy place to evangelize because of the strong presence of various satanic cults, particularly those known as the Macumba and Umbanda. According to EHC's Argentine director, Rino Bello, for every evangelical church in Caseros there are five or six satanic worship centers. Yet through his planned campaign for Caseros, every family in almost 100,000 homes was to be given a personal presentation of the gospel of Jesus Christ in their language, as well as an invitation to view Campus Crusade for Christ's *Jesus* film in one of several locations throughout the community.

Because satanic worship was so prevalent in the city, seven churches of the area had been mobilized to walk the streets of Caseros, declaring the praises of God while interceding in prayer for every household. These churches had agreed to send teams of worshiping intercessors as advance troops for a larger group of believers, from at least 20 churches, who would ultimately visit every home in the city, presenting to each a printed gospel message and witnessing at every opportunity.

The overall strategy involved dividing Caseros into several small districts and targeting those districts one at a time, beginning with an area called Villa Pineral that consisted of about 1,100 homes. First the prayer teams saturated the area with intercessory worship, and then, during a five-day period, every home in this district was personally visited and the residents given a printed gospel message in their language, as well as an invitation to view the *Jesus* film.

UNDER THE OMBU TREE

On Sunday evening, after the door-to-door evangelism had been completed, the *Jesus* film was shown in the public square of Villa Pineral. The large screen had been set up beneath a huge 200-year-old ombu tree, considered a treasured historic site in the community. At the conclusion of the film, 135 people gave their hearts to Jesus. This was in addition to the many who had responded as the result of the home-to-home campaign.

Showing the film under the huge ombu tree was especially significant because for almost a decade this unique tree had been the site of area-wide satanic worship gatherings every week. Friday night was the time set aside for worshipers to bring their sacrifices to Satan. (Quite often these sacrifices included body parts of animals such as chickens, cats and dogs.)

The choice to proclaim the gospel in this particular place set the stage for a spiritual confrontation in the heavenlies, as well as an occasion for evangelism. This became apparent in the days immediately following the Sunday-night showing of the film.

The following Tuesday, without any plausible explanation, the 200-year-old ombu tree mysteriously "exploded" and split in half, falling to the ground. The noise was heard many blocks away. The city engineer, with two of his colleagues, came to examine the fallen tree. It had no visible disease, nor had there been any bad weather (lightning, for instance) at the time that might account for this strange occurrence.

Those believers involved in the evangelistic campaign who had heard the sound and witnessed the fallen tree knew it was an act of God. Our Every Home for Christ director, Brother Rino Bello, explained, "We understood that this tree had fallen as the result of spiritual warfare against the powers of darkness. We knew that God had ordered this to happen as an indication that revival was on its way and that many lost souls would be won to Christ."

But God was not finished yet. These believers were to see a further sign of the impact of their intercessory worship over Caseros. Exactly one month to the day following the first explosion, a second explosion took place—at the exact site where the mighty ombu once stood. This time the very roots of the 200-year-old tree exploded under the ground. If the first explosion was unusual, the second was bizarre!

Later we learned that immediately after the first explosion, one of the satanic leaders in Caseros had instructed his followers to go to the site of the fallen ombu tree and dig up some of its roots so that they might be planted and the original tree, sacred to the satanists, re-grown. Thus, a new point of worship for their cult would be established.

A woman in this cult had responded and was collecting roots at the time of the second explosion. As she lay on the ground, severely injured and waiting for an ambulance, a crew from a national television network in Argentina came and filmed what had happened. The story was televised that night across the region.

The news report showed the lady being rushed to the hospital, where she lay in grave condition. At first it was thought she might not survive. Her neighbor, a committed Christian, recognized the injured woman from the television report and decided to visit her in the hospital. In an amazing turn of events, this satanist who had attempted to dig up the ombu roots received Christ as Savior and totally renounced all ties to the satanic cult. Soon, many others in the city of Caseros received Christ as well.

In the weeks following the two strange explosions, other interesting testimonials emerged. Members of one church reported that for many years it had been common to find parts of sacrificed animals on their church doorstep on Sunday mornings. But after the second explosion of the old ombu tree, those occurrences abruptly stopped.

A THEOLOGY OF GOD'S PRESENCE

There is little doubt that those teams of worshiping intercessors who walked the streets of Caseros had enthroned God in their community. Worship, indeed, provides a place for God to dwell among His people and thereby brings Him into their circumstances in all His fullness. This unleashes explosive potential for the transformation of communities, peoples and even entire nations.

But how do we explain more adequately what transpires when we enthrone God over a situation or region? I believe it concerns the "manifest presence" of God as compared to simply His omnipresence.

We say God is omnipresent because He is, theologically speaking, everywhere present. This is to say that God is always present whether we realize it or not. But it is not to say we always recognize His presence. In fact, at the time of my worship fast I heard that researcher George Barna had found that 7 out of 10 Christians said they had never felt God's presence while attending church.[4]

In this regard we might define God's presence in three ways: (1) God's *intellectual* presence, (2) God's *conscious* presence and (3) God's *manifest* presence. We use these terms to describe how we as believers might view God's presence, not necessarily how God views the reality of His own presence or existence.

By referring to God's *intellectual* presence, I mean our intellectual recognition that God exists everywhere and therefore must always be present. In other words, because we believe God is everywhere, He must be here whether I feel it or not.

This fact was emphasized to me many years ago, when I was preparing to leave on a ministry trip from California to Washington, DC. Our two daughters, Dena and Ginger, were just six and three years old, respectively. It was my custom to go into their bedroom the night before a trip and sit between them on their bed while each prayed a simple prayer. I asked Dena if she would pray first, specifically asking that God would be with me on my trip.

I could tell Dena was thinking about something because of the pause before she prayed. Then, with a quizzical look, the six-year-old queried, "Daddy, can I ask you a question?"

"Sure," I replied.

"Why should I ask God to do something for you that He has already promised to do anyway?"

I was, of course, momentarily dumbfounded, and choked out some sort of answer like, "Well, Dena, that's true, but it still never hurts to ask." Meanwhile I was thinking, *Oh dear, we have a six-year-old theologian on our hands!*

Intellectually, we know God is present at all times. Then there are those times when we sense His presence in such a way that we both know and feel He is near. We might describe this as His *conscious* presence because we consciously feel that He is present. John Wesley, in describing his conversion, said, "My heart was strangely warmed." Of course, Wesley's conversion would have been just as real without that warm feeling, but he was sensing something. To a degree, this is what we might consider the conscious presence of God.

The *manifest* presence of God is something far more intense, though it also involves a sense, or feeling, of His being near. While this is not always the case, God's manifest presence generally has a sweeping impact, touching many people—even whole communities or regions—not merely a single individual. Real revival is frequently—if not always—the result of the manifest presence of God upon His people.

As weak an explanation as this may be, it is worth exploring—and by exploring I mean experiencing, rather than merely studying. But for now we will have to be content with planting seeds for your future experiential exploration.

ENCOUNTERING GOD'S THRONE

Most major revivals and awakenings began as small streams where the manifest presence of God had begun to flow. Soon those streams became rivers. (Part three of this book looks at some of these prophetic rivers.) The Welsh Revival began with a coal miner turned preacher, Evan Roberts, sharing the brokenness of his heart to a few people who stayed late after a Monday-night prayer meeting.

America's Great Awakening of the late 1850s began at a noon prayer meeting at the Old Dutch North Church on Fulton Street in New York City. Only six people had gathered for an hour of prayer, including a layman, Jeremiah Lamphier, who called the first meeting. Within two years, tens of thousands of people were praying weekly in cities up and down America's East Coast, resulting in 50,000 new conversions to Christ every week—a conversion rate that was sustained for months.

Although all such awakenings have had differing manifestations, each seemed to result from an intensely fervent passion for God coming upon His people. Deep repentance, for example, came when people wanted nothing between them and God that would hinder their worship. Fervent united prayer was primarily focused on seeking God so that He would simply "come!"

Today's growing harp and bowl intercessory worship movement is precisely this, possibly taken to new heights in the pursuit of God. You can join this movement daily. It's simple:

Declare in song (worship) and prayer (intercession) that God dwells, or is enthroned, in every situation.

This is the result of all this intercessory worship: God is being enthroned because His people *are* pursuing Him in passionate worship as never before. Throne zones, where God can dwell in all His fullness, *are* being established throughout the earth. Radical, revolutionary, worship-saturated prayer is the result, and a new climate is being created to transform peoples and nations through fruitful evangelism. I'm not at all surprised that some of these movements and their leaders have been heavily criticized, often falsely. The enemy must fear this movement more than mortals can comprehend. It's a wave becoming a tsunami. And this is only the beginning.

3

SECOND REALITY

Worship Encounters God

A Few Kind Words for Silence

"You must begin with God. Then you begin to understand everything in its proper context. All things fit into shape and form when you begin with God," wrote A. W. Tozer, one of the great worship mentors of the past century. He defined "genius" well when he declared, "The wisest person in the world is the person who knows the most about God. The only real sage worthy of that name is the one who realizes that the answer to creation and life and eternity is a theological answer—not a scientific answer."[1]

Tozer brings us to our second vital worship reality as we seek to understand the relationship between intercessory worship and the transformation of nations: *Worship encounters God.*

One might wonder why this reality is not first on our list, since it could be argued that we cannot enthrone God until we first encounter Him. However, I am not speaking here of that initial encounter we have with God in Christ, at conversion, but rather of those ongoing intimate encounters that leave us wanting much, much more.

From these experiences we begin to develop a passion to see others, even multitudes, brought into such encounters as they first meet and then grow in Christ. Thus, this worship reality again leads directly to the harvest and the ultimate transformation of peoples and nations.

Stated as our second intercessory-worship principle:

Worship provides an opportunity to encounter God in all His fullness, firsthand.

ASTONISHED REVERENCE

Encountering God is clearly basic to all true worship, and it is certainly essential to powerful intercession. At the heart of encountering God is a pure, passionate adoration and fear of God.

Tozer, whom I quote often on this subject because worship was such a primary focus of his life, explains:

> I will say that when we adore God, all the beautiful ingredients of worship are brought to white, incandescent heat with the fire of the Holy Spirit. To adore God means we love him with all the powers within us. We love him with fear and wonder and yearning and awe.[2]

Notice Tozer's reference to "fear" as it relates to our encounters with God. There is a significant difference between anxious fear and godly fear. As an example, Tozer discusses how the apostle John reacted in the garden of Gethsemane (see John 18) when Jesus was arrested. John was among those who ran away in *fear*. He was no doubt afraid of being arrested. Tozer suggests it was either a fear of danger, a fear of punishment or a fear of humiliation. But later, when John was exiled on Patmos (see Rev. 1:12-17), he saw an awesome Being standing amid golden lampstands and experienced an entirely different kind of fear.

Tozer observes that in this second situation, John was not afraid and he did not feel threatened. He was, in fact, experiencing godly fear. Thus, a true fear of God is a beautiful thing, for it includes worship, love and veneration all at once. It is encountering God! Tozer concludes: "True worship is to be so personally and hopelessly in love with God that the idea of a transfer of affection never even remotely exists. That is the meaning of the fear of God."[3]

Earlier in this same work, Tozer describes this fear and awe of God as part of a "sweet relationship" and "astonished reverence": "When we come into this sweet relationship, we are beginning to learn astonished reverence, breathless adoration, awesome fascination, lofty admiration of the attributes of God and something of the breathless silence that we know when God is near." The author adds, "You may never have realized that before, but all of those elements in our perception and consciousness of the Divine Presence add up to what the Bible calls 'the fear of God.'"[4]

Absolute silence might well be, in some instances, our greatest act of worship. Tozer referred to our experiencing a "breathless silence" when we know God is near. Not all worship is expressed in words or actions. Indeed, the closer one comes to a true encounter with God, the less appropriate some words or actions become. Our very silence can have a profound impact when it comes to extending God's kingdom throughout the nations.

Note God's dramatic admonition regarding silence. God commands, "Be silent, and know that I am God! I will be honored by every nation. I will be honored throughout the world" (Ps. 46:10, *NLT*). Here we discover that being silent in God's presence, as an act of worship, is linked to impacting the nations, and it is certainly essential to "knowing" God, for the text clearly implies that being silent leads to a deeper knowledge of God.

THE LOST ART OF WORSHIP

All of this brings us back to our second premise: that worship provides the opportunity for us to encounter God in all His fullness, firsthand. Of course, to encounter God is to know Him—up close!

In Proverbs we read, "The reverence and fear of God are basic to all wisdom. Knowing God results in every other kind of understanding" (Prov. 9:10, *TLB*). The *New International Version* reads, "Knowledge of the Holy One is understanding." A. W. Tozer, who also wrote the classic book *The Knowledge of the Holy*, wisely said, "The Christian is strong or weak, depending upon how closely he has cultivated a knowledge of God."[5]

Especially significant is the promise, "Knowing God results in every other kind of understanding." The word "every" is an all-encompassing adjective. All the wisdom we could possibly need is reserved for those who increase their knowledge of God. According to the psalmist, silence and knowing God are linked—"Be silent, and know that I am God!"

This seems a good occasion to offer a few kind words for silence. Silence is a lost art of focused worship in much of the Church today. Sadly, even where there is a measure of it, it is but a small fragment of an otherwise lifeless liturgy.

Worshipful silence takes time and incredible discipline. In the last decade, I have not been in any typical worship setting where more than a token moment was devoted to pure silence. If such a time was appointed at all, it was usually designated for silent prayer, which suggests our minds are still very active—we are just praying under our breath. True silence implies that nothing is happening, and our human nature cries out for things to happen—even in worship.

Silence, however, when properly understood and cultivated, is a power all by itself if God is encountered in the process. Listen again to Tozer: "More spiritual progress can be made in one short moment of speechless silence in the awesome presence of God than in years of mere study."[6]

THE OIL OF EXPECTANCY

I am not good at silence. I think that is why God acted as He did in my personal journey to amplify the importance of this worship reality.

In December 1998, almost a year prior to my 40-day worship fast mentioned earlier, I felt strongly led to set aside an entire month to seek God daily regarding Every Home for Christ's emerging decade-long plan, called Completing the Commission. It was an ambitious plan to see home-to-home campaigns in every nation on earth in our generation.

The more I had studied the complexity and cost of the plan, the more I realized it would be impossible to carry out without a miracle beyond anything any of us could ever imagine.

This was to be the second such month-long prayer experience for me. The first occurred in December 1987, when God burdened my heart with the great need for the gospel in Communist Eastern Europe and what was then the Soviet Union.

Those prayers in 1987 were soon remarkably answered, and over a decade-long period, Every Home for Christ visited and gave the printed gospel to more than 40 million households in this Eurasian region alone. Nearly 2 million people from the former Soviet Union and Eastern Europe have mailed decision cards or written letters requesting more information about Jesus. The majority of those indicated they had received Christ as Savior. Prior to that time, the number of such requests from that region was probably fewer than 200 in more than two decades.

So, here I was, about to enter my second month-long prayer experience. As with my first month of prayer, I felt specifically led to set aside the amount of time daily for prayer that I would normally spend in my office or in planning meetings and preaching assignments. I did not feel it was to be a time of fasting and prayer, as such, but rather a full month of seeking God (sometimes with others)—every day.

For this second month-long commitment, I decided to keep a daily calendar and on selected days invite other intercessors, as well as our staff, to join me for prayer. Among other focuses for the month, for two days we specifically prayed over and anointed with oil the 10-year plan that had prompted this month of prayer in the first place.

Much of those two days was spent literally on our faces in my office. At one point we anointed each of the hundreds of pages of the plan with traditional anointing oil. On the third day, our entire staff spent a day doing the same thing. It was truly a symbolic saturation of the plan with the oil of expectancy and anticipation, and to this day I keep this copy of the plan, with oil marks on each page, in my prayer room at home.

Been There, Done That

The rest of that month held an interesting variety and diversity of prayer experiences. But by Sunday, December 20, a little "warrior weariness" had set in. That night as I sat alone in my prayer closet under the staircase in our basement, I quietly wondered, *What should I do next?* I remember telling the Lord, "I'm not sure if there's anything else I can do to seek You this month that I haven't already done, probably five or six times."

This was not an arrogant statement, but an honest expression of losing steam in my praying. Of course, I knew better, but still there was something of a "been there, done that" feeling. My heart was crying out, "I've run out of ideas, God, and it's only December 20. I've got 11 days to go in this month of prayer and I'm dying down here!"

That is when it happened. As clearly as you read the words on this page, the gentle whisper of God's unmistakable voice filled my mind. It was soft but firm.

No! You haven't done everything, the voice said. *There is at least one thing you've never done in My presence for an entire day.*

For a moment I honestly did not know what the Lord was referring to. What had I never done in prayer for an entire day?

My mind searched my past prayer encounters that had lasted a complete day. I remembered spending an entire day simply praising God. I also remembered how, on another occasion, I had spent a day just lying on my face before God. I had felt led to spend that day thanking God, by name, for every person who had ever blessed me. It was, to be sure, a day of many tears and incredible gratitude.

Then there was that most memorable day in 1987 when a handful of intercessors and I sang to the Lord, spontaneously, in worship for an entire day. None of these occasions had been planned out of a hope to impress God, as if we were climbing a spiritual Mt. Everest. Nor was it because we thought such dedication would prove that we were spiritual giants. These days resulted simply from a desire to get closer to God.

But now, on this twentieth day of my second month-long commitment, I wondered what I had missed. What had I never done for an entire day? What I heard next stunned me.

The gentle voice returned: *You've never spent an entire day in total silence in My presence.*

THE MIRACLE OF SILENCE

God had me on that one! Actually, I had never even spent a single hour in total silence. (Make that 20 minutes!) Silence is just too tough and, frankly, a little unmanly. At least, that was my thinking back then.

Praying prostrate, claiming Scripture, singing praises, breaking strongholds, rebuking Satan—that is where the action is in prayer. *Silence is for sissies*, I reasoned. *Besides, what good would a full day of silence accomplish anyway?*

Then, God amazed me with His Word. He asked, *Is it not the desire of your heart and ministry to help reach all the un-evangelized peoples of the earth with the good news?* My response was, obviously, yes.

God's still, small voice then questioned, *Does not My Word declare, "Be still, and know that I am God; I will be exalted among the nations, I will be exalted in the earth"* (Ps. 46:10)?

I began to weep as I saw the connection between pure, worshipful silence in God's presence and His being exalted in the *nations*. I could never remember reading or hearing someone suggest that simple, focused silence in God's presence was in any way connected to

God being exalted in the nations through the completion of the Great Commission.

Instantly I knew I had to set aside just such a day of silence that month. I determined to do it three days later, on Wednesday, because I had already scheduled Monday and Tuesday to pray with others.

I vividly recall the start of that Wednesday encounter. After several hours of simply being still, during which I battled the myriad rushing thoughts that often seemed louder than if I had spoken them—or even shouted them—I suddenly sensed a uniquely open heaven. Although I was not specifically seeking to hear from the Lord, His voice spoke with unusual clarity, giving me details I had not thought of before about how our plan to reach the world's unreached peoples, home by home, would unfold.

Though space does not allow for the sharing of all those details here, I am convinced my Psalm 46:10 encounter of silence was crucial to unlocking an understanding of this vital reality. My quiet day with God revealed to me that our plan would find its fulfillment through strategic ministry alliances among many evangelism and discipleship organizations, along with business and professional leaders, all coming together to partner through intercessory worship.

All of this, of course, involves encountering God, a clear result of worship. I am convinced that a fundamental and powerful key to encountering God is silence, which, as stated before, provides an opportunity to encounter God in all His fullness, *firsthand*. It is impossible to boast or argue when you are truly silent. In fact, the very miracle at Jericho, when the 12 tribes united to take the city, was first and foremost a miracle of silence (see Josh. 6).

AN APOSTLE OF SILENCE

Years ago I read about the life of Francis of Assisi, one of the few bright lights shining in quite possibly the darkest days of the Church—the Middle Ages. In some ways Assisi might be described as "the Apostle of Silence." The absence of light during that season of the Middle Ages was such that even historians refer to the period as the Dark Ages.

It is said that once, while deep in prayer, Francis heard the audible voice of Christ. The voice said simply, "Go, Francis, and repair my House." One of Francis of Assisi's biographers would later write,

"From then on Francis could never keep himself from weeping." Thomas of Celano, a Franciscan friar and poet, said of this remarkable disciple: "He was always occupied with Jesus; Jesus he bore in his heart, Jesus in his mouth, Jesus in his ears, Jesus in his eyes, Jesus in his hands, Jesus in the rest of his members."[7]

Those who have studied the life of Francis of Assisi know he was first and foremost a worshiper. So remarkable was the impact of his life over so many generations that we can refer to him simply by the name of the Italian city in which he was born, Assisi, and most of the Church knows exactly who we are talking about.

This apostle of silence encountered God to such a degree—and so often—that some say his face literally glowed with God's presence when he came from his usual place of prayer. Oh, that God would raise up a new order of just such apostolic worshipers!

Silence was almost a creed with Francis of Assisi. He understood that words are not the underlying reality of our Christianity, either in worship or in witness. One memorable statement attributed to Francis, and said to have been repeated often as a challenge to the brothers of his order, is: "Go everywhere and preach the gospel to everyone. And if you absolutely must, use words."[8]

Francis of Assisi was indeed a person of few words but a man of great power. Francis encountered God often, it is said, during whole days of almost absolute silence in a cave near Averno, Italy, not far from the city of Assisi where he was born. From those silent worship encounters, Francis went forth as a mighty intercessor—a spiritual go-between—to impact generations of would-be worshipers.

Could it be that God is ready to raise up an entire generation of worshiping intercessors like Francis of Assisi? You can become just such an all-consumed worshiper. Apply this worship reality daily:

> Devote a specific portion of your daily devotional time to encounter God in all His fullness through a specific season of worshipful silence.

Imagine an army of apostolic leaders, filled with God's Spirit, ready to transform neighborhoods, nations and the entire world with the gospel. Does this sound appealing? Do you long to see it happen in our generation? Then continue with me on this journey.

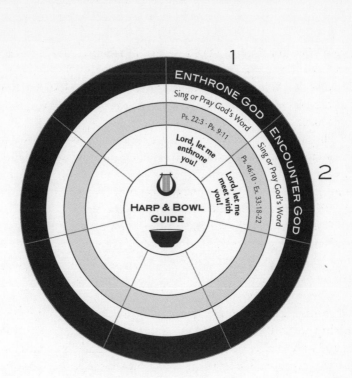

4

THIRD REALITY

Worship Enlarges God

Seeing God Big

Amplifying the necessity of a worship-saturated worldview, John Piper writes, "God is calling us above all else to be the kind of people whose theme and passion is the supremacy of God in all of life." To see God as supreme is to see God *big*. Piper wisely adds, "No one will be able to rise to the magnificence of the missionary cause who does not feel the magnificence of Christ. There will be no big world vision without a big God."[1] Max Lucado, in his inspiring book *Just Like Jesus*, adds this insight:

> Worship is the act of magnifying God. Enlarging our vision of Him. . . . Of course, His size doesn't change, but our perception of Him does. As we draw nearer He seems larger. Isn't that what we need? A *big* view of God? Don't we have *big* problems, *big* worries, *big* questions? Of course we do. Hence we need a big view of God.[2]

These thoughts bring us to a profound truth about the role of worship in fulfilling Christ's mandate to take the gospel to all peoples. The more we worship God, the bigger God becomes in our understanding, resulting in a greater faith to believe He will accomplish His purposes through us. Identified as our third worship reality: *Worship enlarges God!*

Of course, our worship does not actually change anything in or about God. To say that worship enlarges God really means it increases our capacity to know and understand Him in all His greatness. Tozer said it well: "You can't make God big. But you can see Him big."[3]

The psalmist prayerfully pleaded, "Oh, magnify the LORD with me, and let us exalt His name together" (Ps. 34:3, *NKJV*). Later in the psalms we read, "I will praise the name of God with a song, and will magnify Him with thanksgiving" (Ps. 69:30, *NKJV*).

The psalmist longed to discover God in all His greatness. He wanted to see God big, which is at the heart of our third intercessory worship principle:

Worship provides an atmosphere to expand and increase our knowledge and understanding of God in all His fullness.

A BAPTISM OF WONDER

We recall Mary's beautiful song, recorded in the Gospel of Luke and often referred to as the *Magnificat*. Mary said, "My soul magnifies the Lord, and my spirit has rejoiced in God my Savior" (Luke 1:46-47, *NKJV*). Like the psalmist before her, Mary magnified the Lord. She was seeing God big through her worship, an activity that could continue endlessly throughout eternity because God's magnificence is infinite.

When the power of God's Spirit came upon the house of Cornelius, those who observed this outpouring "heard [Cornelius and his household] speak with tongues and magnify God" (Acts 10:46, *NKJV*). Here we discover that the same outpouring that had taken place on the Day of Pentecost among the Jews also occurred at the house of Cornelius among the Gentiles. As the Holy Spirit came, the worshipers began to *see God bigger* through their praise. All who were present were filled with awe and wonder.

A. W. Tozer speculated about what a modern-day baptism of wonder might accomplish in transforming cultures. He wrote:

In the very midst of the myriad of created wonders all around us, we have almost unknowingly lost the capacity to wonder. If the Holy Spirit should come again upon us as in earlier times, visiting church congregations with the sweet but fiery breath of Pentecost, we would be greater Christians and holier souls. Beyond that, we would also be greater poets and greater artists and greater lovers of God and of His universe.[4]

Seeing God bigger also means understanding Jesus better. Joseph Garlington highlights this reality in his book *Worship: The Pattern of Things in Heaven*. Discussing how worship helps us see Jesus more clearly, Garlington suggests:

> Although Jesus Christ won't be "better" than He is now, our understanding of Him, our comprehension of His love and sacrifice, our revelation of Him as God incarnate, and especially *our capacity* to enjoy intimate fellowship with Him will be better, fuller, richer, bigger, and deeper than what we have now.[5]

STUDY THE LIGHT

Seeing God bigger indeed requires our knowing Jesus better. This must go far beyond mere head knowledge to become a passionate heart yearning. We must pursue this study of Jesus by being *with* Him, long and often, not just by reading or hearing *about* Him.

An interesting lesson can be learned from a study of more than 2,000 years of lighthouse technology. The study appeared in *Smithsonian* magazine, in an article titled "Science Makes a Better Lighthouse Lens."[6] According to the author, Bruce Watson, there were no major improvements in lighthouses from about 280 BC, when the famed lighthouse of Alexandria, Egypt, towered 450 feet above Egypt's greatest harbor, until the early 1800s. Even though many scientists and engineers tried their best to design and build a better lighthouse, they failed.

Throughout most of those years, lighthouses burned coal or wood. Finally, by the eighteenth century, oil lamps with mirrors offered a little more light. Still, according to Watson, the shorelines of the world were "littered with the ribs of broken ships" as evidence that little had improved in lighthouse technology over those 2,000 years. True, the glass lantern of the 1690s helped a little, as did the practice of placing mirrors in huge wooden bowls to create crude reflectors. But as maritime traffic increased, so did shipwrecks. The quest was on for a far more reliable light source.

The goal of that quest was reached through the visionary genius of Augustin Fresnel, a frail, 34-year-old French-Swiss scientist who had a passion for optics, the branch of physics that studies how light behaves. Fresnel took a totally different approach from all the others who were seeking to build a better lighthouse. While others tried to improve lighthouse technology, Fresnel decided simply to study the behavior of light itself. His studies not only advanced the understanding of the nature of light, but also led to huge breakthroughs in the effectiveness of lighthouses.

Through his study of light, Fresnel developed a number of formulas to calculate the way light changes direction, or refracts, while passing through glass prisms. This understanding led to the development of the remarkable Fresnel lens and, in the process, to a much better lighthouse. Fresnel arranged different lenses and dozens of prisms at precise angles so that diffused lamplight was redirected into a unified, far-reaching beam.

Today, the concepts behind Fresnel's original lens impact our lives every time we turn on our automobile headlights. That is because headlights use adaptations of a Fresnel lens. The lens in a television studio camera is often referred to as a Fresnel lens. In fact, Fresnel's theories of light form the basis of all modern optics.

There is a lesson in all of this for those who seek to be better worshiping intercessors. We need to study the Light, Christ Himself, if we truly want to see God bigger. Where light shines, we see more clearly. If we want to see God bigger, we need to see Christ more brightly!

MAKING SATAN SMALL

Seeing God bigger through worship leads to bigger and more powerful prayers. The most effective intercessors I have known have cultivated their prayer effectiveness through concentrated, focused worship. Joy Dawson, one of my personal mentors, is such an intercessor.

Joy, associated for years with Youth With A Mission (YWAM), is particularly known for her outstanding teaching on intercession, holiness and intimacy with God. I consider Joy's book *Intimate Friendship with God* a true classic. In my early years of developing an understanding of intercession, I would often spend entire days in my prayer closet, listening to one audiocassette after another of Joy's teachings. Later, I had the privilege of serving with Joy and her husband, Jim, for many years on America's National Prayer Committee.

It was during one of our all-day prayer retreats in Washington, DC, with the National Prayer Committee that Joy uniquely demonstrated how to see God bigger. We were midway through a morning of seeking and waiting on God when Joy began to worship God audibly, praising a variety of aspects of His nature and character. As usual, Joy filled her worship with God's Word.

I learned by praying with Joy over the years that she had developed a lifelong habit of regularly spending many early morning hours saturating herself in the Scriptures. In so doing, she had compiled her own concordance of scores of Bible passages focusing on who God is and what He is like.

Her understanding of God was not just head knowledge. Joy studied the Light! Her prayers were filled with God because she knew Him so well. My prayers too often seemed as if they were reflecting the light of an old, worn-out lantern. Joy's were much more like the powerful beam of a Fresnel lens. Her praise reflected God brilliantly and beautifully.

That day in Washington, the light was reflecting especially brightly as Joy worshiped. All of us felt as if we had been lifted into the presence of God as this precious worshiper filled her prayers with praises of God's nature and character. Repeatedly, Joy spoke that memorable phrase Jesus used in confronting Satan while fasting in the wilderness (see Luke 4:4,8,12). It is a phrase Joy often uses when praying. "It is written," Joy would declare, following that phrase with a bold declaration from some Bible passage about who God is, what He is like, what He has done or what He will do for those who seek Him. I thought to myself, *God always gets bigger when Joy prays!* That morning was no exception.

Suddenly, Joy did something rather startling. She stopped, midsentence, interrupting her praise. What Joy did in that moment I had never heard anyone do before. She spoke directly to the devil and abruptly declared, "Satan, I'm not the least bit impressed by you." Then, with hardly a pause, she continued on with seeing God even bigger through her worship.

Through years of saturating herself in an understanding of God's nature and character, Joy had recognized this vital principle: *The bigger we see God through our worship, the smaller Satan becomes in his capacity to defeat us.* Further, the more we understand Satan's diminished capacity, the more powerful our prayers of intercession become. Worship

makes all this happen, allowing us to expand and increase our knowledge of God, thus providing us with a path to much greater power in
our praying.

PRAYING BIG PRAYERS

Sadly, it seems some believers almost negate—and certainly diminish—the potential power of their worship and intercession by their
own faithless words spoken during prayer. We verbally lament over
the many pressing problems and attacks of the enemy to the point
that we almost lose faith—we can hardly believe that victory is even
possible. Joy Dawson points out that this can be especially devastating to our prayers of intercession.

During that same worship and intercession retreat with the National Prayer Committee, Joy described being invited to participate
in a time of prayer in Europe a few months earlier. A room full of
young, would-be missionaries was waiting when Joy arrived. Soon,
the prayer meeting was underway.

It was not long before Joy realized there was a problem. Participants filled their prayers with too much of the negative. This "bad
thing" and that "horrible circumstance" were the focuses of their
praying. Nothing of God's greatness or power was voiced. There was
little if any praise. This continued for more than half an hour.

Joy tried to be gracious but knew if she continued praying with
these young people for very long, her faith to intercede effectively
would be seriously hindered. She stood up and politely, though
boldly, told the group, "I'm truly sorry, but I've been here only a short
while, and it's already evident you're more impressed with the power
of Satan than you are with the awesomeness of God. So I need to ask
if I may be excused!"

Joy was not being unkind, just responsive to the concerns of her
heart that the unintentional non-focus of their prayers that morning
was making God smaller—at least in her eyes. To Joy, big prayers only
happen through those who see God big. That is why our third worship reality is so critical to this matter of intercessory worship. Worship, indeed, enlarges God; you can apply this principle daily as you:

*Declare in song and prayer God's greatness in comparison to every
attack of the enemy.*

The bigger we see God, the bigger we pray—and the bigger we pray, the greater the answers we receive. To totally transform nations will take some pretty big prayers. To literally reach every family and person on earth with the gospel, while discipling entire people groups in the process, will take huge prayers. (Intercessory worship, particularly in a corporate setting, greatly enhances praying big prayers, as we'll describe more fully in part two of our study.)

So, let's not let the enemy make God small in our thinking, praying or planning! Worship God fervently. Worship Him passionately. Worship Him aggressively and extravagantly. You will soon see God big—and *pray* big prayers. Best of all, you will experience the joy of the Lord that the Bible says will give you strength (see Neh. 8:10). And that leads us to our next key worship reality.

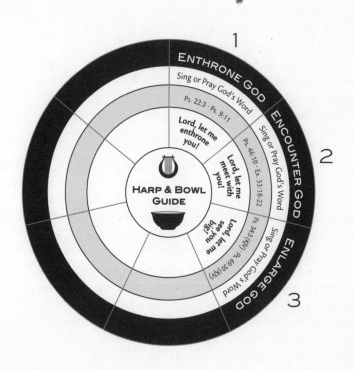

FOURTH REALITY

WORSHIP ENJOYS GOD

THE CLIFFS OF MOLOKAI

It was an early Sunday flight to the Hawaiian island of Kauai, where I was to speak that morning. Hawaii is a favorite ministry destination for my wife, Dee, and me because of the sheer beauty of the location, and also because of the opportunity to minister to believers eager to see God display His glory throughout their islands.

When we had been in the air only a few minutes, the pilot of the small commuter plane commented that just off the lower left wing was the island of Molokai, population 7,000. The dim light of an early dawn oozed through thick clouds hovering just above, creating a deep red-brown haze hanging over the island like a huge rust-colored blanket.

What a desolate place that has to be, I thought. Then I remembered that I once flew to Molokai in a private plane. A pastor from Honolulu, where I was ministering at the time, had just acquired his pilot's license and wanted to fly somewhere. Molokai had a little-used airfield, so that was his choice. It was a quick trip: We flew to the island, landed, stepped out of the plane to stretch, and then took off again. I was not impressed. So brief was the experience that it was hardly an experience at all.

Now, 27 years later, gazing at Molokai from a distance, I remembered I would be going there the following Sunday to speak at a local church. "Maybe I'll see the desolation close up," I said and chuckled to myself.

Over the years, Dee and I had made many trips to Hawaii, most often to spend times of ministry coupled with rest, and we usually went to our favorite island, Maui. Often, when staying on Maui's north shore, we would see Molokai across the Pacific and experience that same sense of desolation. Molokai did not look inviting at all.

The locals on Molokai refer to their home as "the Forgotten Island." For centuries other Hawaiians called it "the Dark Island." It was on Molokai that the famed Flemish priest, Father Damien, died of leprosy in the late 1880s. He was there to minister to the islanders, who were steeped in traditions of witchcraft and superstition.

In fact, Molokai was the island where all the powerful *kahuna* (priests) were trained in the ways of witchcraft. Some *kahuna*, tradition tells us, could "pray a person to death." They clearly understood the supernatural. At the Kahuna school on Molokai, sorcerers were equipped and prepared to be sent to other islands.[1] It truly was the Dark Island!

GETTING CLOSER: A JOURNEY OF JOY

The following Sunday, an inter-island commuter plane took off again from Maui's Kahului airport, this time headed for Molokai. Even close up, my initial impression was the same: This was indeed a desolate island. However, my perception began to change as Pastor Michael Zarle took me on a brief but interesting drive along Molokai's southwest coast.

Soon I was speaking to a small but lively group of worshipers who were keeping the incense of worship rising from this island.

I finished my ministry that morning and boarded the commuter plane departing for Maui. Then something remarkable happened. Immediately after takeoff, the pilot flew the small plane directly over the beautiful cliffs of Molokai. It's hard to describe the awe and wonder of looking straight down those sheer walls of beauty from less than a few hundred feet above. The experience was breathtaking. I cannot recall having seen such a beautiful sight in all the journeys my wife and I have taken around the world in our many years of ministry. I wondered to myself how much of the grandeur and majesty of this island I had missed simply because I had not come close enough to see its beauty. I had almost deprived myself of the view of a lifetime—and the pure joy this view afforded—because I had never come close enough. Getting closer changed everything!

Reflecting on the wonder of that moment, I could not help but think of those who genuinely know God, in Christ, but have not come close enough to really see Him in all His beauty. Worship, of course, is the key to bringing us close. It is a journey of joy that takes us closer and closer to the true beauty and awesomeness of God, revealing to us more fully the pure pleasure of being in His presence.

Madame Guyon, the seventeenth-century French mystic, pursued with an almost defiant passion an inner revelation of the fullness of God. Her quest, which landed her in prison at the hands of the ecclesiastical authorities of her day, led Guyon to remarkable insights regarding prayer. She discovered prayer to be, in its essence, experiencing the joy of who God is.

Tracing her own journey of prayer, and applying what she had learned to all such seekers, Guyon wrote, "In the beginning, you were led into His presence by prayer; but now, as prayer continues, the prayer actually becomes His presence."[2]

What an extraordinary truth! Guyon then amplified this thought by explaining how God's Spirit drives us onward toward this goal: "The Spirit moves us forward, plunging us toward the ultimate end. And what is the ultimate end? It is union with God."[3]

The old Westminster Catechism defines this ultimate goal similarly: "The chief end of man is to glorify God and enjoy Him forever." This suggests that worship is more than merely a means to an end—it is the end itself. Further, this process of cultivating our ultimate end of union with God before we actually achieve it has the capacity not only to transform nations, but also to provide us incredible joy as our journey unfolds.

The psalmist said it thus: "In Your presence is fullness of joy; at Your right hand are pleasures forevermore" (Ps. 16:11, *NKJV*). True, this verse may well picture the believer's ultimate end—our eternal ecstasy with God—but there is another truth revealed in this promise. Great joy is also to be found simply by entering into and waiting within God's presence, a thought that leads to our next worship reality: *Worship enjoys God*. Expanded to our fourth intercessory-worship principle:

> *Worship provides a place of entry into the delights and pleasures of God's presence.*

Few have fascinated me as much in their passion to become consumed with our Lord as has the already mentioned Francis of Assisi, the son of a wealthy twelfth-century Italian merchant. Born Francesco de Pietro Bernardone, this faithful believer made such a global impact through his life that, as stated earlier, generations now know him simply as Francis of Assisi.

What most marked Francis of Assisi's life was his passion for God. His pure enjoyment of God seems almost unmatched since the early apostles. Such was evident when he wrote to his brothers:

> We should wish for nothing else and have no other desire, we should find no pleasure or delight in anything except in our Creator, Redeemer, and Savior; He alone is true God, perfect, good, all good, every good, and the true and supreme good . . . loving and gentle, kind and understanding.[4]

In this same discourse, Francis elaborated at length:

> Nothing, then, must keep us back, nothing separate us from him, nothing come between us and him. At all times and seasons, in every country and place, every day and all day, we must keep him in our hearts, where we must love, honor, adore, serve, praise and bless, glorify and acclaim, magnify and thank, the most high supreme and eternal God, three in one, Father, Son, and Holy Spirit, Creator of all and the Savior of those who believe in him, who hope in him, and who love him; without beginning and without end, he is unchangeable, invisible, indescribable and ineffable, incomprehensible, unfathomable, blessed and worthy of all praise . . . lovable, delightful and utterly desirable beyond all else, for ever and ever.[5]

ABSOLUTE JOY

Francis of Assisi's life was clearly a journey of joy. It was a life that impacted millions, including another worshiping intercessor, the seventeenth-century monk, Brother Lawrence, who personified practicing God's presence. He offered us this insight regarding man's ultimate goal: "The thing we ought to purpose to ourselves in this life is to become the most perfect worshipers of God we can possibly be as we hope to be through all eternity."[6]

Both Francis and Lawrence understood that approaching God through pure worship was to enter an atmosphere of absolute joy! In so doing, their very lives became powerfully intercessory in the sense that God allowed them to intervene in the transformation of multitudes, even long after they were gone.

I want to particularly emphasize the total joy that flooded all they did! This joy is available to any believer who pursues God in worship, because worship enjoys God. The psalmist described such worshipers: "What joy for those you choose to bring near, those who live in your holy courts. What joys await us inside your holy Temple" (Ps. 65:4, *NLT*).

Elsewhere we read, "How lovely is your dwelling place, O LORD Almighty. I long, yes, I faint with longing to enter the courts of the LORD. With my whole being, body and soul, I will shout joyfully to the living God. . . . How happy are those who can live in your house, always singing your praises" (Ps. 84:1-2,4, *NLT*). How many believers today have tasted such joy? Imagine the impact such joyful worshipers would have on those around them!

A.W. Tozer spoke of cultivating this joy and linked it to the fear of God when he wrote: "I believe that the reverential fear of God mixed with love and fascination and astonishment and admiration and devotion is the most enjoyable state and the most purifying emotion the human soul can know."[7]

Imagine a joy that transcends anything we could possibly anticipate or experience in our lifetimes. Picture it as beyond the delight of falling in love or the passion of marital intimacy. Think of it as surpassing the birthing of a child, wildly succeeding in a career, loving a grandchild or growing old in a happy marriage. Imagine all of that together but much, much more. Then, add to it total health with a complete absence of pain, fear, doubt and any form of discouragement. In other words, imagine a joy that is unimaginable. Imagine absolute joy.

Heaven holds just such joy, not because heaven happens to be heaven, but because God will be worshiped "close up" in heaven—and *worship enjoys God.*

THE BEAUTY REALM OF GOD

True, heaven *will* be a place, a very real place, but heaven will only be what it is because of the presence of the person of Christ, the Bridegroom, and the splendor of God's presence around His throne. Our joy will be in our worship, for *worship enjoys God!*

Mike Bickle captures this thought well when he speaks about "the beauty realm of God" that King David experienced in the Tabernacle of David. We, too, can catch glimpses of God's beauty realm even now, although we will only experience it in totality when we spend eternity in God's presence. Bickle writes: "Feasting on the beauty realm of God was a primary desire of David—and one of the secrets of this quality of worship (see Psalm 27:4)."[8]

Bickle adds, "In fact, David was the first man to bring into one context worship singers, musicians and intercessors. I believe that many of the intercessory psalms were written on site in the Tabernacle of David."[9]

This joy of worship surrounding David's tent (or tabernacle) is especially vital because Scripture clearly speaks of an ultimate restoration of what King David once established as being linked to a future massive global harvest of all peoples (see Acts 15:16-18). This text, to be examined in depth in part two of this book, quotes the apostle James, who was restating the ancient prophecy of Amos (see Amos 9:11-15). James declared:

> This conversion of Gentiles agrees with what the prophets predicted. For instance, it is written: "Afterward I will return, and I will restore the fallen kingdom [tent, *NIV*] of David. From the ruins I will rebuild it, and I will restore it, so that the rest of humanity might find the Lord, including the Gentiles" (Acts 15:15-17, *NLT*).

But here I want to primarily emphasize the "joy factor" that becomes so essential in powerful intercessory worship. Further discussing this theme, Mike Bickle refers to the harp and bowl model, that, as mentioned earlier, draws its focus from the picture in Revelation 5:8-10. It is here that we see the living creatures and elders coming before God's throne with "harps" (symbolic of worship) and "bowls" (filled with prayers of intercession), releasing a new worship song of the redeemed who are saved out of every tribe, tongue, people and nation.

Intercession, of course, is a key to this ingathering, but as Mike Bickle contends, if joy does not saturate our intercession, it grows both weak and wearisome. He explains, "I believe the harp and bowl model of intercessory worship is key to the present worldwide prayer movement because it creates the 'joy in the House of Prayer' about which Isaiah prophesied (see Isaiah 56:7)."[10]

Does God call us to wear ourselves down in wearisome prayer? Absolutely not. He invites us to experience His joy! Employ your own harp and bowl daily! It's easy:

> *Declare in song and prayer your delight and joy in God for who He is and what He has done.*

Bickle adds, "Our intercessory prayer furnaces can burn longer and brighter when they are fueled by love songs to God. As music and praise from the beauty realm of God are joined with the prayers of the saints and offered at the throne of God, great spiritual benefits are released on earth."[11]

CATCHING A GLIMPSE

During the second day of my 40-day worship fast, I caught a small but significant glimpse of this "beauty realm of God" and how its resulting joy helps fuel our "prayer furnaces." At God's direction, I had determined on the previous day that each of my daily prayer times for the following 40 days would consist entirely of worshiping the Lord in song—including the singing of all my prayers. However, I had no idea how these worship times would unfold, because I had never before attempted something like this over such a long period of time.

It was now the second day of my fast, and I realized that I had a long way to go. I had decided to work at home that day on some ministry projects. At noon, I went into my prayer closet intending to spend that day's hour of my worship fast alone—a very different experience from the day before, when I had joined hundreds at the World Prayer Center. I was not exactly sure how it would go, but I knew this was to begin the pattern of many days of singing both my worship and my prayers!

It was not that I had never spontaneously worshiped the Lord in song, but on the only other occasion that involved a prolonged time (an entire day), I had worshiped with other intercessors. Now I was to do it alone—and for 39 days! I turned off the prayer-closet light, so I would not be distracted by anything in the room—including maps of various countries as well as pictures of our Every Home for Christ staff and other Christian leaders and their families. I wanted to focus totally on the Lord.

Sitting on my comfortable cushions, I prayed, "Lord, I'm not exactly sure how to do this, but here goes!" and I began to sing. I cannot recall the specific content of those first attempts at spontaneous song, but I vividly remember running out of steam in about 10 minutes. The words made little sense, and the melody, I am sure, sounded pathetic. I started to chuckle in embarrassment, interrupting my song with a barely audible, "This is silly!"

Instantly, a voice within responded, *No, it's beautiful. Your singing blesses Me!*

I knew the Lord was speaking and so I continued, though with some degree of difficulty. I recalled the Bible promise from the day before: "You satisfy me more than the richest of foods. I will praise you with songs of joy" (Ps. 63:5, *NLT*). I felt I was to continue, no matter how uncreative or insignificant my song seemed. Besides, it was not for me; it was unto the Lord. He was hearing my heart, not my lips or my voice.

My goal was to spend at least an hour of worship in song. I decided not to look at my watch for fear of being discouraged if I could not complete an entire hour. The room was dark because the lights were out, so I could not see my watch anyway. Suddenly, it seemed as if the heavens above me opened.

A RAIN OF JOY

Moments after I had decided to continue no matter what, God's glory came. It felt like a rain of joy. My song obviously did not end. For a time it seemed like it never would. Nor did I find myself growing weary.

What had begun with a sense of awkwardness now became an entry into the beauty realm of God. Finally, I stood to leave my prayer closet. As I opened the door, the light from the outside hall nearly blinded me. Once my eyes adjusted, I looked at my watch. I was stunned—what had seemed like only a few minutes had, in reality, been hours.

In that moment I grasped something of an understanding of the pure joy that comes from being in God's presence and observing nothing but glimpses of the unending facets of His beauty. This, I realized, could well be an eternal preoccupation. I had always thought of heaven as a place to do things that we enjoy on earth, only with bodies absent of pain. I recall hearing clever sermons as a youth on how heaven would include such blessings as "fuzzless peaches and seedless watermelon" and how the average score for 18 holes of golf there would be exactly 18. Now it was clearer than ever that the pure joy of heaven would be our enjoying more and more of the beauty of God.

A vital aspect of that joy, I realized, was the incredible delight of making it possible for millions of others from every tribe, tongue, people and nation to join with us in experiencing it.

Making Heaven Happy

Saint Augustine, in his work *Patrologia Latina*, wrote, "In the house of God there is never-ending festival; the angel choir makes eternal holiday; the presence of God's face gives joy that never fails. And from that everlasting, perpetual festivity there sounds in the ears of the heart a strain, mysterious, melodious, sweet—provided the world does not drown it."[12]

David clearly tapped into a never-ending festival of joy. He understood something of its perpetual festivity. There was no drowning of heaven's melody in David's day. He heard heaven's sounds, sensed heaven's joy and entered into it with total abandon.

It is impossible to read through the accounts describing worship related to the Tabernacle of David, and the Temple that followed, without noticing the repeated references to the joyfulness demonstrated in Davidic worship. Joy was central to their adoration. Even when David admonished other worshipers to praise the Lord, he repeatedly instructed them to do it with joy. He declared, "But let the godly rejoice. Let them be glad in God's presence. Let them be filled with joy" (Ps. 68:3, *NLT*). This is a direct command. David is saying: Get happy, and then worship!

Elsewhere David sang, "The LORD is my strength and my shield; my heart trusts in him, and I am helped. My heart leaps for joy and I will give thanks to him in song" (Ps. 28:7). Increasingly, we understand why David was a man after God's own heart. He gazed constantly into the face of God—the face that, according to Augustine, "gives joy that never fails."

Heaven's joy, or what Scripture refers to as "the joy of the LORD" (Neh. 8:10), is clearly essential to effective intercession and, for that matter, to any measure of balanced, practical Christian living. We know that Jesus is interested in our joy. He longs for our joy to be complete in Him.

In the context of sharing His analogy of the vine and the branches (see John 15:1-7), Jesus said, "I have told you this so that my joy may be in you and that your joy may be complete" (John 15:11).

What does the expression "the joy of the Lord" actually mean? During a great revival feast in ancient Israel, Nehemiah said, "The joy of the LORD is your strength" (Neh. 8:10). This is one of the most frequently quoted phrases about joy from the Bible. Most often we highlight the result of our experiencing this joy, rather than what this joy actually is or what it means to the Lord.

The answer might be found in the truth that Jesus shared when He gave His parables of the lost sheep and the lost coin (see Luke 15:1-10). In both of these parables, our Lord talks about the rejoicing that takes place in heaven when just one person repents.

Jesus concludes the parable of the lost coin by describing the joy experienced by the woman who finds the coin. Christ quotes the excited woman and adds His application: "In the same way, I tell you, there is rejoicing in the presence of the angels of God over one sinner who repents" (Luke 15:10). Of the parable about the lost sheep, Jesus says, "Joy shall be in heaven over one sinner that repenteth" (Luke 15:7, *KJV*).

Perhaps the reason there is so much joy in heaven when people are converted is that each time a person repents and receives Christ, there is one more addition to that eternal chorus of worshipers. The apostle Paul amplified this idea when he told the Corinthian believers, "And as God's grace brings more and more people to Christ, there will be great thanksgiving, and God will receive more and more glory" (2 Cor. 4:15, *NLT*). Worship, indeed, enjoys God and enjoys bringing others into that joy. What could possibly be more eternally exciting?

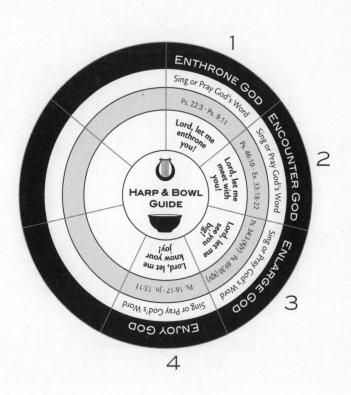

6

FIFTH REALITY

WORSHIP ENLISTS GOD

FIRE FROM HEAVEN

"Whenever the church has come out of her lethargy, rising from her sleep and into the tides of revival and spiritual renewal, always the worshipers were back of it."[1] These words of A. W. Tozer bring us to yet another vital worship reality: *Worship enlists God.*

True revival is always the heart's cry of any committed believer—and central to every revival is worship. It was Tozer who specifically defined revival in terms of worship. He wrote:

> In my study and observations, a revival generally results in a sudden bestowment of a spirit of worship. This is not the result of engineering or manipulation. It is something God bestows on people hungering and thirsting for him. With this spiritual renewing will come a blessed spirit of loving worship.[2]

Worship, then, not only helps bring revival and sustains it but also opens the heavens for more of God so that worship, and the revival itself, can expand further. This results in an even greater increase of our awareness of God, which is the essence of revival.

Additionally, intercessory worship releases something of God's glory into circumstances that otherwise would seem hopeless. When we engage in intercessory worship, we are intervening in the needs of others (intercession) by enlisting the fullness of God to assist us (worship). Summed up as our fifth intercessory worship principle:

> *Worship provides our primary means to mobilize and release the resources of God into the needs of peoples and nations.*

One thing is certain: Transforming peoples and nations through a full revelation of Jesus Christ, accomplished by literally reaching with the gospel all of these peoples specifically and individually right where they live, will require a miracle. Of course, only God can perform true miracles. Thus, we need to include the God of the miraculous in all of our plans and strategies if we hope to accomplish our objective. Intercessory worship is the only means I can conceive of that will help Christ's Body achieve this goal. Yes, we still have to go, but if we go without power we will return without fruit.

How do we tap this power? It is worship that *enlists* God and intercession that *involves* God, together resulting in a release of the spiritual and material resources needed to touch and transform individuals and nations. The psalmist worshipfully pictured the power we need when he sang, "You are the God who performs miracles; you display your power among the peoples" (Ps. 77:14). We worship in the same manner as David when we practice this important act of worship:

> *Declare in song and prayer that God's power is being released into your needs and into the nations.*

All of this, of course, involves spiritual warfare. Our warfare is victorious only if God is in it. Worship, by enlisting God, assures us that He will be in it.

WINNING THROUGH WORSHIP

In both the Old and New Testaments we see evidence of this reality that *worship enlists God*. We recall the familiar account of King Jehoshaphat and the people of Judah facing the humanly insurmountable enemies of Moab and Ammon (see 2 Chron. 20:1-28). A great multitude of God's people had gathered to fast and pray regarding the ensuing battle, crying out to God for victory. As they humbled themselves before the Lord, the prophet Jahaziel stood in their midst, prophesying, "March down against them. . . . You will not have to fight this battle. Take up your positions; stand firm and see the deliverance the Lord will give you. . . . Do not be afraid; do not be discouraged" (vv. 16-17).

It seems this prophecy was somewhat confusing to both the king and his commanders. How does an army "march down" against an enemy and "take up" their positions, all suggesting movement, while "standing firm" and "not having to fight"? It makes little sense. It appears to be a call to step out and do nothing. This no doubt led to some discussion, because the Bible says, "After consulting the people, Jehoshaphat appointed men to sing to the LORD and to praise Him . . . as they went out at the head of the army" (v. 21).

Notice, in particular, the phrase "after consulting the people." It is clear that something prompted this consultation. Could it be that Jehoshaphat said to his captains and commanders, "God has told us to stand still because the victory is His, but He's also told us to move into position! Any suggestions?" I can imagine someone in the crowd responding, "Perhaps, O King, our position ought to be a position of worship, because God says He will come to dwell amid those who praise. Could it be that God is saying we will win through worship?"

Whatever was said during the consultation, we know that worship was the strategy chosen because of what happens next. The passage continues, "As they began to sing and praise, the LORD set ambushes against the men of Ammon and Moab and Mount Seir . . . and they were defeated" (v. 22). So massive was the victory that it required three full days to gather up all the spoils. Worship, clearly, had enlisted God.

Another worship victory can be found in the experience of Paul and Silas while incarcerated at Philippi. They were in a life-threatening situation, but then a miracle happened. The Bible reports, "Suddenly there was such a violent earthquake that the foundations of the prison were shaken. At once all the prison doors flew open" (Acts 16:26). Interestingly, this miracle took place *during* a worship encounter. When the earthquake occurred, Paul and Silas were both singing hymns and offering praise. Again, worship had enlisted God.

A FALLING WALL

A memorable journey my wife and I took with a small team of intercessors to the Buddhist land of Bhutan in 1998 significantly amplified this worship reality. I had been invited to speak at a conference of some 1,500 leaders from throughout the Himalayas who were meeting in Darjeeling, India. Our original plan for the journey included a visit first to Nepal for an Every Home for Christ leadership meeting for South Asia, followed by traveling directly to Darjeeling for the conference. But as my wife and I were making travel plans and looking at a map, I noticed, quite by accident, how very close our trip would take us to the tiny nation of Bhutan. For several years I had felt a burden to go to this closed Buddhist land to pray that it would be opened to the gospel. In late 1987 I had felt a similar burden regarding East Germany and the Berlin Wall.

At that time God had deeply burdened me in a late-night prayer encounter to confront the strongholds of communism in Eastern Europe. Immediately I saw in my mind, as the primary symbolic stronghold of the region, the Berlin Wall. More specifically, I felt God was calling me to go to Berlin and physically lay my hands on the wall, commanding it to come down "in Jesus' name." Interestingly, the total prayer assignment for the entire journey was to consist of a mere five words: "In Jesus' name, come down!"

The trip finally took place (after a month of prayer) in January 1988, and the five-word prayer became a reality. The following year, the wall came down, and Every Home for Christ saw immediate results. In less than six months after the wall fell, our West German EHC office received more than 120,000 requests from East Berlin and surrounding areas for Bible lessons about Jesus.

In the decade following, home-to-home literature campaigns were conducted in all Eastern European countries as well as throughout Russia and the former Soviet republics, touching tens of millions of households in this Greater Eurasia region.

Of course, I realized my prayers alone did not make all this happen, but I felt a small part of the miracle. Later I would hear a remarkable account of how, eight days before the first bulldozer broke through the Berlin Wall, a group of teenage worshipers from a West Berlin church climbed up on the wall and began singing choruses. West German soldiers were about to remove them when one of their officers said, "They're only singing songs about God, leave them be."

When the first bulldozer arrived, just over a week later, to break the first opening into the wall, it hit the same spot where the youth had been singing. I have often wondered, though I cannot confirm it, if that was the same spot where I placed my hands when praying my five-word prayer. I would not be surprised if it was!

FIRE AND THE DRAGON

As I realized how very close we would be to the border of Bhutan as we traveled to Darjeeling, I had a strange sense that this tiny "Dragon Kingdom" (the name given it by the people of Bhutan) would prove key to the ultimate evangelization and even transformation of all of the Himalayan nations, including China, Tibet, Nepal, India, Pakistan and even deeply troubled Afghanistan.

I contacted our director in Nepal to see if we would have enough time to travel to Bhutan—even if our visit was only an hour long. At least that would allow a few moments for prayer.

Our director's response came promptly; we learned that if we traveled an entire day by Jeep from the border of Nepal when our EHC meetings ended, we could reach Bhutan late that same evening and spend the night there. But only one night—it would be necessary to depart early the following morning for Darjeeling.

I asked about getting visas for Bhutan and received more encouraging news. Normally such visas take months to obtain. But our director explained that an international town, named Phuntsholing, on the border between India and Bhutan required no visa. Because the border runs down Main Street, a free flow of traffic was permitted back and forth at this particular point.

Bhutan's main border, with much more restrictive customs and immigration requirements, lies some 25 miles farther into the nation. So, praise God, no visas would be required to plant our feet on the soil of the Dragon Kingdom.

Following a grueling nine-hour drive from Nepal's eastern border, we finally arrived in Phuntsholing, Bhutan, late on a warm and misty Sunday night. It was April 19, 1998. The first building we saw was an ornate Buddhist temple and monastery. We knew immediately that this was to be the focal point for prayer later that evening. We quickly located a hotel (that had exactly the number of rooms we needed for our small team), and we dropped off our luggage so we could return to the temple.

We paired up and began walking quietly around the temple, declaring our prayers and praises over this tiny Dragon Kingdom of Bhutan. Although it's hardly a speck on a map, with a population considerably less than a million, I felt once again that Bhutan was somehow a key in God's plans for all of the Himalayas and that we were there as part of His purpose for the region. Even the fact that Bhutan is known as the Dragon Kingdom seemed significant. It reminded me that we were confronting the Prince of Darkness, who is referred to in Scripture as "the great dragon" (Rev. 12:9).

The youngest member of our team prayed an especially interesting prayer that night. He asked God to send fire from heaven to burn away the scales from the eyes of those who were bound in spiritual darkness by the spirit of Tibetan Buddhism. The young man could not recall what prompted those specific words, but they soon proved to be prophetic.

We returned to our rooms late that evening and wakened early enough the following morning to return to the temple for another season of prayer. This time we circled the temple seven times in intercessory worship. Interestingly, Buddhist priests and devout worshipers also were prayer walking around the temple. But their prayer walks included the spinning of small cylindrical prayer wheels that looked like colorfully painted, oversized tin cans. These were adorned with perhaps hundreds of hand-painted prayers to their gods.

In addition there were perhaps 20 such prayer wheels on each of the four walls of this beautifully decorated temple. A short staircase led to a portion of the temple that included two huge cylinders the size of giant oil drums, again colorfully decorated with prayers to their gods. These also could be rotated, but required considerably more effort.

CONFRONTING THE COMPETITION

Tibetan Buddhists believe that each time a wheel is spun, it sends these printed prayers into the heavenlies and to their gods. But now, even as these Buddhist devotees were circling their temple time after time, we also were prayer walking—engaging in intercessory worship. We were confronting the competition by enlisting God through our prayers and praises for all the people of the Himalayas.

Just before our departure from the temple, I climbed the stairs to the huge drums and placed my hands on them, just as I had done at the Berlin Wall a decade earlier. I was keenly aware that something significant was happening in the heavenlies.

We left Bhutan on schedule and traveled throughout the day over the treacherous one-lane roads heading up through the Himalayan foothills toward the mountain town of Darjeeling. More than once, I put my head out the window of our Jeep and looked straight down more than a mile and a half into the valley below. This was not too difficult to do as my side of the Jeep was actually hovering near the edge of the cliffs! I am sure we all learned some new ways to pray during that eight-hour journey up the mountain.

The conference in Darjeeling was inspiring and significant, involving more than 1,500 leaders representing 52 ministry strategies and organizations with a burden to evangelize the Himalayas.

I represented Every Home for Christ's specific contribution to the goals of the conference. Our part included working with several of these groups to take the gospel, in print or audio form, to every home in every village throughout the Himalayas. I also addressed the gathering on the role of prayer in completing the Great Commission.

It seemed unusually significant that the Lord sent us by way of Bhutan to declare His glory over this dark region before bringing us to Darjeeling to discuss ways to transform the Himalayas through the gospel. I had little idea, however, how truly significant that brief Bhutan encounter would prove to be.

THE FIRE FALLS

Dee and I left Darjeeling for New Delhi, India, where we had planned to set aside a few days for rest before heading to Europe for additional meetings. We especially looked forward to our first visit to the famed Taj Mahal, just a few hours' drive from India's capital.

Arriving at our hotel in New Delhi, I quickly went in search of the *International Herald Tribune*, anxious to see what news I had missed during the previous two weeks. Not only did I purchase the English edition for that particular day, but, being something of a "news nut" (to quote my wife), I also bought two older issues the bookshop had on hand. However, I only read that day's copy, setting aside the other two, intending to read them later.

After some much-needed rest and our day trip to the Taj Mahal, it was time to leave for Europe. We were hastily packing to head for the airport when I noticed the two unread newspapers, now more than a week old. I bent over to drop them into the wastebasket—and stopped abruptly.

I felt a strange impression, in the form of a question, *What if something important happened during those days that I was without a newspaper, and I missed it?* I paused momentarily above the trash basket and opened one of the folded papers. It was the older of the two unread editions, from Thursday of the previous week. My eyes instantly focused on a headline that leaped from the page. It read: "Fire Destroys a Famed Buddhist Shrine in Bhutan." I could hardly believe my eyes. Had not one of our team members actually prayed for fire to come down?

The paper certainly captured my attention. The article began: "The Taktsang Monastery in Bhutan, one of the oldest and best-known shrines in the Himalayan Buddhist world outside of Tibet, was destroyed by fire Sunday night, Bhutanese officials have announced."

The fire happened on the very night, April 19, when we had prayed around another temple monastery not far away, the one at the Bhutanese border town of Phuntsholing. That was where one of our team had prayed for fire to fall from heaven. The young brother had specifically asked God to send His fire to burn away the scales from the eyes of those blinded by the darkness of Tibetan Buddhism.

Little did I know at that time how significant the Taktsang monastery was to the practice of Buddhism throughout the Himalayas.

A DISAPPEARING DRAGON

The Taktsang temple monastery was built centuries ago on the face of a 2,500-foot cliff high above the road from Paro in Bhutan. This monastery, located on the Tibetan border near Mount Chomo Lhari, had existed since at least the ninth century.

According to the region's mythology, in the eighth century, a famous Buddhist saint from India, Guru Rimpoche, landed at the spot where the temple was later built, arriving on the back of a flying tiger and miraculously bringing Buddhism into the Himalayas from the plains of India. The word *Taktsang*, meaning "tiger's den," is derived from this legend. Buddhist historians believe that Rimpoche's teachings then spread to Tibet, perhaps along that very road from Paro to Mount Chomo Lhari. In other words, this temple was no ordinary temple. It is thought to be the primary point of entry of the spirit of Buddhism into all of the Himalayas, and particularly Tibet, the seat of Tibetan Buddhism.

The *Tribune* article concluded by quoting Kinley Dorji (editor of *Kuensel*, Bhutan's only newspaper), who had been to the Taktsang Monastery on the Tuesday following the fire. He described the monastery as "totally gone."[3]

Within days of the Taktsang fire, a team of Every Home for Christ workers began ministering in the mountainous regions of Tibet near the border of Nepal. In the very first villages visited, two Buddhists openly responded to the gospel and received Christ. Two days later, in a nearby village, two Buddhist priests, one the head of the local monastery, heard the gospel and also believed.

Then, following a nonstop, 14-hour trek at 17,000 feet, those same Christian workers came to a small village. In this single town, 70 villagers listened to the gospel and 4 made a public decision to accept Christ as Savior. The workers were later told that several others had received Christ but were afraid to declare their faith publicly.

The scales, indeed, seemed to be coming off the eyes of those who had been blinded by Buddhism. One year later I picked up a copy of the *Denver Post* and read an article that further convinced me that our prayers had had a continuing effect. Once again, the headline immediately grabbed my attention: "Bhutan's Monarch Embraces Democracy, Himalayan Style." The article began, "King Jigme Singye Wangchuck, leader of the Himalayas' last Buddhist monarchy, boasts four wives, a passion for basketball and a gilded throne. His latest infatuation is democracy."[4]

After explaining how the king enjoys watching NBA basketball via satellite television, the article continued, "In a series of dramatic moves, the king has charted a course aimed at preparing this fabled land of myth and magic for the tedious realities of self-rule." Realizing that our intercessory worship experience in Bhutan had been exactly one year earlier, I was especially stirred by the next statement:

> *Since last year,* the ruler of the Thunder Dragon People has fired his top advisers, surrendered day-to-day control of his government, and, most important, given a group of longtime yes-men the right to throw him off his own throne.[5]

Could there be a correlation between that intercessory worship encounter at Phuntsholing and the "since last year" of the newspaper article? More recently, while at a missions conference in Australia, I decided to share the story of my team's worship experience in Bhutan. To my amazement, before I was able to share my news, the host church's missions pastor presented a report of the congregation's past 12 months of missionary outreach—including a testimony about the miraculous planting of 14 New Testament fellowships within Bhutan in just the previous year.

Could it be that we are seeing the beginnings of a disappearing dragon in Bhutan? Is Satan, "the great dragon" (Rev. 12:9), starting to lose his grip on this tiny yet strategic stronghold called Bhutan? Could this mean the burning away of the scales from the eyes of multitudes of nonbelievers in all the Himalayas?

One thing is certain: Worship, when linked to intercession, does indeed enlist God. And enlisting God is essential to the transformation of nations through the gospel of Jesus Christ. Imagine how all this must excite the heart of God!

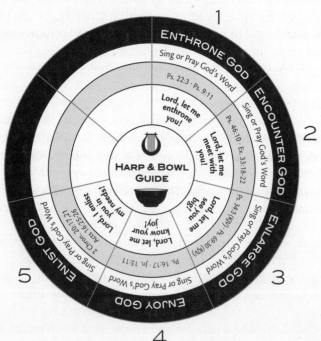

SIXTH REALITY

WORSHIP EXCITES GOD

A DANCE OF DELIGHT

A chill settled over the small wooded area near central Washington, DC, where I had been sitting beside a huge rock, somewhat uncomfortably, praising the Lord audibly for eight hours. Several years earlier, while reading the writings of A. W. Tozer and others on worship, I had felt an urge to someday set aside an entire day, from sunrise to sunset, just to praise God—audibly. I wanted to see what would happen if the only words I spoke for an entire day consisted of praise.

Now that day had arrived and most of it had passed. The goal of continuous, audible praise had nearly been achieved. By 4:30 in the afternoon, my voice was getting weary, and the wooded area I had discovered at 7:30 A.M. (I needed a place where I could be secluded for the entire day) was getting cool as the sun began its descent.

Little could I have known that I was about to be introduced, firsthand, to what I would later come to see as one of the most significant of these worship realities: *Worship excites God.* This reality is more fully described in a simple 14-word intercessory worship principle:

> *Worship provides the only true position from which we might bring God pure pleasure.*

THE WARMTH OF WORSHIP

My day of continuous praise came about when I traveled to Washington, DC, for America's National Day of Prayer, scheduled for the first Thursday in May. I arrived in the DC area in time to speak on the preceding Sunday at the Church of the Apostles, an Episcopal church where I was to conduct our Change the World School of Prayer the following Saturday.

As I prepared for the activities of that week, I realized Tuesday was free of all meetings. Nothing was on my schedule. No luncheon, dinner or appointments were planned for the day. I knew it would be the perfect occasion to fulfill my dream of a day of praise.

When Tuesday arrived, I arose early with my list of praise Scriptures in hand and set out to find a quiet place somewhere near our nation's Capitol to spend the day in praise.

Driving along the George Washington Parkway, I spotted a large wooded area not too far from the center of the city. I parked my rental car beside the road and, with my Bible and praise list, headed into the woods. I was encouraged when I found a small clearing, quite secluded, with a huge rock where I could sit (or stand) and praise the Lord for the rest of the day.

This was not to be a day of meditation, contemplation or quiet Bible reading. It was to be a day of nothing but audible praise. I had even begun compiling numerous pages of praise Scriptures to help me fulfill this dream if and when this day came.

Now it was almost five o'clock in the evening, and a heavy chill had settled in. As I looked toward the center of the clearing, a ray of sunlight streaked its way through the thick trees, making that part of the clearing look a bit warmer. So I stood and walked toward the warmth. But more than anything, I wanted to experience the warmth of God's presence through my worship.

By now my voice had grown hoarse and weak from this day of praise. I was running out of expressions of praise. I had spoken every Scripture on my list at least twice. I also had exhausted various praise postures, though I am sure this did not matter to God. I had *sat* in praise, *stood* in praise, *knelt* in praise and even *walked* the clearing several times in praise. The thought, *What else can I do?* crossed my mind.

DELIGHTING GOD

As I stood in the clearing, trying to catch the sun for a little warmth, I inwardly longed to reach up and touch God. This desire that seized me is hard to express in words. On the one hand, I wanted to feel God, but on the other, I merely desired to please Him.

Then a rather surprising thought came to my mind. I longed to do something I had never done before in worship, public or private. I looked toward the top of the clearing and said, "Lord, there is one act of worship I've read about often in Scripture but have never done." I added, "Lord, I know King David did it, and You said he was a man after Your own heart."

Oddly, I felt as if I needed to explain all this to God, as if He had no idea what I was thinking. So I continued, "Father, David danced before You with all his might, and I know this is something I've never done."

Somewhat ashamed, I added, "In fact, You know I've often considered people who do stuff like this overly emotional or even strange. Besides, I'm not even sure I know how to do it properly."

My explanation was really more to myself than it was to God, as I continued: "Lord, I do know the Hebrew word for dance means to 'whirl about,' so I guess that's what I'm supposed to do." Tearfully I added, "Lord, I'm just running out of words to praise You, so I think I'll just whirl about for a few minutes. Here goes!"

What happened next was totally unplanned on my part, and it was probably humorous to God. I started moving my feet up and down as I spun about. Then I started hopping. Soon I was whirling, hopping and spinning—with a periodic awkward leap thrown in for good measure. At one point I honestly thought I might hurt myself. Plus, I was quickly running out of breath.

My dance had lasted probably only 7 to 10 minutes when I started to laugh. The entire experience suddenly seemed hilarious. I was sure that if a passerby had seen me they would have thought I was a lunatic. Yet, I continued dancing, leaping and now laughing. Then, I stopped and looked up, asking, "God, is this right?"

I really wondered if what I was doing mattered. What I felt next I will never forget—and it moved me immediately to more tears. I knew God was speaking as I heard, *You'll never know the joy you're giving Me. You delight Me with your dance.*

I fell to my knees in that clearing, weeping. Nothing could have meant more to me than the sense that my worship had excited the heart of God. Indeed, in spite of those theologians who explain that God does not actually need our worship, I knew I was making God happy. Worship, I now understood, truly excites God. It is the only thing that really brings Him pure pleasure.

A SACRIFICE OF DELIGHT

To this point, each of our worship realities has focused primarily on the impact worship has on *us*—our personal growth and spiritual warfare, as well as our mission in life. Here we examine how our worship brings delight to the heart of our Lord.

Notice these words of the psalmist as he describes the focus of God's delight: "Praise his name with dancing, accompanied by tambourine and harp. For the LORD delights in his people; he crowns the humble with salvation" (Ps. 149:3-4, *NLT*).

Here God's delight in His people is described in the context of their worship. Further, this theme is linked to spiritual warfare as it impacts the nations. The psalm continues: "Let the praises of God be in their mouths, and a sharp sword in their hands—to execute vengeance on the nations" (Ps. 149:6-7, *NLT*). As in numerous other places in the psalms, praise and worship are described in a context of touching all the earth, which is surely a reason praise so delights the heart of God (see Pss. 66:1-4,8; 67; 96:1-3,7-10; 98:1-4).

Generations later, the author of the book of Hebrews would explain more clearly why praise delights God. He wrote: "Through Jesus, therefore, let us continually offer to God a sacrifice of praise—the fruit of lips that confess his name" (Heb. 13:15). *Praise-filled worship is a sacrifice.* Hebrews 13:15 makes this clear. It is choice fruit offered to God. Thus, worship becomes the one true sacrifice we can give God that truly brings Him delight. It's simple to apply this principle daily:

> *Declare in song and prayer your desire to excite the Lord through your worship and obedience.*

Of course, God has all He needs within Himself and, in that sense, needs nothing. However, we also recognize He had a reason for creating humankind. Indeed, the powerful picture of praise around God's throne in Revelation 4 concludes with the living creatures and elders prostrating themselves, declaring, "You are worthy, our Lord and God, to receive glory and honor and power, for you created all things, and by your will they were created and have their being" (Rev. 4:11). The *New Living Translation* reads: "You created everything, and it is *for your pleasure* that they exist and were created" (emphasis added).

It is obvious, here, that all creation exists for God's pleasure, which naturally suggests there is something special about God's purpose in creating humankind. Of all creation, only human beings have the capacity to reason and understand what praise and adoration are all about. In addition, we have been given the ability to sing this adoration as well as to see and comprehend the beauty of creation.

Animals might show forth God's beauty by their very existence, or, as in the case of the birds, glorify God through their songs, but they don't have the gift of reason to recognize what they are actually doing. Neither can they comprehend the true beauty of what they see with their eyes.

A. W. Tozer believed that God made the flowers and the birds, and, indeed, all the wonders of creation, simply so that we might delight in Him. This wise worshiper explained that any ordinary believer could tell you that God created those flowers to be beautiful and the birds to sing so that we might enjoy them. Scientists, however, will suggest that a male bird sings primarily to attract the female so they might nest and procreate—it is really all just instinctively biological. Tozer responds with this conclusion:

> It is at this point that I ask the scientist, "Why doesn't the bird just squeak and groan or gurgle? Why does he have to sing and warble and harmonize as though he had been tuned to a harp?" I think the answer is plain—it is because God made him to sing. If I were a male bird and wanted to attract a female I could turn handsprings or do any number of tricks. But why does the bird sing so beautifully? It is because the God who made him is the Chief Musician of the universe. He is the Composer of the cosmos. He made the harp in those little throats and the feathers around them and said, "Go and sing."[1]

Singing is God's idea!

HEAVENLY MUSIC

What about God Himself? Does He only enjoy listening to music, or does He make music? One of the most fascinating passages of Scripture concerning God's delight in His people is found in Zephaniah.

Here the prophet records, "For the LORD your God has arrived to live among you. He is a mighty savior. He will rejoice over you with great gladness. With his love, he will calm all your fears. He will exult over you by singing a happy song" (Zeph. 3:17, *NLT*). The *New International Version* translates that last sentence: "He will take great delight in you, he will quiet you with his love, he will rejoice over you with singing."

Compare Zephaniah 3:17 with Revelation 4:11, mentioned earlier, where we are told that everything God has created is for His "pleasure" (*KJV, NLT*). God clearly delights in His children and seems to be especially delighted as we worship Him. In fact, it appears that God delights in Himself in delighting in us even as we are delighting in Him—something you may want to think about for a moment before reading on!

Author John Piper helps tie all this together and links it powerfully to fulfilling the Great Commission in his provocative book *Let the Nations Be Glad*. Piper writes:

> The most passionate heart for God in all the universe is God's heart. This truth, more than any other I know, seals the conviction that worship is the fuel and goal of missions. The deepest reason why our passion for God should fuel missions is that God's passion for God fuels missions. Missions is the overflow of our delight in God because missions is the overflow of God's delight in being God. And the deepest reason why worship is the goal in missions is that worship is God's goal. We are confirmed in this goal by the Biblical record of God's relentless pursuit of praise among the nations. "Praise the Lord, all nations! Extol him, all peoples!" (Ps. 117:1). If it is God's goal it must be our goal.[2]

No doubt God delights in our worship precisely because such worship ultimately will establish His purpose for all of humankind—that the earth will be "filled with the knowledge of the glory of the LORD, as the waters cover the sea" (Hab. 2:14; see also Isa. 11:9). In other words, worship leads to even more and greater worship.

John Piper further addresses the theological challenge of God's passion for Himself causing Him seemingly to require our worship—something that over the centuries has caused some to wonder if God is a bit egotistical in His quest for worship. Concerning this enigma, Piper points us again to the old Westminster Catechism:

> What I am claiming is that the answer to the first question of the Westminster Catechism is the same when asked concerning God as it is when asked concerning man. Question: "What is the chief end of man?" Answer: "The chief end of man is to glorify God, and enjoy him forever." Question: "What is the chief end of God?" Answer: "The chief end of God is to glorify God and enjoy himself forever."[3]

Piper expands on this thought by explaining the impact the Puritan revivalist Jonathan Edwards had on his thinking:

> God's passion for God is unmistakable. God struck me with this most powerfully when I first read Jonathan Edward's book entitled *The Dissertation Concerning the End for Which God Created the World*. There he piles reason upon reason and scripture on scripture to show this truth: "The great end of God's works, which is so variously expressed in Scripture, is indeed but ONE; and this one end is most properly and comprehensively called, THE GLORY OF GOD." In other words, the chief end of God is to glorify God, and enjoy himself for ever.[4]

IGNITING THE FLAME

All of this serves to underscore the reality that *worship excites God*. It excites God because God is excited with Himself and knows that humankind can only experience ultimate excitement *in Him*. It is that simple! This reality is also precisely why intercessory worship is so important in carrying out God's plans.

Someday, indeed, from every village on earth, even from every dwelling, the smoke of the incense of worship will rise in adoration to our heavenly Father. As John Piper dreams, "When the flame of worship burns with the heat of God's true worth, the light of missions will shine to the most remote peoples on earth."[5]

Recognition of God's true worth, then, ought to ignite within us a flame of such fervent intercessory worship that we are overwhelmed with a new zeal to touch and transform our families, neighbors and nations. Toward this end, let us risk something of our "religious" dignity in a humble attempt to excite the heart of God. I feared hurting myself—or at least, embarrassing myself—while dancing in those woods in Washington, but I knew my praise delighted God. Even history's great worship mentors sometimes struggled in their worship. Tozer said it well: "I cannot sing a lick, but that is nobody's business. God thinks I'm an opera star! I mean it when I say that I would rather worship God than do anything else on earth."[6]

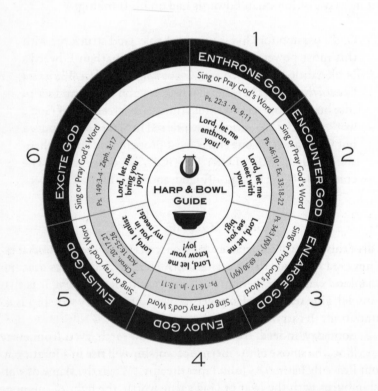

8

SEVENTH REALITY

WORSHIP EXALTS GOD

CATCHING THE WAVE OF WORSHIP

"What on earth is that?" my wife asked as she looked at a map of the world that was taped to the steering wheel of our car. It was December 1975.

"It's a map of the world," I answered—as if she couldn't tell what it was from two feet away.

"I can see that," she added, "but why would you tape it to the steering wheel?"

So began my daily prayer journey to the nations that has continued joyously for more than three decades. It is a deeply personal journey that I have been reluctant to describe in print, though it seems appropriate here as it relates so clearly to our final worship reality. (More about this unusual daily prayer journey to the nations in a moment!)

All that has been discussed in the previous chapters, I believe, can be summed up in this final worship reality: *Worship exalts God!* In exalting God through intercessory worship we not only *enthrone* Him and *encounter* Him, but also *enlarge, enjoy, enlist* and *excite* Him.

All of this results in exalting God, which is at the heart of all true worship and leads to the ultimate fulfillment of God's plan for humankind. That plan, I am convinced, is the completion of Christ's Bride and all the earth being filled with God's transforming glory (see Isa. 11:9; Hab. 2:14).

FURNACE-ROOM ENCOUNTERS

The psalmist lays this important foundation for worship reality seven: "I will praise you, O Lord, among the nations; I will sing of you among the peoples. . . . Be exalted, O God, above the heavens; let your glory be over all the earth" (Ps. 57:9,11). As mentioned in the previous chapter, we find many similar expressions throughout the psalms where praise is pictured as impacting the nations. In this particular admonition, these words stand out: "Let your glory be over all the earth."

Stated succinctly as our final intercessory worship principle:

Worship provides the platform and power necessary to exalt God in the nations.

John Piper again provides insight: "Worship . . . is the fuel and goal in missions. It's the goal of missions because in missions we simply aim to bring the nations into the white-hot enjoyment of God's glory. The goal of missions is the gladness of the peoples in the greatness of God. Missions begins and ends in worship."[1]

Piper concludes, "Missions is not the ultimate goal of the church. Worship is. Missions exists because worship does not. The Great Commission is first to delight yourself in the Lord (Ps. 37:4) and then to declare 'Let the nations be glad and sing for joy' (Ps. 67:4)."[2]

Interestingly, it was God's reminder to me, during the first day of my 40-day worship fast, that I was to delight in Him over the nations that set in motion all that I am sharing in these pages. Prior to that time, I'm not sure I ever equated delighting in the Lord with fulfilling the Great Commission.

That brings me back to the map on the steering wheel.

Very early in my ministry, I began sensing a special burden for the nations of the world. This burden grew out of prolonged seasons of seeking God simply for the sake of seeking God. In other words, my passion for the nations began with a passion just to know and seek the Lord. The church in southern Wisconsin where Dee and I served as youth leaders, long before the map experience, had a furnace room that I quickly commandeered for prayer because it was a warm place to sit alone during our freezing Wisconsin winters. Interestingly, it also was the coolest place to pray in Wisconsin's steamy summers.

I would retreat to this furnace room for extended times of prayer when I felt I needed to be alone and unhindered. It was in that room that a burden for the lost and for the nations slowly began to saturate my praying. It seemed that the more I sought the heart of God, the more I had a heart for the nations. The nations were clearly on God's heart!

A particularly powerful passage of God's Word that significantly impacted those early years was the psalmist's declaration of intercessory worship in Psalm 67. We read:

> May God be gracious to us and bless us and make his face shine upon us . . . that your ways may be known on earth, your salvation among all nations. May the peoples praise you, O God; may all the peoples praise you. . . . God will bless us, and all the ends of the earth will fear him (Ps. 67:1-3,7).

The Living Bible paraphrases that last verse: "Peoples from remotest lands will worship him," a thought that would become my lifelong obsession and so became a personal "life passage" of Scripture.

JACK'S MAP

The morning that I taped the map to my steering wheel, Dee and I and our two young daughters, Dena and Ginger (at the time just six and three), were preparing to visit Dee's sister and brother-in-law in Portland, Oregon, for the Christmas holidays. Six months earlier I had met Jack McAlister, the founder and president of Every Home for Christ. The ministry was then known as World Literature Crusade.

Jack was pretty much responsible for the whole map episode. He had added significant fuel to the fire of my heart for the nations. When I first met Jack, I had no idea that a year later I would join him and his worldwide organization as their director of prayer mobilization. Nor could I have known that 12 years later I would become the ministry's international president.

For years, Jack had annually produced what he called the World Prayer Map, a simple map of the world that could be folded up and placed in one's Bible. Jack's map listed all the 210 nations of that time in various strategic categories (e.g., all the communist nations in a group, all the Arab-Muslim nations together, and so forth).

In my first meeting with Jack, in May of 1975, he handed me one of these maps and rather pointedly asked me how many nations of the world I prayed for daily. I told him two—China and America—which was stretching the truth a bit, because I probably prayed for China every third or fourth day.

My prayers up to that time were much more geographically general—for souls and missionaries wherever they might be. My petitions were vague in other ways as well. I prayed many "bless 'em" prayers: bless the lost, bless the missionaries and bless all the churches in the whole wide world! Jack did not seem impressed.

Not one to skirt issues, Jack suggested, with a bit of a smile, "Maybe that's why so little is happening in so much of the world! You're only praying for 2 nations out of 210."

This unique leader, whom I had only met about 30 minutes earlier, concluded more seriously, "You know, Dick, God answers specific prayers because praying specifically requires faith. Here, take this map. Maybe it will help you pray more specifically."

I had never met someone quite so blunt, and that one encounter with him changed my prayer life. Conviction settled that day, and I determined I would pray for many more countries in the future. Because a systematic plan always helps me remain faithful, I decided to pray for a grouping of 30 countries each day. I divided the 210 countries by seven, one group for each day of the week, and marked off these listings on the map accordingly. (I counted 30 nations and drew a line in ink, then counted another 30, and so on.) This all began in the early summer of 1975.

About midway through the following December, as I prayed over my 30 countries for a particular day, an overwhelming concern for the 180 nations I had not prayed for came over me.

Tears came as I held the map in my hands, praying. I proceeded to pray for all the remaining nations and then clutched the map silently for a few moments. Quietly I prayed, "God, if you'll just give me the strength and desire, I'll try to make this a daily habit for the rest of my life."

I knew it was a challenging commitment, but I felt I had to try.

Next, I decided to commit these countries to memory to help my prayer be more than merely reading a list, and I felt that a good time to do this would be during the long drive from Sacramento to

Portland, and back, over the holidays. I knew that I could glance down periodically at the map and memorize the countries during the trip. By the time we returned from Portland, I had indeed committed all 210 country names to memory. It was less of a challenge than one might think. Thus, the map taped to the steering wheel!

A Journey to the Nations

So began my daily journey of prayer to the nations—a journey that has continued, as of this writing, for more than 35 years. Little could I have known how Jack's challenge and this world focus would impact my life and ministry. When I first memorized these nations, I did not learn them in alphabetical order, but rather committed them to memory according to Jack's geographical and political listings.

As I mentioned earlier, Jack grouped all the communist nations in one list for special prayer. He did the same for all the Arab-Muslim nations. Then, all the islands and smaller nations with populations of fewer than a million people each appeared on a separate list. These various listings were added below the map itself, which showed all the continents and their respective nations. Each nation in these various categories also had a number that corresponded to its location on the map itself.

When I began praying for all these nations, I was not even working for the EHC ministry. But within a year, at Jack's invitation, I had joined the EHC staff as the director of prayer mobilization (a position few ministries had at that time) and soon became a part of the answers to the very prayers I had been praying.

I specifically recall an experience that took place 17 years after I memorized the nations from Jack's map. It was 1992. By that time, Jack had long since retired, and I had been appointed the international president of EHC and was still praying daily for all the nations.

So here I was in my prayer closet in Colorado, where the ministry had relocated in 1991, praying once again for all the nations, in the same order that I had first memorized back in 1975. As I came to my mental list of the communist lands, I began praying for each by name. Tears unexpectedly began to flow as I was overwhelmed by a sudden realization of the power of simply exalting God over the nations, day by day, year after year.

You see, when I had begun that daily discipline some 17 years earlier, none of the communist lands was open to any free expressions of religious faith. Home-to-home evangelism of a systematic nature, such as Every Home for Christ conducts, was strictly forbidden in each of them. What little evangelism was happening in those nations was highly clandestine. By 1992, all but two were open to some degree. Only Laos and North Korea still seemed totally closed.

Not only were all but these two nations open to the gospel in some measure, but Every Home for Christ was also working directly in all of them but those two. A few years before, the Berlin Wall had come crashing down, and all of Eastern Europe was suddenly open to the gospel. Just in the former Soviet Union, more than 2 million households were reached by Every Home for Christ in the first twelve months after that dramatic event!

A few days before my 1992 prayer encounter, word had reached our headquarters in Colorado Springs that an Every Home initiative had been officially approved in the once highly restricted communist nation of Albania.

We were especially amazed to hear that Albania's new president had actually invited our newly appointed EHC coordinator for Albania to his home and personally served him afternoon tea. The Albanian president also gave EHC his personal blessing to launch an effort to take the printed gospel message to every home in Albania (eventually touching some 800,000 homes where 3.5 million Albanians live).

Seventeen years earlier, when my daily prayers for all the nations had begun, Albania was a place in which it had been a capital crime to be a Christian or even possess a Bible. Now it was being saturated with the good news of Jesus!

FORTY DAYS OF DELIGHT

Something else special and unexpected was to happen as my 40-day worship fast began in March of 2000.

You will recall that God impressed on my heart that I was to spend my times of daily prayer, for 40 days, entirely in worship. I was to sing all my prayers. This posed for me an interesting dilemma. For 25 years (at that time), I had prayed daily for all the nations, in addition to my usual focuses of prayer. Now it seemed God was leading me to worship Him purely in song during these times of prayer.

"Lord," I asked, during the first day of my worship fast, "are you asking me to suspend my usual daily intercessory prayers for the nations for the next 40 days?"

The Lord responded with His own question: *Did not My servant David sing among the nations?*

Immediately, I recalled that passage in the psalms where King David declared, "I will thank you, Lord, in front of all the people. I will sing your praises among the nations" (Ps. 57:9, *NLT*).

The Lord then spoke again: *Instead of praying for the nations each day during these coming 40 days, I want you to sing over the nations, daily, declaring My glory in song among all these peoples.*

So it was that 40 days of delightful, if unusual, intercessory worship followed. Each day my made-up song was different, as I exalted God by singing over the 227 nations that Every Home for Christ now lists on its updated World Prayer Map.

A Many-faceted Movement

Intercessory worship is central to the accelerated harvest taking place throughout the world today. I agree with Mike Bickle, who wrote:

> The Holy Spirit is orchestrating a global strategy far eclipsing any other prayer movement in history. This movement will be comprised of many diverse models and streams within the Body of Christ. This many-faceted prayer movement will result in an unprecedented harvest of souls and the completing of the Great Commission. It will become common to hear [of] "intercessory worship" ministries that continue non-stop 24 hours a day.[3]

In addition to the International House of Prayer in Kansas City, the growing prayer movement simply named "24/7" also reflects a passionate worship emphasis. Born in Chichester on England's south coast among mostly young students, 24/7 has spread to scores of nations. The ministry has been described in various ways: as a non-stop global prayer meeting, as a new monasticism for the twenty-first century and, perhaps most uniquely, as "a virus spread around the world as a result of God's holy sneeze." Out of this movement have been born literally hundreds of "day and night" prayer rooms in which participants take set times of one hour (or more) to form unbroken chains of prayer.

Another notable example of this spreading 24/7 fervor featuring prayer and worship combined is occurring throughout Indonesia. According to John Robb, chairman of the International Prayer Connection, Indonesia's greater prayer movement has grown to at least 5 million intercessors involving some 500 city and ministry prayer networks. Additionally, there is a strong, well-coordinated Indonesian children's prayer network (called Children in Prayer) representing some 100 cities and involving 200,000 trained child intercessors.

Indonesian Christians also have pioneered "prayer towers" in numerous cities, many of which are manned 24/7. According to Robb, one Indonesian leader known across the region simply as Pastor Niko leads a growing network estimated at 200,000 intercessors involving as many as 800 churches. Niko's ministry has recently completed a 12,000-seat World Prayer Center in Sentul City near Indonesia's capital, Jakarta. It features a 13-story tower with an area devoted exclusively for 24/7 intercession.

Project Luke 18, yet another emerging 24/7 prayer movement (unrelated to the UK movement), has already established more than a thousand day and night prayer ministries on college and university campuses across America. Their goal is to see all 2,600 four-year accredited campuses in America have day and night intercessory worship. Led by a young leader named Brian Kim, Project Luke 18 doesn't intend to stop there—they have already begun training teams to take their intercessory worship vision to the nations. (More about this unique vision is shared in part two of this book.) Interestingly, in all of these places a wide range of streams from throughout Christ's Body are becoming involved. You, too, can join this movement daily:

Declare in song and prayer that God is exalted over every need, opportunity and nation on earth.

A SHOCKWAVE OF PRAISE

Could it be that this growing river of intercessory worship—the harp and bowl model inspired by Rev. 5:8-10—will lead to what some refer to as a global "Christ Awakening" that heralds a literal completion of the Great Commission?

Joseph Garlington, one our nation's gifted worship leaders, offers this provocative observation: "One of the things undergirding the expansion of the Kingdom of God is a new concept of praise. Something mighty is taking place in the earth. Praise and worship are at the center of what is happening. . . . The shock wave of our praise is unaffected by distance, different time zones, or different languages, cultures, and political systems. It is a spiritual force to be reckoned with, and the Church is just now catching on to this truth."[4]

Has there been any specific evidence that any of this has already begun? You'll recall the vision that I described at the outset of this book: smoke wafting from thousands of villages across the Gwembe Valley of southern Zambia and beyond. God showed me this was the incense of worship rising from vast numbers of villages turning to Christ. At the time of my vision, the people of that region were among the most unreached in all of Africa. Our ministry had no work there and did not know of a single church in the 920 villages of the Gwembe. Today, almost every known village of the Valley has been visited (home by home and hut by hut), and new churches have been planted in more than 600 of the villages. This all began, not long after my vision experience, when an Every Home for Christ leader led the paramount chief of the region to faith in Christ. That chief would later hold his Bible high on different occasions and say boldly, "I'm your number one evangelist in the Gwembe Valley!" Since that time, hundreds of young pastors and evangelists have been trained and continue to plant even more churches in the remaining villages. The smoke of the incense of worship is indeed rising from all parts of the Gwembe Valley. (Visit Every Home for Christ's website, www.ehc.org, to view a brief video simply titled "Zambia" for a greater picture of this miracle.)

Elsewhere we have seen equally encouraging harvest advances. Consider how the following statistics have changed since we began embracing this intercessory worship model. In 2000, our ministry followed up with approximately 750,000 people who responded to our home-to-home campaigns. At the time of this writing, about a decade later, we are seeing considerably more than that number respond *every month*. Indeed, in the past 12 months the total exceeded 13,500,000. (This number represents the number of follow-up Bible courses given to those who indicate they have prayed to receive Christ as Savior or want to know how to become a Christian.)

Every Home for Christ's church planting initiatives have grown dramatically in this same time frame. In 2000, we were seeing approximately four fellowships of new believers (we call these "Christ Groups") established daily, or some 1,500 for the year. We rejoiced in that number at the time but could not have imagined what was yet to come. In the past 12 months (again, as this is being written), the number has increased to 58 a day, or almost 22,000 for a 12-month period. Other ministry leaders report similar advances that at times are difficult to explain. A Southern Baptist leader told me they had seen 27,000 new fellowships planted in the most recent year.

The one thing that I see as creating a climate for such an impact is the rise of intercessory worship during this same decade-long period. Consider that at the start of the new century, ministries like the International House of Prayer in Kansas City were only a few months old, and the 24/7 movement out of the UK mentioned earlier was just being birthed. The now highly regarded annual Global Day of Prayer (with as many as 300 million people praying and worshiping each Pentecost Sunday) was yet to be born (that occurred in 2001), and Every Home for Christ wouldn't build its Jericho Center, where intercessory worship would ultimately rise day and night, until 2003. It seems like an earthquake (or should I say heaven-quake?) of divine proportions is causing a supernatural tsunami of signs and wonders now sweeping across the shores of needy nations.

Intercessory worship is, indeed, a wave of transformation—and a big one at that. Nothing short of re-formation and reform in the attitude and understanding of the Church when it comes to what we're referring to as intercessory worship is clearly underway. It is happening today, as I mentioned briefly earlier, in what some refer to as "the restoration of the Tabernacle of David." It's the theme of part two of this book. It took me nearly a lifetime to see its significance, and that finally happened through a song. It was my song, never sung before and never to be sung again. It was arguably (technically speaking) the worst song ever sung. I sang it to an audience of one, and soon afterward my eyes were opened to what I now believe is a vital key to the great harvest yet to come. This is how it happened . . .

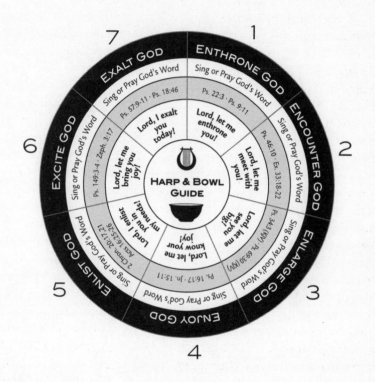

PART TWO

REFORMS

Worship Transformation

A Song for a Stranger

"Is this a joke?" I asked the Lord as I looked at my watch lying on the nightstand. It was past midnight. I was lying in a bed I had never slept in before, at the home of a businessman I had met only a few hours earlier.

Now God was instructing me to do something in worship that seemed odd—if not bizarre—in the presence of this stranger I was visiting.

This is not a joke, came the strong impression in my heart—an impression I have come to recognize over the years as the still, small voice of God.

The voice continued, *I want you to do it right after breakfast, when you share Every Home for Christ's* Completing the Commission *ministry plan with Bill.*

Bill Williams is unique—a delightful man, never married, who has a radical, though quiet, passion for God.[1] I first met Bill through Ruth Mizell, a board member for Every Home for Christ who had served as a White House aide to the first President George Bush. Ruth's husband, the late Wilmer "Vinegar Bend" Mizell, a congressman and former Major League baseball player, had previously served on our board. When Wilmer passed away, Ruth agreed to take his place.

One Stream

It was during Ruth's first board meeting that she heard the plans and details for our international ministry project, The Jericho Center. It was but a dream at the time. Our ministry had felt compelled to build this facility to host consultations with organizations seeking to establish strategic partner alliances among ministries, churches and other organizations, thus helping to fulfill the Great Commission. It was also to be a center for non-stop intercessory worship to cover these alliances and strategies for impacting the nations. Jericho, of course, was where God's tribes, though known for their bickering, murmuring and arguing, came together as one to obey God in a divinely given worship strategy that resulted in His supernatural intervention.

I shared with our EHC board my conviction that God was about to do a new work in Christ's Body, bringing its many tributaries together as one river and that we needed to be a part of it. I was careful to explain that although there had been many attempts to do this very thing (some with modestly positive results), nothing compared to what was yet needed had been done. This could only happen, I explained, with God's supernatural intervention. It had to be a Jericho-like victory—complete unity, saturated in worship and welcoming God's involvement.

As I stressed at that meeting, it takes a supernatural work just to get a few core leaders united to pray about meaningfully working together. Many are too busy doing their own thing, as if they could finish the task alone. The fact is that these ministry efforts, if strategically woven together as one and bathed in sustained worship, could accomplish the task—practically overnight. At least that is what I believed.

I anticipated the question: "How would this center be different from other similar projects?" I responded with what I felt was the key. The center and its vision, I proposed, needed to be built around 24-hour-a-day intercessory worship—a combination of both intercession and worship that would saturate every consultation and planning session with God's presence and power. All these plans needed to be God-saturated, and intercessory worship was vital to seeing this happen.

I reminded the board of something I mentioned in an earlier chapter of this book: One Japanese translation of Psalm 22:3 reads, "When God's people praise Him, He brings a big chair and sits there."[2] We need God to bring a big chair (i.e., His throne) into our planning meetings and sit there, I suggested. Continuous worship will help make this happen.

Providing a further foundation for the board to understand the need for both worship and intercession at The Jericho Center, I drew their attention again to Revelation 5:8-10, that passage describing the Harp and Bowl theme of intercessory worship that I explained in depth earlier in this book.

I highlighted again how heavenly worshipers came before Jesus, the Lamb, holding harps and bowls—the harps representing worship and the bowls intercession. A new song was then sung that unmistakably focused on the harvest. The song included these words: "You were slain, and with your blood you purchased men for God from every tribe and language and people and nation" (Rev. 5:9).

"That is what we are about," I told the board, "and not just us, but all of Christ's Body! History's greatest harvest is yet to be gathered in, and the Church is about to unite as never before, saturated in a harp-and-bowl intercessory worship atmosphere. Intercession, saturated in worship, will create a climate for the most productive evangelism advances in history."

Ruth Mizell took it all in and, as is typical for Ruth, began to think of all the acquaintances with whom she felt the need to share this vision.

"Have you ever heard of Bill Williams?" Ruth asked me during a break in our meeting.

I responded, "Not that I recall, Ruth."

"He has continuous worship music playing in his homes, both here in the States and in his residences in Jerusalem."

Ruth then explained that in addition to Bill's residences in America, he had two houses side by side in the heart of Jerusalem, one of which was devoted specifically to worship.

"I really think you should share this vision with Bill," Ruth suggested. I told her I would be more than happy to do so, and she offered to contact him on my behalf.

A Sleepless Night

Ruth called Bill that weekend. Three weeks later, I found myself struggling to fall asleep in Bill's guest room at one of his residences, a condominium in South Texas. But sleep was not to come that night; I was still wide awake when the sun rose over the warm Gulf waters of Galveston.

I am not sure I can do this, I thought, reflecting on what I was certain God had told me in the middle of the night to do. *How did I get myself into this?* I wondered.

I had arrived the night before just in time for dinner with Bill. After we ate, I shared briefly some of the plans Every Home for Christ had for the immediate months ahead—as well as our ambitious long-term goal to take the gospel to every home on earth. I suggested to Bill that I would like to share more about our plans, including details about how the proposed Jericho Center might help facilitate the vision, just after breakfast the following morning. Bill agreed.

Then we retired for the night. As I lay in bed, I could hear the soft worship music playing in the background. Ruth had been right—it never stopped. *What a beautiful, restful atmosphere,* I thought as I tried to drift off to sleep. That is when I heard God speak.

I have a special message I want you to give Bill, came the impression. *My message includes two passages of Scripture: Psalm 27 and Psalm 149. I want you to share them as a gift for Bill right after breakfast.*

This seemed like a relatively easy thing to do, not unlike other assignments I have felt the Lord impress upon me when visiting people. But as I lay there thinking about reading these two passages to my new friend, the Lord added something startling.

I don't want you to read these passages to Bill, came the impression. *I want you to sing them over him—in his presence. I want you to do it right after breakfast.*

That is when I thought, *Is this a joke?*—a question to which I knew the answer as quickly as I had thought the question.

Understandably, I did not sleep the rest of the night. You do not go into the home of someone you have met only a few hours before and sing a song over him—one that you have never sung before. At least, I had never done that or known anyone who had. Also, I am not a singer. I was sick the entire night.

As Bill and I sat down for breakfast, my heart was racing with the thought of the assignment given in the night. After breakfast I suggested the possibility of our praying together, and Bill graciously agreed. I was inwardly wrestling with just how to explain to Bill the impressions I had received the night before. Finally the courage came, and I told my new friend what had happened.

"Bill," I said somewhat haltingly, "I believe God spoke to me in the night with a message for you."

Bill, not one for a lot of words, nodded and said simply, "That's good!"

"Actually, Bill, God gave me two messages for you. Both are passages from Psalms."

Bill smiled and commented, "That's even better."

The difficult part had arrived.

"Bill," I said after a brief pause, "I believe God has told me I'm not to read these passages to you, but I'm to sing them over you."

With an inquisitive look, Bill just said, "That would be interesting."

I offered a brief spoken prayer, inviting God's presence, which really was an attempt at stalling until a little more courage came for me to sing. It is not uncommon for me to sing alone to the Lord, making up songs as I go. I actually do this daily with the psalms. But to do it in front of a stranger was a stretch.

SUDDENLY SINGING

Suddenly I was singing, verse by verse, through the first psalm assigned, Psalm 27. I sang of David's one desire—that which he sought so passionately: to dwell in God's presence all the days of his life, beholding the Lord's beauty (see v. 4). Then I sang about David's intention to shout for joy in radical worship at God's tabernacle (see v. 6). I was, however, totally oblivious to the unusual significance of what I was singing over this gentle brother whom I had met only the night before.

Turning quickly to Psalm 149, I continued my song. Now I was singing about God's people dancing before Him, making music with tambourine and harp, speaking His praises as they hold double-edged swords to carry out God's plan for the nations (see vv. 1-6).

How I ended my song I do not recall. I was numb. I looked up and observed a rather interesting expression on Bill's face. Again, his words were few. With a slight smile he said, "That was different." What an understatement. Before I could say a word, and as I was nervously wondering if Bill thought he had an oddball on his hands, he spoke once more, asking one of those out-of-left-field questions that one is not at all prepared to answer. Yet, as you respond to it, you try to convey a small sense of understanding—even though you really aren't sure what you're talking about.

"Dick," Bill asked, "have you ever thought much about what the Bible says in Acts 15 about the restoration of the Tabernacle of David in the last days?"

Like any disciplined believer who reads his or her Bible through on a regular basis in the course of the year, I knew it is not unusual to read passages repeatedly and still miss things of significance. Such was the case regarding the passage Bill referred to—Acts 15:16-18. I just didn't remember it, although the phrase "Tabernacle of David" seemed vaguely familiar.

I turned quickly to the passage to see exactly what Bill meant while he began his own brief explanation. He referred to the fact that the apostle James, at a council in Jerusalem, talked about a time in the future when David's Tabernacle, or tent as it is sometimes translated, would be restored, leading to a great Gentile harvest.

Still clutching my *New Living Translation* Bible from which I had just sung, I glanced down and read the passage even as Bill continued speaking:

> Afterward I will return, and I will restore the fallen kingdom [tent, *NIV*] of David. From the ruins I will rebuild it, and I will restore it, so that the rest of humanity might find the Lord, including the Gentiles—all those I have called to be mine. This is what the Lord says, he who made these things known long ago (Acts 15:16-18, *NLT*).

Frankly, I was surprised that I had not caught the significance of this passage before, especially the remarkable correlation between David's kingdom (i.e., tent or Tabernacle) being restored "so that the rest of humanity might find the Lord" (v. 17). That last phrase especially captivated my attention. The rest of "humanity" (which I later learned referenced "all the Gentiles") would "find the Lord" as the Tabernacle of David was restored. *What did all this mean?* I thought. Whatever it meant, it was surely a key to the great end-time harvest of lost souls yet to come. I was about to experience a "worship transformation." "Transform" means "to change markedly," and that was what was about to happen to me. Hopefully, it will soon happen to the global Church.

DAVID'S SPIRIT

Shortly I would understand that the Acts 15 quotation by James was originally spoken by the prophet Amos, who had declared centuries earlier,

" 'In that day I will restore David's fallen tent. I will repair its broken places, restore its ruins, and build it as it used to be, so that they may possess the remnant of Edom [the Gentiles] and all the nations that bear my name,' declares the LORD, who will do these things" (Amos 9:11-12).

The passage continues, " 'The days are coming,' declares the LORD, 'when the reaper will be overtaken by the plowman and the planter by the one treading grapes. New wine will drip from the mountains and flow from all the hills' " (v. 13). I especially like *THE MESSAGE*'s paraphrase of this passage:

> "Yes, indeed, it won't be long now." God's Decree. "Things are going to happen so fast your head will swim, one thing fast on the heels of the other. You won't be able to keep up. Everything will be happening at once—and everywhere you look, blessings! Blessings like wine pouring off the mountains and hills" (Amos 9:13).

As I gazed at the Acts passage, wondering about its relationship to the great end-time harvest I was certain was coming, Bill shared something of his own journey regarding Acts 15 and the Tabernacle of David.

"Twenty-five years ago," Bill explained, "a strange but deep longing came over me to ask God to place the spirit of David on me. I even asked my Episcopal priest at the time if it was wrong to pray this, but he thought it was a good request."

Bill continued, "At that time God told me I would somehow be a part of seeing David's Tabernacle restored just as it says in Acts 15."

Caught even more off guard, I was attempting to form a coherent comment when I felt God speak to my heart again: *I brought you here because Acts 15:16-18 is the key to the fulfillment of My plans for the nations. You are to be a part of the answer to the prayer Bill prayed many years ago.*

Within a few months of this experience, Dee and I were able to travel to Jerusalem to spend time worshiping with Bill in the beautiful place God had given him as a part of fulfilling his burden of 25 years earlier.

While I was in Jerusalem, God significantly increased my understanding of the role of David's fallen tent and how its restoration is already underway—not as a physical structure, but as a spiritual edifice.

David's Tabernacle would be, I felt, a global movement of passionate praise and powerful prayer that would lift a canopy of God's glory over every nation and people group on earth.

While in Jerusalem, I had the opportunity to visit various sites that were important in the life of David. I began researching every aspect I could of David's lifestyle of worship—especially the significance of the small tent he set up in Jerusalem where the Ark of the Covenant was placed (see 2 Sam. 6:12-23; 1 Chron. 15).

Through my research, clear characteristics and needed reforms began to emerge that helped me understand just what we might expect if this spirit of intercessory worship, which I believe saturated David's original tent, were to be restored globally. These critical reforms, which I will describe shortly, will happen, not only on a small scale on some tiny hill in Jerusalem, but in every city, town, village, rural area, people group and nation on earth. The very climate, I believe, will be one of total transformation. To understand all this, we need to take a close look at David's Tabernacle itself.

10

WORSHIP REFORMATION

A CLASS OF ONE

It is a fascinating phrase—one of the most quoted of any description in the Old or New Testaments. Rare is the study of the foundations of biblical leadership in which you do not hear it: *a man after God's own heart*. What follower of Jesus, man or woman, does not desire to become a person "after God's own heart"?

Biblically speaking, however, those who qualified for this distinction represent a class of one. Only of David, the shepherd king who "danced before the LORD with all his might" (2 Sam. 6:14), do we read this description (see 1 Sam. 13:14; Acts 13:22).

What made David so special? A look at other Old Testament characters and the space allotted to them in the Scriptures helps us see how David stands out. Fourteen Old Testament chapters tell Abraham's story. Eleven describe the events of Jacob's life, and some 14 relate the story of his son Joseph. Only 10 chapters are needed to detail the lives of Elijah and his protégé, Elisha.

Then there is David. At least 66 chapters tell his story! There are about 1,200 references to David in Scripture, including 59 in the New Testament—written hundreds of years after his death.

Kevin J. Conner, who provides the above facts in his remarkably detailed book, *The Tabernacle of David*, adds this insight:

> If we think of a character who speaks of faith, we think of Abraham, the father of all who believe. If we think of a man of meekness, we speak of Moses. . . . If we look for a man of miracles, we think of Elijah, or Elisha. But when we look for the Bible character for praise and worship, we speak of King David. He is the man after God's heart. The Psalms of David are primarily worship Psalms.[1]

Conner adds this interesting insight:

> While other ceremonials and ritualisms of the Old Testament
> pass to the cross and are abolished there, expressions of worship
> pass to the cross and through the cross into the New Covenant.
> Through the cross they become purified. Worship and praise
> will never be abolished. Worship and praise are eternal.[2]

A GOD-SATURATED LIFE

There is, of course, the enigma surrounding David's life: How could
a man guilty of such deep personal failure be described as "a man after God's own heart"? Most Bible students are familiar with David's
adultery with Bathsheba and his conspiracy to murder Bathsheba's
husband, Uriah, a commander in David's army (see 2 Sam. 11:1-17).
But David would repent, and God would hear his powerful prayer of
repentance as recorded in Psalm 51:

> Against you, you only, have I sinned and done what is evil in
> your sight. . . . Create in me a pure heart, O God, and renew
> a steadfast spirit within me. Do not cast me from your pres-
> ence or take your Holy Spirit from me. Restore to me the joy
> of your salvation and grant me a willing spirit, to sustain me
> (Ps. 51:4,10-12).

This is David, and somehow David is different, in ways not always easy to understand. If there is a secret to David's life, a key
that explains his description as a man after God's own heart, it
clearly has something to do with his all-consuming passion for the
Lord. Philip Yancey perhaps explains it best in his book *Reaching
for the Invisible God*:

> David's secret? The two scenes, one a buoyant high and the
> other a devastating low, hint at an answer. Whether cartwheel-
> ing behind the ark or lying prostrate on the ground for six
> straight nights in contrition, David's strongest instinct was
> to relate his life to God. In comparison, nothing else mattered
> at all. As his poetry makes clear, he led a God-saturated life.[3]

A Picture of Praise and Power

This is the man who pitched a tent in Zion and who put within it the Ark of the Covenant. This tent would come to be known as the Tabernacle of David—a picture of praise and power, providing guidelines of reforms for the end-time Church. Read again that passage from Acts 15 introduced earlier:

> After this I will return and will rebuild the tabernacle of David, which has fallen down; I will rebuild its ruins, and I will set it up; so that the rest of mankind may seek the LORD, even all the Gentiles who are called by My name, says the LORD who does all these things (Acts 15:16-17, *NKJV*).

The subject of this portion of the book is the incredible prophetic significance of David's Tabernacle (or tent) being restored in the end times, and the clear patterns (or reforms) of Davidic worship (what we've been describing as *intercessory worship*) that will be essential to this restoration.

Central to this study is the extraordinary harvest of humankind pictured in the Acts 15 promise "that the rest of mankind may seek the LORD, even all the Gentiles" (v. 17, *NKJV*). The *New Living Translation* renders the passage: "that the rest of humanity might find the Lord, including the Gentiles."

Before exploring in depth this interesting biblical picture and the various worship reforms I see as related to it, some brief historical background regarding David's tent might prove beneficial. Attention to a few details now will be significantly helpful later. If the spirit of David's tent is indeed to be restored globally in the last days, it is important to know what that means and what precisely is to be restored. Further, how are we to be involved in a practical way in seeing this happen?

J. T. Horger, writing in *Fundamental Revelation in Dramatic Symbol*, explains that it was approximately 1490 BC when Moses erected a temporary Tabernacle, which served until he built God's prescribed Tabernacle the same year.

This tent and the Ark of the Covenant within it were transported by the Israelites throughout their wilderness wanderings for 40 years, and the Tabernacle with its Ark continued to serve as their worship center for the next 350 years in Canaan. Then, for at least 20 years, the Ark was neglected and left in a Gibeonite city in the house of Obed-Edom. Finally, David retrieved the Ark and placed it in a temporary tent on Mount Zion, in the southwestern corner of Jerusalem.

David's tent, of course, would have been entirely insignificant without the Ark of the Covenant inside it. Of all the furniture in Moses' Tabernacle, the Ark was the most important. Its meaning to ancient Old Testament Israel was much like what Jesus means to His New Testament Church. Mentioned 180 times in Scripture, the Ark was the very throne of God on earth. To Israel, the Ark represented God's presence, and His glory, among His people.

So David was desperate to bring the Ark home. To him it was the essence of God's presence. There even seems to be a sense of urgency in his setting up a mere tent for the Ark. He did not want to wait until he could build some glorious edifice to house the Ark that God had long before told Israel was the specific and literal place where He would dwell (see Exod. 25:22).

In the Acts 15 passage cited earlier, and also in its Amos 9 source, the Greek and Hebrew words for "tabernacle" suggest a simple tent. The Hebrew word used in Amos 9:11 is *sookah*, meaning "a tent, tabernacle, pavilion, booth or cottage" or even "a hut made of entwined boughs."[4] The Greek word used in Acts 15:16 is *skene*, meaning "a tent or cloth hut."[5]

The Hebrew word used in 2 Samuel 6:17 to describe the tent David sets up is different from the one that appears in Amos 9. Here the Hebrew word *ohel* is used, but it similarly has the meaning of a tent, tabernacle, dwelling place, home or covering. The term generally describes a covering or dwelling used by nomadic people (see Gen. 4:20; 13:5).

A COMING COVERING

It is the definition of "covering" that holds interesting significance when considering the Acts 15:16-18 prophecy and the end times. These verses picture a coming season when the Tabernacle of David will be restored "so that the rest of humanity might find the Lord" (v. 17, *NLT*). As we shall see shortly, I believe that this covering relates to David's Tabernacle and that it is most certainly a covering of Davidic-style intercessory worship in a season just ahead for the global Church. In fact, I believe there is irrefutable biblical proof that the restoration of David's Tabernacle, as referred to in Acts 15 and first prophesied by Amos, could not have occurred before the very times in which we live today. I'll share this biblical evidence shortly. Before we get to that, let's consider what we know about the historical tent of David.

First of all, we know this tent (*ohel*) was not fancy, because the Bible says simply that David "pitched a tent for [the Ark] in Jerusalem" (2 Chron. 1:4). Of this same event, we also read an earlier account: "They brought the ark of God and set it inside the tent that David had pitched for it" (1 Chron. 16:1).

Of course, one doesn't "pitch" a building, much less a temple! This was, as the text indicates, a simple tent, even though the word used also can be translated as "tabernacle." It was something of a portable shrine, perhaps only 10 to 15 feet high.

Of the Hebrew word *ohel* used to describe this tent, Kevin J. Conner writes, "*Ohel* . . . is used of a covering, a dwelling place, a home, a tabernacle or tent for cattle, for man, for families or for God Himself. It has both secular and sacred uses as a dwelling place for either man or for God."[6]

Citing the significance of this term's use in reference to David's Tabernacle, Conner adds, "The very fact that the ARK of the Covenant, where the Lord dwelt between the cherubims (2 Samuel 6:2), was placed in the Tabernacle of David (2 Samuel 6:17) shows that the '*ohel* of David' was God's house, God's dwelling place, God's home."[7]

Conner also reminds us that the real truth of the Hebrew and Greek words used in the prophecy of Amos and the reference to that prophecy in Acts is the fact that they are fulfilled, first and foremost, in Jesus Christ, the Messiah.

According to Conner, Christ "is God's TENT (Ohel). He is God's TABERNACLE (Mish-kan). He is God's BOOTH (Sook-kah). He is God's HABITATION. . . . He is the fulfillment of the Tabernacle that David pitched." Citing John 1:14, Conner adds, "He [Christ] took upon himself a human body, a human tabernacle, and 'pitched His tent among us.'"[8]

The symbolism of David's Tabernacle is obviously vital to God's plan for the ages. Further, it is essential that we see the significance of Amos's prophecy that it would be rebuilt, or restored, at some point in the future, which James reiterates at that critical council in Jerusalem, highlighting its purpose: "so that the rest of humanity might find the Lord" (Acts 15:17, *NLT*). It is that purpose that we cannot overlook.

But why did God say He would rebuild David's Tabernacle? Why not Moses' Tabernacle or even the far more glorious Temple of Solomon? Indeed, David's worship structure was little more than a tent. It was but a stretch of canvas over a few tent poles. To God, however, it represented radical worship and passionate praise. That is why God chose to restore that one rather than Moses' original Tabernacle or Solomon's grand Temple!

THE DAYS OF OLD

Two additional historical observations are essential to our understanding of what it is about David's Tabernacle that God desires to be restored and why. First is the historical and biblical context for the apostle James's referring to the future restoration of David's fallen tent; second are the particulars of the Amos prophecy itself (e.g., when was, or is, all of this to take place?). Specifically, what exactly did Amos mean when he prophesied that David's fallen tent would be built "as it used to be" (Amos 9:11), or "as in the days of old" (*NKJV*)?

Kevin J. Conner, to whom this author is grateful for his detailed analysis of both the Acts and Amos passages, poses an interesting series of questions about why James was prompted to cite the Amos prophecy in the first place, especially as it relates to all the world (Gentiles) receiving the gospel message. Conner asks, "Why did the Apostle James quote this passage of Scripture from the Prophet Amos? It seems to have absolutely nothing to do with the immediate context, either before or after. It seems that James takes it right out of context altogether in his use and application of it." Conner further queries, "Then, what has the rebuilding of the Tabernacle of David got to do with the Gentiles coming into the Gospel Dispensation? What is the Tabernacle of David? Why not have the Gentiles come into the Tabernacle of Moses?"[9]

It is clear that the primary reason James cites the Amos prophecy is to quell the dissension surfacing at the Council of Jerusalem regarding the growing number of Gentile converts and the question of whether they should be circumcised (see Acts 15:1-3). It was about AD 50-51 when the events of Acts 15 occurred. The Early Church was obviously advancing, with whole cities and regions being impacted by the gospel (see Acts 13:44,49; 14:1,3,21).

Tensions, however, began to arise over issues of Gentile conversions and which aspects of Jewish law applied to them. As Kevin Conner reminds us, the Early Church was in a significant period of transition, growing out of the Old Covenant with its heavy restrictions, laws and ceremonials, which often tended toward spiritual bondage. They were now coming into the New Covenant with liberty in Christ.

Conner writes, "It looked as if the whole of the Early Church would be rent into two factions, two churches—a Jewish Church and a Gentile Church, thus dividing the Body of Christ."[10]

We must remember that the Early Church had only the Old Testament as a basis for what was unfolding. This was their guide, or as Conner observes, "their only infallible court of appeal." They had to "discover the New Testament in the Old Testament."[11] Thus James, clearly inspired by the Holy Spirit, refers back to the Amos prophecy to build a case for the future Gentile harvest.

A VITAL KEY

The Holy Spirit's prompting of James to cite the prophecy of Amos is critical. James was no doubt familiar with the Amos prophecy, which reads, "In that day I will restore David's fallen tent. I will repair its broken places, restore its ruins, and build it as it used to be" (Amos 9:11).

Note especially the phrase "build it as it used to be," or as rendered in the *King James Version*, "as in the days of old." Again I borrow heavily from Kevin Conner, who reminds us that Amos gave this prophecy during the days of Uzziah, who reigned as king of Judah while Jeroboam II was king of Israel (see Amos 1:1). This was more than 750 years before the birth of Christ.

Although the prophecy involved several surrounding Gentile nations as well as the Southern Kingdom of the house of Judah, it primarily concerned the Northern Kingdom of the house of Israel.

As Conner conveys, the house of Israel was in a backslidden condition; it had become a culture of almost complete apostasy. For 200 years, each king in Israel had perpetuated the golden calf system of worship established under Jeroboam I (see 1 Kings 12:25-33). It is with this historical understanding that Amos prophesies, "I will restore David's fallen tent . . . repair its broken places . . . and build it as it used to be" (Amos 9:11).

Here is a key to understanding this whole prophecy—and a vital key at that! To quote Conner, "Undoubtedly, in the minds of that generation, [the people of Amos's day] would understand this utterance to speak of a restoration or revival of true and proper worship as was established in the days of King David."[12] I refer to this restoration in terms of a series of "reforms" that I see coming in the Church globally through intercessory worship. Seven of these reforms will be examined in this portion of my book.

A COLLAPSING TENT

The people of Amos's day clearly had strayed far from the practice of Davidic worship. There was no doubt that the Tabernacle of David, as far as worship was concerned, had crumbled. They knew Amos was not speaking of God raising up, or pitching, another literal tent. He was speaking of something having to do with the purity and passion of the worship associated with David's tent. That is what God would someday restore.

Sadly, it did not take long following David's death for the tent pegs of his spiritual house to loosen. Sin would soon topple it altogether.

When did David's tent (as a symbol of worship) actually begin to fall? We find a hint in these instructions of the Lord to Solomon:

> As for you, if you walk before me in integrity of heart and uprightness, as David your father did, and do all I command . . .
> I will establish your royal throne over Israel forever, as I promised David your father. . . . But if you or your sons turn away from me and do not observe the commands and decrees I have given you . . . then I will cut off Israel . . . and will reject this temple (1 Kings 9:4-7).

Unfortunately, Solomon's encouraging beginning (see 1 Kings 3:5-14) had a sad conclusion (see 1 Kings 11:1-13). Already during Solomon's reign, the tent had begun its collapse. We read:

As Solomon grew old, his wives turned his heart after other gods, and his heart was not fully devoted to the LORD his God. . . . So Solomon did evil in the eyes of the LORD; he did not follow the LORD completely, as David his father had done. . . . So the LORD said to Solomon, "Since this is your attitude . . . I will most certainly tear the kingdom away from you" (1 Kings 11:4,6,11).

Such was the spiritual condition of God's people and the beginning of the decline of Davidic worship for many generations. But, according to Amos, all that was to change—and change remarkably—at some future point in history. "In that day," God said through Amos, "I will restore David's fallen tent" (Amos 9:11). The next question is, when is "that day"?

THAT DAY!

There is irrefutable biblical evidence that we are living in the time that Amos referred to as "that day." The evidence is irrefutable because of the Amos prophecy itself. To fully grasp this, we must read the rest of what Amos foretold:

> "The days are coming," declares the LORD, "when the reaper will be overtaken by the plowman and the planter by the one treading grapes. New wine will drip from the mountains and flow from all the hills. I will bring back my exiled people Israel; they will rebuild the ruined cities and live in them. They will plant vineyards and drink their wine; they will make gardens and eat their fruit. I will plant Israel in their own land, never again to be uprooted from the land I have given them," says the LORD your God (Amos 9:13-15).

The expression "the days are coming" here refers to the same biblical context that Amos talked about two verses earlier when he prophesied about what would happen "in that day" (v. 11).

Clearly God is looking toward a specific point in future history when whatever the Amos prophecy means would begin to unfold. It was to be a restoration, or reforming, of all that David's tent once represented. Of this future time, God didn't say "one day" or "some-day," or that this would happen "at a future yet-to-be-determined point when certain conditions are just right"! He says very specifi-cally, "in that day." Key to determining when "that day" would come is to look at the concluding statement of God in the Amos proph-ecy: "I will plant Israel in their own land, never again to be uprooted from the land I have given them" (v. 15).

Thus, David's fallen tent (a covering of global intercessory wor-ship) will be restored when (and only when) the exiled people of Is-rael are brought back from being scattered everywhere and are planted forever in their own land.

Who can dispute the fact that May 14, 1948, is the most likely possibility (if not the only possibility) for the beginning of this ulti-mate fulfillment of the prophecy of Amos? This was the day it was announced publicly that a new nation of Israel had been established.

Today, most of us see that special day in 1948 simply as a remark-able historical fact and easily miss the totality of the miracle. As a wise student of Israel's history explains, "If you were to talk to an an-thropologist or historian who studies history, cultures and societies, you'd find that in thousands of years of recorded human history, there is one anthropological anomaly. There is one unprecedented thing that has happened throughout all of recorded human history. It is the re-gathering of Israel into her land."[13]

BELIEVING THE UNBELIEVABLE

Think of how unbelievable this 1948 miracle would have seemed to historians just a century ago. I thought of this as I read an English edition of a book titled *Science and Faith: A Letter to Intellectual Friends*, originally published a few years ago in Chinese.

Written by Dr. Edward W. Li, a brilliant Chinese scientist who had come to faith in Christ, *Science and Faith* was originally a lengthy and comprehensive letter explaining to his unbelieving intellectual friends in mainland China how he had come to believe the Bible and accept Christ as his personal Savior.

In detail, Li explained how accurate the Bible is, particularly its many prophecies. He specifically highlighted Israel becoming a new nation as an example:

There is no other nation that can compare with the Jews in the tribulation and disasters they have suffered. Besides the distresses of war caused by Assyria, Babylon and the Roman Empire, the persecutions that they suffered at the hands of European nations were almost as relentless.[14]

Li points out that in 1881, the czar of Russia was assassinated, and one million Jews were slain in retaliation. Later, during World War I, the Russian government compelled the Jews to leave; anyone refusing was slain by machine gun or grenade. Then, of course, there was the massacre of Jews by Hitler during World War II. Of the nine million Jews under Hitler's influence, six million were killed.

Dr. Li offers this conclusion:

> Israel, as a nation that suffered tremendous calamities, was diminished in population, scattered to many different countries, stripped of its own land and nation, yet was never assimilated or destroyed. It . . . survived as a peculiar tribe preserving its special national tradition. This is a marvel in all of human history. Commonly in history, once a nation was conquered by others, it would not last over five hundred years. Powerful countries in history such as Babylon, Egypt and Rome, could not escape this fate. So, why was this weak and small country of Judea an exception? Historians cannot give an explanation.[15]

Biblically, however, we do have an explanation. God had set aside a particular day to bring the people of Israel back to their land. We have the extraordinary privilege of living in "that day."

Having said all this, I want to emphasize the totality of the Amos prophecy that James later cites during the Council of Jerusalem. Central to the prophecy is the restoration of David's Tabernacle "so that the rest of humanity might find the Lord, including the Gentiles" (Acts 15:17, *NLT*).

This means that just as the prophecy of Israel's return from exile as recorded by Amos has been fulfilled quite literally, so will the part about David's Tabernacle being restored be fulfilled. Further, this restoration will involve an unprecedented harvest of souls being brought into the Kingdom.

Could it be that the ultimate restoration of the Tabernacle of David, as described in Acts 15:16-18, actually refers to a supernatural tent, or covering, of worship and intercession that will be raised up by the Church in our generation over every tribe, tongue, people and nation on earth as pictured in Revelation 5:8-10 and 7:9-12? Could it be that the global Church is on the threshold of a true worship reformation?

If so, what can we learn from worship in David's day that we might expect will mark this movement? "Reform" simply means "to change for the better" or "to improve." It's not that all worship in the Church today is deficient, but perhaps God wants to take us to higher heights and deeper depths of His glory. What reforms, then, might be required to see the restoration of His Tabernacle become a practical reality? How will all of this bring in history's greatest harvest? For starters, let's look at seven reforms, or characteristics, that appear as we revisit David's ancient Tabernacle.

REFORM ONE

CONTINUOUS WORSHIP

A FLAME UNENDING

There was something special about David's Tabernacle that seems to have caught the fancy of God's heart. It was no doubt the unending flame of fervent worship at David's tent. That flame, from the first-ever 24/7 worship movement, was destined to burn brightly for some three decades. God seems to be saying, *Someday I'll restore that unending flame, and with it, gather in history's greatest harvest of lost souls.*

One of the most distinctive characteristics of the worship surrounding David's tent in Jerusalem was the fact that it was continuous. We see this in the description of the Ark when it is initially placed in David's tent: "So he left Asaph and his relatives there before the ark of the covenant of the LORD to minister before the ark continually, as every day's work required" (1 Chron. 16:37, *NASB*).

We likewise read, "[David] left Zadok the priest and his relatives the priests before the tabernacle of the LORD in the high place which was at Gibeon, to offer burnt offerings to the LORD on the altar of burnt offering continually morning and evening, even according to all that is written in the law of the LORD, which He commanded Israel" (1 Chron. 16:39-40, *NASB*).

Here we discover that worship before the Ark in David's tent was continual. Although some translators render the Hebrew word here *tamiyd* as "regularly," the essence of the word's meaning is "constantly."

Tamiyd literally means "to stretch." When used as an adjective, the word means "constant." As an adverb, it means "constantly" or "continually." *Vine's Expository Dictionary of Old Testament Words* says that *tamiyd* "signifies what is to be done regularly or continuously without interruption."[1]

A study of the use of the word *tamiyd* in the Hebrew texts reveals it is first used in Exodus 25:30: "And thou shalt set upon the table shewbread before me alway" (*KJV*). The *New American Standard Bible* translates this phrase "at all times." The fact that the word denotes uninterrupted activity is seen in other Scriptures where *tamiyd* is used. Isaiah's watchman said, "My lord, I stand continually [*tamiyd*] upon the watchtower in the daytime, and I am set in my ward whole nights" (Isa. 21:8, *KJV*).

Interestingly, it is this same Hebrew word that we find translated as "always" when God's visible presence is described as appearing at the Tabernacle of Moses. We read, "So it was always: the cloud covered it by day, and the appearance of fire by night" (Num. 9:16, *NKJV*). "Always" here does not mean that the cloud came every morning at a particular time and then promptly departed, nor that the fire came for but a short time at nightfall and then quickly left. "Always" (*tamiyd*) here means that while the cloud was there, it was there continually, as was the fire at night.

When God said of Jerusalem, "Your walls are continually [*tamiyd*] before Me" (Isa. 49:16, *NKJV*), He did not mean just at a particular time during the day, such as once in the morning and perhaps once at night, but continuously.

We see further substantiation of this thought of never-ending worship in 1 Chronicles 9, which describes worship in the Temple being restored, according to the order David had earlier established, following the Babylonian captivity. We read, "The musicians, all prominent Levites, lived at the Temple. They were exempt from other responsibilities there since they were on duty at all hours" (1 Chron. 9:33, *NLT*). The *New International Version* translates the expression "at all hours" as "day and night."

It seems quite logical that if the musicians lived at the Temple and were on duty "at all hours," the worship was continuous. Indeed, these worshipers actually were exempted from all other responsibilities because this was their specific focus.

We also see this emphasized in Psalm 134, which declares, "Praise the LORD, all you servants of the LORD who minister by night in the house of the LORD" (v. 1). This suggestion of ministering by night supports the idea that constant worship was being sustained.

A NEVER-ENDING PURSUIT

This theme of continuous worship dots the landscape of David's journey of intimacy toward the heart of God. When we read David's various psalms, we see his constant passion for continuous worship. On one occasion he sang, "I will extol the LORD at all times; his praise will always be on my lips" (Ps. 34:1).

In an earlier psalm, we read one of David's most powerful declarations of desire: "One thing I ask of the LORD, this is what I seek: that I may dwell in the house of the LORD all the days of my life, to gaze upon the beauty of the LORD and to seek him in his temple" (Ps. 27:4). It's little wonder that God called David a man after His own heart (see Acts 13:22). David wanted nothing more than to sit all day long and simply gaze upon his Lord!

A. W. Tozer captured something of this Davidic desire when he wrote, "It does not seem to be very well recognized that God's highest desire is that every one of his believing children should so love and so adore him that we are constantly in his presence, in Spirit and in truth."[2]

This wise worshiper adds, "True worship of God must be a constant and consistent attitude or state of mind within the believer."[3] So it was with David. David's pursuit of God was never-ending.

It is this David who sets up a tent, brings in God's Ark and institutes unending worship. Surprisingly, David's tent doesn't appear to have had a veil that kept on-lookers from seeing the Ark of God's presence. It was an open tent that created an open heaven. The worshipers were gatekeepers standing at-the-ready to allow entry into the fullness of God's presence.

Today's intercessory worshipers, I believe, are these gatekeepers who hold open the gates of heaven. It is interesting to note that many Bible scholars (e.g., Matthew Henry, Adam Clark, John Wesley, and others) believe that Psalm 24 is a song David sang when the Ark was brought into his tent in Jerusalem. That song declared:

> Lift up your heads, O you gates; be lifted up, you ancient doors,
> that the King of glory may come in. Who is this King of glory? The
> LORD strong and mighty, the LORD mighty in battle (Ps. 24:7-8).

David's song was a call to worship, no doubt inviting many other worshipers to help him lift up these gates through praise. Perhaps it was this very song that first began the continuous worship in his tent.

A Case for Continuing

Years ago, when I was first called into ministry, the Lord used a passage of Scripture in Isaiah to influence me regarding this matter of continuous prayer. It would lead my wife and me to begin a prayer center in Sacramento, California, for college-aged youths. (I recount the details of these early years, and what has followed since, in my book *The Purple Pig and Other Miracles*, Charisma House, 2010.) A committed group of young adults continued in prayer day and night for five years—more than 43,000 continuous hours! These words of Isaiah birthed that vision:

> For Zion's sake I will not keep silent, for Jerusalem's sake I will not remain quiet, till her righteousness shines out like the dawn, her salvation like a blazing torch. The nations will see your righteousness, and all kings your glory; you will be called by a new name that the mouth of the LORD will bestow.... I have posted watchmen on your walls, O Jerusalem; they will never be silent day or night. You who call on the LORD, give yourselves no rest, and give him no rest till he establishes Jerusalem and makes her the praise of the earth (Isa. 62:1-2,6-7).

As in so many other passages, we again see worship and watching linked to God's glory touching the nations. Note particularly the phrases "The nations will see your righteousness, and all kings your glory" (v. 2) and "till he establishes Jerusalem and makes her the praise of the earth" (v. 7). The goal, according to this admonition, is to watch continuously: "never be silent day or night" and "give yourselves no rest" (v. 6). Such watching in worship (which we are describing here as *intercessory worship*) will no doubt help make possible an open heaven over the earth, so that the nations might see, as the text declares, "[God's] righteousness, and all kings [his] glory" (v. 2).

David certainly understood this key when he brought God's Ark into his humble tent and commissioned continuous worship. One might argue, I believe rightly, that David created an open heaven over Israel for nearly four decades.

What specifically were the benefits of this open heaven? Prosperity and blessing accompanied David's rule, unlike those experienced during the reign of any king before or after. It is indeed noteworthy that David's kingdom grew beyond all other kingdoms of those times. I believe this was the result of David's passion for God, demonstrated through his lifestyle of praise and worship. In fact, more scriptural insight on praise, worship and hungering after God's heart is attributed to David than almost all other Bible writers combined.

Something in David did not want the flame of worship to die out in his Tabernacle. Perhaps he remembered the Levitical directive that the flame was to burn continuously in the Tabernacle of Moses (see Lev. 6:13). The end result for David was the extraordinary extension of his kingdom.

A TASTE OF THE TABERNACLE

Something similar to what David initiated happened many centuries later, in the 1700s, with the amazing extension of the Moravian movement in one of the great missionary advances in Church history. The Moravians, under Count Nikolaus von Zinzendorf, began a prayer watch before the Lord that continued for more than 100 years. It was, to a small degree, a foretaste of the ultimate restoration of David's Tabernacle that I believe is unfolding in our generation.

The Moravian prayer watch began in late August 1727, after revival broke out among several hundred people who lived in a place called Herrnhut in Saxony (modern Germany). Populated by persecuted Christians from Bohemia and Moravia, Herrnhut—meaning "watch of the Lord"—was founded in 1722 at the estate of the wealthy and devout Count Nikolaus von Zinzendorf.

For the first five years of its existence, Herrnhut hardly lived up to its name, being wracked by dissension and open hostility. In early 1727, Zinzendorf and several others agreed together to seek God fervently for revival. The revival they sought came gloriously on May 12. The entire community was transformed. Later Zinzendorf would write, "The whole place represented truly a visible habitation of God among men."[4]

A hunger for God intensified in the weeks following, and on August 27 a decision was made to cultivate this attitude and atmosphere, so that it might continue. That day 24 men and 24 women covenanted together to spend one hour each day, at different times, in scheduled prayer. This was no short-term commitment, and they fixed no date for concluding.

Historian A. J. Lewis later wrote, "For over a hundred years the members of the Moravian Church all shared in the 'hourly intercession.' At home and abroad, on land and sea, this prayer watch ascended unceasingly to the Lord."[5]

Some 95 years after this unique watch commenced, a journal was published documenting the growth of the Moravian movement. Titled *The Memorial Days of the Renewed Church of the Brethren*, the journal cited an Old Testament typology as a basis for this continuing watch: "The sacred fire was never permitted to go out on the altar (Leviticus 6:13); so in a congregation [which] is the temple of the living God, wherein He has his altar and fire, the intercession of his saints should incessantly rise up to Him."[6]

FRUIT FROM THE FLAME

What is most amazing about this continuous prayer watch is the extraordinary fruit it produced. Most mission historians refer to William Carey, the eighteenth-century British missionary to India, as the father of modern missions. However, Carey himself, when proposing his first mission to India in 1792 before a Baptist mission board in Kettering, England, used the Moravians as his example of extraordinary missionary advance. The Moravians had already sent out 300 missionaries to all parts of the world.

At the Kettering meeting, Carey, trying to build his case for a new missionary thrust to the East Indies, actually tossed on the table before his fellow Baptists a copy of a small booklet titled *Periodical Accounts of Moravian Missions*. Boldly, he challenged his brothers, "See what these Moravians have done. Can not we follow their example, and in obedience to our heavenly Master, go out into the world and preach the gospel to the heathen?"[7]

One example of fruit borne from that flame of 100 years of unending Moravian intercessory worship came in 1738, just 11 years after the prayer watch began. A small Moravian group had formed in London and was meeting regularly when a young, searching sinner attended one of their meetings.

Something deeply moving occurred that night as this young man came to understand what it was that he had so desperately been seeking. Years later he would define that experience as his personal conversion, testifying that in that meeting his "heart was strangely warmed." This convert's name was John Wesley, and he went on to lead one of England's greatest-ever spiritual awakenings, which ultimately spread well beyond Britain's borders and blessed the entire world.

As we will discover in looking more carefully at the additional reforms, or characteristics, of David's Tabernacle, something of what the Moravians began is about to be remarkably restored. I believe this emerging movement will be marked with an even greater understanding of the role of worship-saturated prayer in reaching the nations and will involve far more of the Church than the Moravian prayer watch did. It will represent a flame of white-hot worship from every tribe, tongue, people and nation and will, indeed, send an unending flow of "incense-laced prayers" for the nations to God's throne (Rev. 8:4, *THE MESSAGE*). That will be just the beginning! You certainly won't want to miss the finish!

12

REFORM TWO

Skillful Worship

In Pursuit of Excellence

"We are what we repeatedly do," Aristotle wrote. The philosopher added, "Excellence, then, is not an act but a habit."[1]

Long before the Greek philosopher offered this observation, Israel's King David practiced this axiom in his approach to worship. Prior to setting up his tent in Jerusalem, and much more so after, David desired that the worship he offered before the Lord would achieve a clear degree of excellence. He made certain all the musicians involved were skilled and well trained.

Perhaps David linked his understanding of the various Hebrew words used to describe God's glory—*kabowd, hadar, howd*—to his desire for the very best in worship at his tent and later in the Temple (which his son Solomon would complete almost 40 years afterward).

Kabowd, for example, literally refers to the "weight" of God's presence or the substance of all He is and has.[2] It is associated with God's excellence. *Hadar* could be variously translated "glory," "magnificence," "excellence," "beauty" or "majesty."[3] But when David spoke of God's glory being present as the Ark was put into his tent on Mount Zion (see 1 Chron. 16:1,27), he used the word *howd*. *Howd* means "grandeur, majesty or excellency."[4] At least two other times in Psalms, where God's glory is referred to using the Hebrew word *howd*, we see it linked to the excellency of His Name. Note these passages:

> O Lord, our Lord, how excellent is Your name in all the earth, who have set Your glory above the heavens! (Ps. 8:1, *NKJV*).

Let them praise the name of the LORD: for his name alone is excellent; his glory is above the earth and heaven (Ps. 148:13, *KJV*).

Everything about or related to God is truly excellent. When God's glory (*kabowd*) filled the temple (see 2 Chron. 5:14), the suggestion is that the full weight of His excellency saturated His house.

Of course, God's excellence is His perfection—His absolute holiness. Our problem with the term "holiness" is the way we equate it to a standard of conduct (which, to an extent, it certainly does involve), rather than to how the expression relates specifically to God.

God is not holy merely because He does not smoke, drink, dance, go to the movies or wear lipstick. I mention these behaviors because in the earliest days of my upbringing, according to a sometimes rigid evangelical "holiness" theology, they were considered unholy. In our thinking, holiness meant not doing these things—plus a long list of additional things. Bowling was actually once on that list! Later it was removed and our church joined a bowling league. We were the "Holy Rollers!"

THE PERSONIFICATION OF EXCELLENCE

In reference to God, however, holiness is all about His absolute perfection. It is excellence with a capital E. He is excellence personified. God is uniquely perfect. Unique means "unlike any other; different from all others; having no like or equal."[5]

Snowflakes are unique (no two are exactly alike), and the same can be said of people. But only God is uniquely unique. It is His perfection, or excellence, that makes this so.

It is interesting that the glorious angelic beings, those cherubim and seraphim worshiping around the throne, choose but one aspect of God's nature and character to verbalize endlessly. It is not His mercy or His grace (both beautiful aspects of who He is). It is not His power, might or majesty; nor is it His faithfulness or truth.

Actually, it is all of these put together. It is all of God's attributes (and those missing from this brief list) that make up His perfection, or completion. The angels cry "Holy, holy, holy" (Rev. 4:8; Isa. 6:3). They are declaring it right now—as you read these words—and they were voicing the exact same praise when David set up his tent. Think of that! It is a never-ending declaration of God's excellence.

David clearly yearned to emulate God's glory and excellence. We see something of this desire manifested in his careful attention to make worship before God the very best it could be. Consider David's selection of worship leaders:

> All these men were under the direction of their fathers as they made music at the house of the LORD. Their responsibilities included the playing of cymbals, lyres, and harps at the house of God. Asaph, Jeduthun, and Heman reported directly to the king. They and their families were all trained in making music before the LORD, and each of them—288 in all—was an accomplished musician. The musicians were appointed to their particular term of service by means of sacred lots, without regard to whether they were young or old, teacher or student (1 Chron. 25:6-8, *NLT*).

Several things are highlighted in this passage that are essential to our understanding of the worship offered at the Tabernacle of David and what this might mean for us as this atmosphere is restored, dramatically and globally, in the last days.

1. MENTORED

First, the worshipers were mentored. There is something significant in the expression "All these men were under the direction of their fathers as they made music at the house of the LORD" (v. 6).

Mentoring has become a buzzword in recent years, and the term has possibly been overused, if not misused. It certainly means more than casual contact, such as a Big Brother who takes a fatherless child to a ball game or a movie once a month. True mentoring is more like close-in (or even "live-in") discipleship.

The origin of the word "mentor" might help us understand its intended meaning. Mentor was actually a character in Homer's poetic classic *The Odyssey*. Mentor was a loyal friend and adviser to Odysseus, the king of Ithaca. Mentor became the teacher and guardian of the king's son, Telemachus, while Odysseus went on his 10-year odyssey. Mentor did not spend just a few hours a week with the king's son—he lived with him in Ithaca while the king was gone.

It is this kind of close-in mentoring that our text suggests. Note especially the phrase "under the direction of their fathers." To me this suggests constant, almost in-your-face mentoring.

As David's Tabernacle is restored in these last days, we should not be surprised to see considerably more attention given to training and mentoring worship leaders. I see the greatest and most skillful of our present worship leaders setting aside blocks of time from their busy schedules to teach other potentially gifted worship leaders their so-called trade secrets.

2. RESPECTED

Second, the worshipers were respected. The worship leaders at David's tent (and in the subsequent Temple of Solomon) were highly regarded for their work. This was not some auxiliary function of Tabernacle activity. Consider this easy-to-overlook detail: "Asaph, Jeduthun, and Heman reported directly to the king" (v. 6).

In today's political culture, this would be equivalent to a person serving in a president or prime minister's Cabinet. The fact that they reported directly to the king suggests they may even have been key advisers, not merely loyal subjects who periodically gave the king a report of their activities.

If the spirit of David's Tabernacle is to be restored in remarkable ways as this present generation unfolds, we should expect an amplification of this reality from David's day. Worship must be made central to every new endeavor, not seen as just a segment of time set aside in a worship service.

3. EQUIPPED

Third, the worshipers were equipped. Note the expression "their responsibilities included the playing of cymbals, lyres, and harps" (v. 6). Later it says they "were all trained in making music" (v. 7).

This orchestral array of instruments indicates a significant investment in worship and those who led it—an investment not only of resources (to provide the instruments), but also of time (for their training).

In considering this observation as it relates to a last-days restoration of David's Tabernacle, we can expect much more attention to be given to equipping, supporting and training intercessory worshipers.

This, of course, takes time—considerable time.

I'm thankful that a growing number of worship leaders and pastors are catching this concept and devoting time to developing intercessory worship. I have watched worship practitioners like Mike Bickle at the International House of Prayer and Murray Hiebert on our staff at The Jericho Center do this, and I have often wondered why it is not done more!

4. SUPPORTED

A fourth observation is noteworthy and relates directly to the previous point—the worshipers were supported. This insight stands out in our text: "All these men were under the direction of their fathers as they made music at the house of the LORD. . . . They and their families were all trained in making music" (vv. 6-7).

Often it is easy, in a casual reading of a biblical passage, to overlook brief, yet key, statements. Here we see just such a phrase: "They and their families" (v. 7). The *New International Version* translates this verse, "Along with their relatives—all of them trained and skilled in music for the LORD—they numbered 288." Some might interpret this to mean that worship was a family activity, passed on from generation to generation. One thing is clear: Some means of support had to be provided by the king to sustain all these families, or clans. These musicians were not merely trained and provided instruments and told to go play as they felt led; they were housed and fed by the king. David had an all-encompassing worship strategy. It was the only way he could assure both continuous and skilled worship.

Again, let's contemplate how this might impact the global Church of our generation.

I see God deeply touching the hearts of successful businesspeople and others blessed with resources to help them recognize the strategic value of supporting such sustained intercessory worship. Some already understand the missionary enterprise and the costs required to effectively sustain it. Sadly, however, too many view worship and intercession as purely auxiliary—even secondary. Expect this to change as the spirit of David's Tabernacle is restored throughout the world.

At Every Home for Christ this already is happening. We have a growing team of young worshipers who are supported by partners who give generously so these warriors can serve full-time. These 20-something leaders form teams of "intercessory missionaries" who sustain, at our headquarters, day and night worship and intercession over all the nations of the world. They lead the many volunteers who join us from the local community, as well as those who drive or fly in from distant places just to be a part of this harvest-focused worship.

Interestingly, as we have increased this ministry of intercessory worship, doors have opened remarkably around the world (even in so-called closed nations), and the harvest has increased overall in our ministry some 1,500 percent over the past several years. In one of these "closed" nations—a relatively small country where it is said that our kind of systematic evangelism is impossible—we saw 260,000 people come to Christ and be baptized secretly in just the past 12 months! This harvest has resulted in the establishing of more than 600 new church fellowships, meeting in secret and multiplying as I write these pages. I believe we can further anticipate that as our intercessory worship grows, the harvest too will grow.

5. FOCUSED

Fifth, we discover that these skilled worshipers were focused. Like several other items on this brief list, this thought warrants a much closer look later, in our overview of coming reforms of Davidic worship in the Church. For now, I will simply highlight the phrase "music before the LORD" (v. 7). The focus was not on the worshipers' gifts or the music itself—and it was certainly not on entertaining others. Their focus was on the Lord.

As the spirit of David's Tabernacle is restored, I strongly suspect that worship times in many settings of varied traditions will move increasingly toward a God-centered, Christ-saturated focus.

6. APPOINTED

Another interesting fact stands out in this brief passage: Worshipers were appointed. This is mentioned in another easy-to-overlook statement in our text: "The musicians were appointed to their particular term of service by means of sacred lots" (v. 8).

The fact that these worshipers had terms of service may well suggest this was some kind of a mission. Today, it is not uncommon to see missionaries appointed to specific terms of service. After a certain number of years, the missionary takes a furlough. This is generally necessary because the worker needs a break. The missionary calling demands such an intense focus that time is needed for restoration.

The day has come when musicians, singers and other worshipers are beginning to sacrifice periods of time, whether short or long, simply to minister to the Lord in worship. At Every Home for Christ, our worship teams are already pursuing a goal of 24/7 intercessory worship. Our vision is to cover all the nations of the world, by name, in prayer every 24 hours. Some of these intercessors are being trained to go out as teams into dark and difficult regions of the globe, where they will participate in raising up a covering of day-and-night intercessory worship over indigenous leaders, missionaries and national churches.

7. DIVERSE

A seventh observation can also be made from our text: Worshipers were diverse. Note the statement "The musicians were appointed . . . without regard to whether they were young or old, teacher or student" (v. 8). Of particular interest is the expression "without regard."

Look also at these two combinations of contrasting words in the passage: "young or old" and "teacher or student." This clearly describes diversity. According to Webster, "diversity" means "difference or variety."[6]

Imagine every tongue, tribe, people and nation bringing their songs and sounds together as we worship around God's throne (see Rev. 7:9-10). Further imagine these sounds blending miraculously to form one unique universal sound to bring God incredible glory. I say this with at least a modest measure of experience, since I have danced with passionate Christ-seeking pygmies of the rain forests of central Africa and swayed with weeping worshipers of the South Pacific island nation of Fiji. Trust me—just hearing the Kwaio pan-pipers of the Solomon Islands exalt the Lord on their bamboo flutes will make heaven profoundly beautiful. I'll never forget that sound.

8. SKILLED

The last of our several observations from the text cited above is really the subject of this entire chapter: Worshipers were skilled. We read of David's worship leaders, "Each of them—288 in all—was an accomplished musician" (v. 7).

Earlier we highlighted this statement from the text: "They . . . were all trained in making music" (v. 7). We might even assume from this passage that some or all of these worshipers played numerous instruments. One thing is certain: They were "accomplished" (v. 7), or "skilled" (*NIV*), in making music before the Lord.

David clearly pursued excellence when it came to worship. We see this when he finally brings the Ark from Gibeon and places it in his tent. We recall how the first attempt ended in failure and the death of Uzzah (see 1 Chron. 13:9-10), a fact we will look at more closely shortly. But when the Levitical priests treated the Ark properly, they did it with incredible attention to detail.

Here I simply highlight David's commitment to excellence in worship. Among other areas, we see this in the king's choice of a person to head the whole operation of bringing the Ark to Jerusalem. David appoints Kenaniah, a Levite specifically chosen because of his musical abilities. Scripture reports that "Kenaniah, the head Levite, was chosen as the choir leader because of his skill" (1 Chron. 15:22, *NLT*).

Excellence in worship was always on David's mind. In one of his many psalms, we read, "Sing to him a new song; play skillfully, and shout for joy" (Ps. 33:3).

As this intercessory worship movement continues to grow throughout the world, lifting a covering of fervent prayer and passionate praise globally and continually adding excellence to its intensity, it should not surprise us to see very skilled musicians devote their talents entirely to intercessory worship.

Some strategists even believe that God may have something to do with placing a desire on the hearts of so many youths—including masses of teens among the unconverted—to develop musical skills. When revival does finally come, and large numbers of these young people find Christ, a huge army of skilled worshipers will be ready to help restore David's fallen tent.

Others are equally committed to seeing this army of skilled warriors rise up globally—something I am convinced will lead to history's greatest harvest of souls. I will build upon this thought substantially in the pages that follow.

13

REFORM THREE

Creative Worship

Wired for Worship

"Music is the gift of God to man!" Evangeline Booth wrote. The Salvation Army leader added, "[Music is] the only art of heaven given to earth and the only art of earth we take back to heaven. But music like every gift is only given to us in the seed. It is for us to unfold, and cultivate, that its wondrous blossoms may bless our own path and bless all those who meet us upon it."[1]

David certainly understood this gift and carefully sought to cultivate it. Worship surrounding the Tabernacle of David was clearly creative. This fact surfaces in an interesting observation, recorded in 1 Chronicles, regarding the moving of the Ark of God from the house of Abinadab. We read, "They transported the Ark of God from the house of Abinadab on a new cart, with Uzzah and Ahio guiding it. David and all Israel were . . . singing and playing all kinds of musical instruments" (1 Chron. 13:7-8, *NLT*).

The expression "all kinds of musical instruments" is not without significance. David and those who served with him in developing their worship must have had a desire to be creative. It appears that they understood the beauty of combining the sounds of a variety of instruments in order to give God even more glory through their music.

Jack Hayford speaks of this creative diversity in his inspiring book *Worship His Majesty*. Hayford observes:

There is a full spectrum of purposes and practices of song in worship. The breadth of style, the endless melodic possibilities, the delicate nuances of choral dynamics, the brilliant luster of instrumental arrangement, the soul-stirring anthems of anointed choirs, the rumbling magnificence of giant organs—all seem clearly to be God-given means for our endless expansion and creativity in worship.[2]

Heaven's Sound

Creativity in music does, indeed, have endless possibilities. Strangely, more than a century ago, a noted church leader suggested the probability that all of the music in the world "would be used up" because there were only a "finite number of notes." He seemed convinced that if we were not careful, somehow no new music would be possible.[3]

David clearly lacked this fear. In fact, sometime after initially setting up his tent of worship, the king significantly expanded that worship in preparation for the Temple that his son Solomon would eventually build. The Bible says that David made elaborate plans regarding those who would participate in the Temple building project—including a vast contingent of worshipers.

Consider this biblical observation: " 'Four thousand [Levites] will work as gatekeepers, and another four thousand will praise the LORD with the musical instruments I have made' " (1 Chron. 23:5, NLT). It is the expression "with the musical instruments I have made" that amplifies this idea of creativity. For some reason, David felt that the existing instruments of his day were simply not sufficient to do justice to the worship God deserved. So he created new musical instruments.

Consider especially the Hebrew word *asah* that is translated "made" in 1 Chronicles 23:5. We note the use of this word in Genesis 1:7: "God made [*asah*] the firmament" (NKJV). *Asah* means "to create, to do, to make or fashion." It is possible that David was hearing sounds during his times of worship and sought to make instruments that could duplicate these sounds.

We can only speculate as to what sounds David may have heard or even if he heard such sounds in the first place. What is clear is that he created instruments to make specific sounds. It is also clear that heaven is the source of music. We see this at the beginning of creation (see Job 38:4-7), and we will see it again—saturating all of creation—at the culmination of this present age (see Rev. 5:13).

CREATION'S SONG

Concerning the creation itself and the earth being established, the Lord asks an interesting question of Job: "On what were its footings set, or who laid its cornerstone—while the morning stars sang together and all the angels shouted for joy?" (Job 38:6-7). The very universe came alive in song as God spoke creation into being. Indeed, the whole of creation seems born of a song!

As we look toward the culmination of God's plan for this present age, we see something remarkable: Virtually everything created in the universe sings. We discover this universal song immediately after reading about that heavenly worship ensemble (the elders and living creatures) who hold harps and bowls and worship with "thousands upon thousands" of angels (Rev. 5:11). Together they sing, "Worthy is the Lamb, who was slain, to receive power and wealth and wisdom and strength and honor and glory and praise!" (v. 12).

Next, a truly unique thing happens. The text says, "Then I heard every creature in heaven and on earth and under the earth and on the sea, and all that is in them, singing, 'To him who sits on the throne and to the Lamb be praise and honor and glory and power, for ever and ever!'" What is amazing about this song is that every living creature sings it! Notice again the words, "I heard every creature in heaven and on earth and under the earth and on the sea, and all that is in them, singing" (v. 13)!

Other passages of Scripture likewise suggest the whole of creation entering into worship. The psalmist said, "Everything on earth will worship you; they will sing your praises, shouting your name in glorious songs" (Ps. 66:4, *NLT*). King David himself sang, "Praise him, O heaven and earth, the seas and all that move in them" (Ps. 69:34, *NLT*). Later in Psalms we read, "Let the heavens be glad, and let the earth rejoice! Let the sea and everything in it shout his praise!" (Ps. 96:11, *NLT*).

All of these passages validate the reality that God brought all creation into being for the purpose of worship. I am convinced it is for this reason He places within the hearts of His children a longing to be creative in worship. Indeed, it seems all of humankind is wired for worship—it is our intended destiny.

MIND MELODIES

A visit to Sandra Trehub's lab in Toronto, Canada, just might convince you that music is already on our minds, even at birth. According to a

Newsweek article titled "Music on the Mind," if you did happen across Trehub's lab, your first impression would be that you had wandered into one of those obnoxious preschool "superbaby" classes. You would see babies six to nine months old sitting silently, almost transfixed, in their parents' laps as classical music pours from speakers.[4]

According to the article's author, the University of Toronto psychologist is not attempting to teach these infants some kind of introductory music appreciation class; rather, she is "trying to shed light on whether the human brain comes preloaded with music software the way a laptop comes preloaded with Windows."[5]

When the pitch, tempo or melodic contour of the music varies, these babies, according to Dr. Trehub, can detect the changes. The researcher adds that the fact that infants recognize that a melody whose pitch or tempo has changed is still the same melody suggests they have at least a "rudimentary knowledge of music's components."[6]

Other research has determined that the temporal lobes of the brain (located just behind the ears) act as a sort of music center. When a neurosurgeon stimulates these areas with a probe, patients sometimes hear tunes so vividly that some have asked, "Why is there a phonograph in the operating room?" The *Newsweek* article concludes, "The brain seems to be a sponge for music and, like a sponge in water, is changed by it."[7]

CORPORATE CREATIVITY

There seems little doubt that we are wired to worship and are connected to that purpose from the moment Christ comes into our hearts. Still, that natural inclination must be cultivated so that it grows and flourishes. Practice is a key to creativity. As I mentioned in an earlier chapter, Brother Lawrence, the well-known seventeenth-century monk, referred to his life of worship as a continual conversation with God. Of this life of worship he said, "Those only can comprehend it who practice and experience it."[8] I believe creativity will begin to flow in our worship if we follow the advice of Brother Lawrence. We must "practice and experience it." When David's Tabernacle was being established, worship was creative. All kinds of instruments blended together, and David even made some new ones (see 1 Chron. 13:8; 23:5).

As David's Tabernacle is being restored globally in the last days, we should expect awesome creative worship to flood the nations. This, of course, can only happen through God's people. I sometimes wonder what new sounds are yet to be born through today's worshipers!

Another sign of creativity in worship might be described as "corporate creativity." We see this type of creativity in emerging styles of corporate worship at the International House of Prayer in Kansas City (that have spread to scores of places globally) and even at our Jericho Center in Colorado Springs. I describe this model in more detail in an appendix to this book titled *Intercessory Worship: A Harp and Bowl Practicum*. This model of sustained intercessory worship basically consists of a worship team (which can involve as few as two persons) leading in spontaneous singing of Scripture or phrases that flow from a particular Bible passage. The words are sung in an antiphonal style (i.e., one singer, usually the lead singer, sings a brief phrase—either a prayer or an expression of praise based on a biblical passage—several times, and then another singer picks up the same brief theme and repeats it in song). This continues as the entire group joins in. We see a picture of this style of worship in a description from Nehemiah's day; Scripture gives an account of a group of worshipers who "stood opposite" one another "to give praise and thanksgiving, one side responding to the other, as had been directed by David the man of God" (Neh. 12:24, *THE MESSAGE*).

Such worship not only leads to unusual spontaneity but also fosters heightened creativity. Throughout the prayer time, people in the group may be invited to come to a microphone or simply stand where they are (in smaller settings) to read and pray a passage of their choosing. After each reading, the singers select a biblical theme (usually a simple phrase from the passage just read), and the worship continues, all the while including prayers of intercession, either spoken or sung, that relate to issues and needs of the day. Because this deserves a fuller explanation, I encourage you to read the appendix. Also, visit the Every Home for Christ website (www.ehc.org) and click on "Intercessory Worship: A Practical Workshop" to view how this can work functionally in a corporate setting.

ALL THE WORLD WORSHIP

Another tool Every Home for Christ has produced to aid in focused worship over every nation on earth is our *"All the World" Worship Experience*.

This unusual DVD (which makes an excellent companion to this book and is available from Every Home for Christ) features a pictorial prayer journey to every nation on earth, along with beautiful instrumental music to enhance one's prayerful worship over these nations. This tool can be used corporately in a prayer time to worship and intercede for every nation in the world in as little as 70 minutes (or even less, if necessary). It can also be used for more extended times of intercession. If you simply allow the DVD to run, each nation will appear on the screen for approximately 15 seconds, but a leader can pause the presentation at will to allow worshipers more time to intercede for areas of particular concern. The DVD menu also has seven 10-minute segments, allowing individuals to use this tool to pray and worship over every nation on earth weekly during personal devotional times of prayer.

Numerous Scriptures related to the nations appear on the screen throughout the presentation to help participants declare God's Word over these nations. Recently I used this tool for an entire day of intercessory worship with a worship team in Hong Kong. A roomful of worshipers of multiple nationalities declared God's Word and their creative worship over every nation in the world. We sang spontaneous songs for each nation as beautiful pictures appeared on the screen, and I paused the presentation at appropriate intervals to allow participants to come to a microphone for "rapid-fire" (15 to 20 seconds) prayers for the nations that had just appeared on the screen. It was a remarkable day, to say the least. Our ministry is now planning to devote time every day of the year for similarly focused prayer sessions led by our various worship teams.

NEW SONGS AND SOUNDS

When God was confirming in my heart the necessity of having 24-hour intercessory worship with both spontaneity and creativity at EHC's Jericho Center, a unique picture came to my mind as I described this vision to a group of young people. At the time, the Center had not yet been built. These youth were participating in an intensive month-long discipleship/training program. I explained that I believed God was going to send many youth groups, in addition to church worship teams, to spend entire nights in worship when our Jericho Center facility was finally completed.

When I told them that I felt God was about to raise up a mighty army of radical, passionate, youthful worshipers, the room exploded with applause and even cheers. I explained that I saw these worshipers coming from all over the world, bringing with them their unique styles and, in some cases, exotic instruments.

As I continued speaking, I sensed God's gentle whisper in my heart. He was saying, *I will give the young people who come for worship new songs—even songs in the night. They will be songs as beautiful as any you have ever heard—and these songs will bring Me great glory to the ends of the earth.*

Immediately I thought of Jack Hayford, who had shared with me one day how, as an 11-year-old boy, he had heard a well-known composer of that day, Phil Kerr. The composer was honoring God with songs born out of his own personal worship. In that moment, young Jack Hayford sent a desire heavenward: "Oh God, someday let me honor you throughout the world with a song like that."

Many choruses and hymns have been born out of Jack Hayford's life, but most memorable is his anointed anthem "Majesty." To my amazement, while visiting a house church in a remote mountain area of southern China in 1985, I heard the believers there singing "Majesty" in their own dialect. I was told it was being sung all over China. Jack's youthful desire had been granted. Few modern anthems have traversed the globe the way "Majesty" has.

As I spoke to that room of praising young people, I thought of Jack's prayer as an 11-year-old, and I saw in my heart an explosion of similar passionate creativity coming upon youthful worshipers as they help restore David's fallen tent.

Reflecting on all this some days later, I read the words of Isaiah, who once looked toward a future remnant of diverse worshipers:

> But all who are left will shout and sing for joy. Those in the west will praise the Lord's majesty. In eastern lands, give glory to the Lord. In the coastlands of the sea, praise the name of the Lord, the God of Israel. Listen to them as they sing to the Lord from the ends of the earth. Hear them singing praises to the Righteous One! (Isa. 24:14-16, *NLT*).

The prophet Zephaniah paints a similar picture:

> The LORD will be awesome to [the nations] when he destroys all the gods of the land. The nations on every shore will worship him, every one in its own land (Zeph. 2:11).

David's Tabernacle is indeed being restored, and new sounds and songs are certainly coming. One can almost hear them in the distance.

14

REFORM FOUR

Extravagant Worship

Exceeding the Limits

With 134 musicians, the Vienna Philharmonic Orchestra is the largest major symphony in the world. The next largest is the Berlin Philharmonic with 112 players. The rest of the top 10 include the Orchestre de Paris with 111, the Chicago Symphony Orchestra with 110, the New York Philharmonic with 109, the Cleveland Orchestra with 108, the London Royal Opera with 106, the Los Angeles Philharmonic with 105, the Philadelphia Orchestra with 104 and the Boston Symphony Orchestra with 98.

If you combined all these musicians into one vast symphony, there would be 1,097 participants. Then add to their number the members of the 30 next largest orchestras in the world (each with at least 80 musicians), and you would have an extraordinary symphony consisting of more than 3,500 musicians.

You would, however, come up hundreds of musicians short of the 4,000 David employed for his worship (see 1 Chron. 23:5). David clearly was an extravagant worshiper!

"Extravagant" means "exceeding the limits" or "excessively elaborate." It is derived from the Latin words *extra*, meaning "outside" or "beyond," and *vagari*, meaning "to wander." Thus, "to wander outside" means "to exceed the limits" or "to go beyond normal bounds."[1] "Extravagant" is synonymous with "lavish," "unrestrained," "exorbitant" and "fantastic." Applied to the Tabernacle of David, extravagant worship meant radical, lavish worship.

One of the more interesting aspects of the worship related to David's Tabernacle, and Davidic worship in general, is its extravagance.

Perhaps, to some degree, all of these "reforms," or facts, about the Tabernacle of David that we are examining are summed up in this one observation: Everything about the worship David inaugurated and sustained was extravagant.

A CELEBRATION OF EXTRAVAGANCE

Notice what the Bible says regarding David's first attempt to move the Ark of God back to Jerusalem: "David and all Israel were celebrating before God with all their might, singing and playing all kinds of musical instruments—lyres, harps, tambourines, cymbals, and trumpets" (1 Chron. 13:8, *NLT*).

True, the sad episode including the death of Uzzah (when priests moved the Ark of God improperly) occurred in this context, and there were vital lessons for David to learn through that mistake. We will examine those lessons later; in the meantime, it is hard to overlook expressions in this passage like "celebrating . . . with all their might" and "playing all kinds of musical instruments" (v. 8). Can you recall any other leader in Israel doing anything like this before David?

This is not the only instance when Davidic worship is described in connection with such expressions of extravagance as "all their might" or "celebrating." Later in 1 Chronicles, we read the following description of moving the Ark: "Then David and the leaders of Israel and the generals of the army went to the home of Obed-Edom to bring the Ark of the LORD's covenant up to Jerusalem with a great celebration" (1 Chron. 15:25, *NLT*).

When examining this extravagance in the context of Davidic worship, one can only imagine all that the expression "with a great celebration" really entails. We do know that David didn't just encourage such celebrating—he led the way.

When the Ark finally reached Jerusalem, the exuberant worship described in this familiar passage took place: "And David danced before the LORD with all his might, wearing a priestly tunic. So David and all Israel brought up the Ark of the LORD with much shouting and blowing of trumpets" (2 Sam. 6:14-15, *NLT*). More extravagance! Here something is said of a king in Israel that is never said of another. Nowhere else in the Old Testament do we read of a king dancing before the Lord with all his might. One can hardly wonder at God describing David as "a man after my own heart" (Acts 13:22). David led the way in extravagant worship. Davidic worship was a celebration of extravagance.

Perhaps one of the most interesting insights regarding the moving of the Ark of God into Jerusalem in David's day was the remarkable extravagance that some believe accompanied the move itself. Before we get to that, however, we must backtrack somewhat and recall that the Ark had been in Gibeon for many months because David was afraid to move it after the first and improper attempt had failed, and some of David's key leaders had died because of his mistake.

A FAILURE IN WORSHIP

For that first attempt, David had a cart constructed to carry the Ark (see 2 Sam. 6:3-4), no doubt to expedite the journey. He seems to have wanted the move to happen quickly. Perhaps David was anxious, even desperate, to obtain the Ark from the house of Abinadab, and it just made sense to take this shortcut. It was, of course, not the way God had instructed that the Ark be moved. Then, too, the Ark was probably extremely heavy, being overlaid with pure gold, including the two solid-gold cherubim sitting up top. David no doubt knew that the Philistines had moved the Ark in this manner. Why couldn't he do the same?

David never sought God about this matter (see 1 Chron. 15:13); if he had, God would have told him it was being handled improperly. At other points in David's life, we see him asking God for guidance in such matters, and God very specifically answering (see 2 Sam. 5:17-20,22-25). But this time he did not bother to ask.

At the threshing floor of Nacon, God allowed the oxen to stumble, and the Ark suddenly shifted (see 2 Sam. 6:6). Because the Ark appeared to be slipping and might have crashed to the ground, Uzzah reached out to steady it.

It is not a pleasant picture, and a phrase in the text is troubling: "God struck him down and he died" (2 Sam. 6:7). The *New Living Translation* is equally blunt: "Then the LORD's anger blazed out against Uzzah for doing this, and God struck him dead."

If this troubles your theology, imagine how David must have felt! He decided to leave the Ark at the home of Obed-Edom and went back to Jerusalem discouraged. For three months he brooded, perhaps complained, and no doubt asked God why this tragedy had occurred. He learned that God had long before given specific directions for how the Ark was to be moved: Poles were to be attached to the Ark, and sanctified Levites were to carry it on their shoulders (see 1 Chron. 15:15). If David knew all this and simply disobeyed, it is easier to understand God's displeasure. If such was the case, perhaps the several months before that final move were spent by David in careful reflection and repentance.

After a season, David's courage returned, and he headed for the home of Obed-Edom in Gibeon to bring the Ark back properly. It is here that we see something potentially remarkable about David's extravagance in worship.

EVERY SIX STEPS

There's an easy-to-overlook statement in the text of this event at Gibeon that has unusual implications. We read, "After the men who were carrying it had gone six steps, they stopped and waited so David could sacrifice an ox and a fattened calf" (2 Sam. 6:13, *NLT*).

It is at least six miles from Gibeon to where the Ark was finally placed in Jerusalem, and it may have been as much as a 10-mile journey.[2] For the purpose of illustration here, we will use the six-mile figure.

Some Bible teachers have suggested the possibility (though others question the inference) that David did not merely stop once after the first six steps to offer a sacrifice, but that he was so afraid of not honoring God properly in this second attempt of moving the Ark that he stopped every six steps for the entire journey of at least six miles. This theory suggests that at every stop he would have offered similar sacrifices.[3] Eugene Peterson's Bible paraphrase *THE MESSAGE* clearly embraces this thought. The paraphrase reads: "David . . . went and brought up the Chest of God from the house of Obed-Edom to the City of David, celebrating extravagantly all the way, with frequent sacrifices of choice bulls" (2 Sam. 6:12-13, *THE MESSAGE*). Peterson uses the word "frequently" in place of the original "after the men . . . had gone six steps."

My conclusion in the matter is that it is at least possible that David's contingent actually did pause every six paces, or steps, for the entire journey, simply because of David's tendency toward extravagance when it came to his worship. Nothing was cheap or second-rate with this worshiping king.

Further, if David intended to make only one sacrifice, it is far more logical that he would have done it at the very outset of the trip. Why wait to do it just one time after going six paces? To me, this is not the David I have discovered in my studies of his passion and pursuit of God.

If the processional did stop every six steps, this adds even more interesting speculation to the potential extravagance of David's worship. Allow me to explain.

If we consider that an average step covers just over two feet of ground, we could conclude that six steps would be approximately 13 feet, give or take a foot or two for tall Levites! Stopping every six steps for six miles would have required an amazing 2,437 stops, breaking down to about 406 stops per mile. Here I have some sympathy for those who believe David stopped only once; it just seems impossible that he would have stopped so often.

But what if this did indeed happen? Further, imagine the number of sacrifices necessary and the total time required to accomplish such a feat. It would require 2,437 oxen and an equal number of calves. Assuming it would take at least 30 minutes to perform each dual sacrifice, the total time required would be 1,218 hours, or 51 days!

We must also consider that the group that accompanied this processional would certainly have needed pauses to eat and sleep if indeed the journey occurred over so many days. If we estimate eight hours for sleep each night and three hours for daily meals, then 1,031 additional hours, or 43 more days, would be required.

With all of these stops factored in, moving the Ark just six miles from Gibeon to Jerusalem would have required 94 total days. I can understand those who consider this unlikely, but knowing David, it would not surprise me in the least. Whether or not David actually stopped every six steps to offer a worship sacrifice, the point is still obvious: David was an extravagant worshiper. All that David did in regard to worshiping God was "beyond normal bounds."

A LIFE OF LAVISH GIVING

As David's life neared its end, he continued to demonstrate this same extravagance. He gave his son Solomon detailed instructions regarding the building of a permanent Temple. David himself then offered a lavish gift toward this task. His own testimony reads, "And now because of my devotion to the Temple of my God, I am giving all of my own private treasures of gold and silver to help in the construction" (1 Chron. 29:3, *NLT*).

The text goes on to explain that 3,000 talents of gold, which amounts to approximately 112 tons, were given. Additionally, some 262 tons of refined silver were a part of David's extravagant sacrifice (see v. 4, *NLT*). Imagine the value of this gift today, given that the price of gold as I write this is approximately $1,500 per ounce.

The king then issued an invitation for those willing to join him in giving. David declared, "Now then, who will follow my example? Who is willing to give offerings to the LORD today?" (v. 5, *NLT*). The results were astounding. Not only had David's worship been extravagant, but now the people's worship in giving also became extravagant. It was lavish, even fantastic!

The *New Living Translation* tells us the total offering included some 188 tons of gold, 10,000 additional gold coins, 375 tons of silver, approximately 675 tons of bronze and about 3,750 tons of iron (see v. 7, *NLT*).

Could it be that as the spirit of David's Tabernacle is restored globally in the last days (i.e., as an extraordinary movement of intercessory worship takes place), we will not only see lavish worship released, but also witness a resulting extravagance in giving? I saw just a glimpse of something like this when I first taught these Davidic worship reforms at a Harp and Bowl intercessory worship conference in Hong Kong.

A WINDOW FOR WORSHIP

Dee and I had been invited to Hong Kong during the Easter season to help lead what was announced as a Harp and Bowl intercessory worship conference. I had been in Hong Kong some time earlier for a conference focusing intercession on the 10/40 Window—that geographic area of the world so designated by its longitudinal lines (10 degrees north and 40 degrees north) and stretching from West Africa to Japan, and including the Middle East. The 10/40 Window has been home to 95 percent of the world's least-evangelized people groups and became a well-known prayer focus throughout the evangelical community during the 1990s.

As we contemplated returning for this follow-up prayer conference, those involved in the planning agreed that the gathering should carry the Harp and Bowl intercessory worship theme. The theme of the first conference had been "Pray Through the Window"; this time participants would be encouraged to "Worship Through the Window."

That first Harp and Bowl conference, for both Dee and me, was a highlight of our (at the time) almost four decades of marriage and ministry. From the onset of the planning, we decided that we would set aside larger blocks of time to actually practice what we would be teaching.

Because it was our intention to have prolonged seasons of worship, including focused intercession, a special worship team was developed to help sustain the worship. The team's work was largely experimental, because we had never attempted something like this in a large multi-church setting. Most, but not all, participants would be from traditional mainline denominations in Hong Kong.

A Spirit of Extravagance

As the conference began, I wondered how successful it was going to be. I deliberately taught very short sessions, from 20 to 30 minutes in length, including time for translation into Chinese. Then the worship team and I would lead the congregation into what I hoped would become seasons of intercessory worship.

However, as we went into our first worship segment, it seemed to be nothing more than a typical time of worship—not unlike what many contemporary churches experience every Sunday morning.

Then something happened. At the conclusion of a particularly worshipful chorus, spontaneous singing began. As the musicians followed along, we heard the blending of a thousand voices, each singing his or her personal song, creating an unusual atmosphere of worship that would recur throughout the conference and build as each day progressed. These worshipers were also beginning to create what I now believe was a spirit of extravagant worship.

Because the Harp and Bowl symbolism of Revelation 5:8-10 focuses on a great harvest of souls coming from "every tribe and language and people and nation" (v. 9), the host of the conference, Dr.

Agatha Chan, expressed her desire to take up a special offering whose purpose would be to spread the gospel throughout the nations, especially the 10/40 Window. Agatha asked me when I felt it might be appropriate to receive such an offering. I suggested perhaps it would be good to do it on the day I taught specifically about the Tabernacle of David being restored (see Acts 15:16-18), because this prophecy speaks of all the Gentiles (nations) being given the gospel. Little did I realize how significant that decision would turn out to be.

The day of the offering just happened to be Easter Sunday, the fourth day of the conference. I had intended to teach all of these "reforms" of Davidic worship in two brief segments that afternoon. Because the entire session was to be three hours long, I thought I would share several aspects for about 30 minutes, then lead in an hour of intercessory worship and then do the same with the remaining reforms (half an hour of teaching followed by an hour of worship).

Agatha and I agreed that we would take the offering sometime in the middle of the afternoon, but we decided to make it a part of the worship, rather than stopping everything for an offering. After all, giving is clearly an act of worship. Passing offering plates seemed too formal and would, we felt, interrupt the worship, so the idea came to us to set cardboard boxes at the front of the auditorium and let people bring their gifts as an act of worship, if they so desired.

I initially thought this might hinder the offering because not everyone would respond, but both Agatha and I agreed it would be less disruptive because it would not involve interrupting our praise to have ushers pass offering plates.

WANDERING IN LAVISH WORSHIP

As I very briefly taught the fourth aspect of worship at David's Tabernacle—that it was extravagant—I mentioned that we would soon go into a sustained time of intercessory worship and that during that time, all those who wanted to give "willingly" (1 Chron. 29:6), just as the people did in David's day, specifically to bless the nations, could bring their gifts and place them in the boxes. But first, I told them, we wanted to devote considerable time to identifying with the first aspect of Davidic worship, which I had taught a few minutes earlier in that session: the fact that worship at David's tent was continuous.

I explained, of course, that we would not be doing this for 24 hours continuously but that we could imagine over the next hour or so joining with those exalted angelic beings around the throne who continuously praise God purely for His holiness (see Isa. 6:2-3; Rev. 4:8).

I explained that the worship team would come to lead us into worship. Then, at a given point, we would once again be invited to sing spontaneously, as we had done often during those days, but during these moments our many personal songs would consist of only one word: "holy." We would sing this word, I further suggested, to melodies that would come from each heart individually and yet blend together corporately.

This was to be yet another experiment in intercessory worship, but I was certain the Lord was leading us. As the worship team members took their places, I briefly reminded participants about the cardboard boxes that would be there later in the worship if they felt led to give a gift for the nations, as an act of worship.

Soon we were singing a chorus of praise that before long led us into a time of spontaneously singing the word "holy." It was difficult for me to tell when the transition initially occurred because the hundreds of participants were singing in Cantonese, the Chinese dialect of Hong Kong.

Suddenly the auditorium was filled with a sound of beauty unlike any I had ever heard. Later, Dee would confirm that she too had heard this heavenly sound. It was as if a new instrument had been created through the voices of these many worshipers.

The sound rose, subsided and rose again. At times, it would be sustained for 10 to 15 minutes, subside and then rise again for an even longer period. I had not specifically suggested that we worship God extravagantly (I am not sure I even knew how), but that was clearly what transpired. This was lavish worship. In keeping with the Latin root for the word "extravagant," everyone seemed to be "wandering outside" the usual limits of worship—if there are such limits. These believers were wandering in lavish worship.

THE EXTRAVAGANCE OF DAVIDIC WORSHIP

But that was not the end of the extravagance. Soon participants began moving toward the cardboard boxes with their gifts. What started with just a few givers exploded into a display of extravagant sacrificial giving. It seemed that every person participated. Some literally ran forward with their gifts. Others danced before the Lord as they came to a cardboard box.

The worship team, recognizing this spirited worship, began singing a song of celebration. The whole scene reminded me of a journey I had taken into Africa's equatorial rain forest five years earlier. On that occasion, newly converted pygmies had danced freely before the Lord in worship. They especially loved to dance during the offering time. Offerings in the forest, I was told, often took as much time as the sermon. Pygmies, it was explained, just could not seem to stop dancing. Now Hong Kong was catching this spirit of unrestrained extravagance.

The following morning, Agatha excitedly told me the amount of the offering. It was the largest she had ever seen at such a gathering: $390,000 in Hong Kong currency (or $50,000 U.S.). As she shared the news with conference participants later that morning, they applauded with delight. Realizing that some participants had missed the Sunday session because it was Easter, Agatha mentioned that additional offering envelopes would be available at the registration table.

The next day, as Agatha met us at our hotel to take us to the airport for our trip home, she reported that an additional HK$100,000 (almost $13,000 U.S.) had been given in those extra envelopes.

It was lavish, unrestrained, exorbitant and fantastic. It was Davidic extravagance! I suspect that as the spirit of David's Tabernacle is raised globally, we will see much more such extravagance, both in intercessory worship and in sacrificial giving.

15

REFORM FIVE

EXPRESSIVE WORSHIP

TO DANCE OR DIE

"This may be hard for some to admit," A. W. Tozer taught, "but when we are truly worshiping and adoring the God of all grace and of all love and of all mercy and of all truth, we may not be quiet enough to please everyone."[1]

At David's Tabernacle we see no absence of exuberance. Silence has its place, and earlier in this book I built a case for more of it (see chapter 3). But we miss something vital about David's Tabernacle if we fail to see the expressive nature of its worship. Look again at this description of the Ark being brought from Gibeon into David's tent:

> David, wearing a linen ephod, danced before the LORD with all his might, while he and the entire house of Israel brought up the ark of the LORD with shouts and the sound of trumpets. As the ark of the LORD was entering the City of David, Michal daughter of Saul watched from a window. And when she saw King David leaping and dancing before the LORD, she despised him in her heart (2 Sam. 6:14-16).

Another account tells us:

> But as the Ark of the LORD's covenant entered the City of David, Michal, the daughter of Saul, looked down from her window. When she saw King David dancing and leaping for joy, she was filled with contempt for him (1 Chron. 15:29, NLT).

DRIVEN BY DELIGHT

Although there is a vital lesson, to be dealt with later, in the sad reaction of David's wife, Michal, to the king's worship intensity, here I
simply want to highlight David's exuberance. He was "dancing and
leaping for joy" (1 Chron. 15:29, *NLT*). The account in 2 Samuel 6
tells us that David "danced before the LORD with all his might" (v. 14).
He put all his emotion into his worship.

This emotion-driven expressiveness is seen on numerous occasions in David's worship. Once David sang these words: "No wonder
my heart is filled with joy, and my mouth shouts his praises!" (Ps.
16:9, *NLT*). David's worship was clearly driven by his sheer delight in
God. Everything around him seemed to fuel that delight. A. W. Tozer
highlighted this thought when he wrote, "Go to the Psalms and you
will find David literally dancing with ecstatic delight as he gazes out
upon the wonders of God's world."[2]

On another occasion, David admonished, "Sing praises to God
and to his name! Sing loud praises to him who rides the clouds. His
name is the LORD—rejoice in his presence!" (Ps. 68:4, *NLT*).

David was into *loud*! He told of offering sacrifices in his Tabernacle with "shouts of joy" (Ps. 27:6) and instructed musicians to
praise God with "loud clanging cymbals" (Ps. 150:5, *NLT*).

Some might say that all that emotion was just a cultural thing—
the Hebrew way of worshiping. Jack Hayford deals with this argu-
ment in his book *Worship His Majesty*. Regarding expressive worship,
Hayford suggests, "Opponents of expressive worship will occasion-
ally concede that the New Testament does contain a few references to
forthright, open praise. Still, the presumption is that expressiveness
in worship went out with the blood-sacrifice system or that such un-
abashed physical exuberance was only a cultural trait passed down by
Hebrew tradition."[3]

He goes on to correct this fallacy, explaining that the essence of
sacrifice never really left worship, and it never will. He cites the author of Hebrews: "Therefore by Him let us continually offer the sacrifice of praise to God, that is, the fruit of our lips, giving thanks to
His name" (Heb. 13:15, *NKJV*). [4]

Hayford then concludes, "The New Testament contains more direct references to expressive worship than usually meet the eye.
Singing, praising, upraised voices, lifted hands, kneeling, offerings and

reading of the Scriptures are all mentioned" (see Luke 24:50; Acts 2:46-47; 4:24; 20:36; 1 Cor. 14:15; 16:1-3; 1 Tim. 2:8; 2 Tim. 2:15).

Worship related to David's tent clearly was expressive. If we expect to see a significant restoration of Davidic worship in the last days, we should not be surprised by a growing movement of exuberant praise.

JOINING THE DANCE

Dancing as a form of expressive worship is one example of exuberant praise that is growing among churches worldwide. I believe this is a sign of at least the beginning of David's Tabernacle being restored. It is truly a welcome reform. Perhaps some brief biblical background regarding dancing would be in order.

When we read of Miriam and the other Israelite women singing and dancing before the Lord following the miracle at the Red Sea (see Exod. 15:20-21), the Hebrew word used for "dance" is *mecholah*, whose other form, *machowl*, means "a round dance."[5]

When the Bible describes David dancing before the Lord as the Ark was brought into his tent (see 2 Sam. 6:14-16), the Hebrew word used is *karar*. It means "to dance, to whirl about."[6] In a parallel account of this event where David danced before the Ark (see 1 Chron. 15:29), the word used for "dance" is *raqad*, meaning "to stomp or to spring about wildly for joy."[7] *Raqad* is variously translated "dance, jump, leap, skip." (You may recall my attempts to do this in the woods near Washington, DC, as described in part one of this book.)

The use of two different Hebrew words to describe the same event may suggest a combination of these expressions. Can you picture King David leaping and stomping, jumping and skipping, as he whirls about wildly in worship?

Interestingly, the word "rejoice" (in Greek it's *agalliao*) similarly means "to jump for joy"[8] (see 1 Pet. 1:6,8; Rev. 19:7). It is derived from the Greek words *agan*, meaning "much," and *hallomai*, meaning "to jump, leap or spring up."

Thus, *agalliao* literally means "to jump or leap much." According to a Bible concordance, it would properly be translated "to jump for joy." This suggests that even in the New Testament we see expressiveness by those who encounter the Lord.

This is not to suggest that all worship must involve such ecstatic expressions, but neither should we reject or avoid them. Feelings can be a vital part of worship. A. W. Tozer once wrote, "I have had people tell me very dogmatically that they will never allow 'feeling' to have any part of their spiritual life and experience. I reply, 'Too bad for you!'" That wise worshiper continued, "I say that because I have voiced a very real definition of what I believe worship to be: *worship is to feel in the heart!*"[9]

Tozer carefully cautions those who would avoid any feelings of emotion in worship. He wrote:

> If you wake up tomorrow morning and there is absolute numbness in your right arm—no feeling at all—you will quickly dial the doctor with your good left hand. Real worship is, among other things, a feeling about our God. It is in our hearts. And we must be willing to express it in an appropriate manner.[10]

Look again at that consummate worshiper, King David. He danced expressively—even wildly—because he couldn't help himself. He interrupted the processional as the Ark was coming into Jerusalem and danced before it with ecstatic delight.

A sad and tragic endnote to the occasion, mentioned in passing earlier, is the response of David's wife, Michal. She watched from a distance, behind closed doors. Why she was not with the worshipers is a fair question.

The Bible says she "despised [David] in her heart" (1 Chron. 15:29)! Michal's motivation is mystifying; her behavior is baffling. The text does not fully address the reasons behind her reaction, but the fruit of her bitterness is made clear: She would be barren for life (see 2 Sam. 6:23). No children would be born of her womb.

As David's Tabernacle of intercessory worship is restored, we will face this question: Do we dance like David or despise like Michal? Said another way: Do we dance or die? I'm not suggesting, of course, that every follower of Jesus must dance to be a true worshiper, but I am suggesting that we not criticize (or worse, despise) those who do. We cannot afford to miss what God desires to do as the spirit of David's Tabernacle is restored. The fruit to be gained or lost is the fruit of the harvest.

Do you feel like dancing?

16

REFORM SIX

OPEN WORSHIP

A BREAK WITH PRIESTLY PROTOCOL

A fascinating observation about David's Tabernacle, implied by much of the context surrounding it, is that the tent was open for public view.

Of David's Tabernacle, and the Ark it housed, Mike Bickle wrote, "A tabernacle is a portable shrine. The tabernacle of David . . . was a small tent—only about 10 or 15 feet high and long (1 Chronicles 15:1; 16:1). The glory of God rested on the Ark, yet it was enshrined in a simple tent."[1]

Bickle adds, "In Moses' time, the glory that rested on the Ark was well hidden in the Holy of Holies, behind a thick veil. In David's tent, there was no veil to keep the people from seeing the glory of God. It was completely unprecedented—David laid the Ark of the Covenant in open view."[2]

We reach this conclusion of an open tent by inference from the description of the tent being set up in Jerusalem and the Ark being brought in. Notice this biblical account of those final moments of the Ark being brought from Gibeon to Jerusalem:

So they brought the Ark of God into the special tent David had prepared for it, and they sacrificed burnt offerings and peace offerings *before God*. . . . David appointed the following Levites to lead the people in worship *before the Ark of the* LORD by asking for his blessings and giving thanks and praise to the LORD, the God of Israel (1 Chron. 16:1,4, *NLT*, emphasis added).

Two expressions here are vital: "before God" and "before the Ark of the Lord." There is nothing here that suggests the Ark was hidden as it was in Moses' day.

No Need for Bells and Whistles

At Moses' Tabernacle, the Ark was well hidden—concealed behind a thick veil in the holy of holies. We recall that Moses' Tabernacle had three specific areas: the outer court, the inner court (the holy place), and the most holy place (the holy of holies). There was a large veil or tapestry that separated the holy place from the holy of holies, which prevented both access and view by anyone except the high priest—and even the high priest could enter that special place only once a year.

David radically changed all this. It was not a mere paradigm shift—it was more like a tectonic shift. Spiritually speaking, it was an earthquake of enormous proportions.

In David's Tabernacle, we see the Levites ministering directly before the Ark continuously. Furthermore, all of the people, as our text declares, join them "in worship before the Ark" (v. 4, *NLT*).

There was something different about David when it came to a worship protocol. He enjoyed radical worship. He did not just march to the beat of a different drummer; he danced to the beat of his own drum—his heart pounding passionately after God. In all this, he seems to have wanted everyone to join him.

David wasn't a king who took an interest in worship. *David was a worship leader who had a side job as king.* On one occasion he sang to the Lord, "I will thank you in front of the entire congregation. I will praise you before all the people" (Ps. 35:18, *NLT*). David led the way in worship.

It is easy sometimes to read through our Bibles and miss simple statements of profound significance. A brief phrase in 2 Samuel 7:18 falls into this category. We read, "David went in and sat before the Lord." No big deal, we might say—except for the facts of who David was and where he sat down.

David was in God's presence. He was in his tent, sitting in front of the Ark. Yet David was neither a priest nor a Levite. Under Jewish law only a Levite could minister in this holy place, and only the high priest could go into the holy of holies to minister before the Ark. Further, the high priest did not sit. He stood—and he kept moving. The sounds of the bells on his garment signaled to those outside that all was well (see Exod. 28:33-35). Today we might refer to this as worship with "all the bells and whistles." David's break with priestly protocol pictures a greater priesthood coming in Christ. One day, the way God's people came before Him would be grounded in worship, not in ritual! We don't need the bells and whistles. And we certainly don't need wooden arms. We need Jesus!

A Look Past the Veil

David, indeed, seemed to break all the rules set by those who preceded him. This man after God's own heart wanted everyone to catch a glimpse of the heart of God. I believe he intentionally kept the tent open—and God allowed it. Some 1,000 years before Christ would die on the cross and the veil in the temple would be permanently split in two, God allowed David to lift the veil for a relatively short pre-resurrection view. This is significant because David's Tabernacle was the only ancient home of God's holy Ark that had no veil. At least, there is no biblical record to suggest any other such open place of worship. Certainly neither the Tabernacle of Moses nor Solomon's Temple was like David's tent in this regard.

Concerning that veil, we know that on "Good Friday" God supernaturally ripped it in two at the moment of Christ's death. This was following our Lord's statement, "It is finished"—arguably the greatest three-word declaration of emancipation in the history of humankind. Finally, there was a sacrifice for humankind's sin providing direct access to God's presence forever.

In all of this discussion, a question still arises: Why was David apparently given this veil-exemption a thousand years before Christ's death? Mike Bickle suggests that God was allowing the worshipers themselves (some 4,000 musicians plus 288 singers) to replace the veil for that particular season (see 1 Chron. 6:31-32; 15:16-24; 23:4-19). Bickle writes, "Instead of the thick veil Moses used, David made musicians and singers into a human veil around the Ark."[3] Some likely think this is a theological stretch, but Bickle may be right.

Among today's worshipers, although we are aware that this veil has been lifted and we have free and full access to God through salvation in Christ, it sometimes seems as if we do not fully understand the totality of this access. It is for us much more than a one-time visit, even though Christ's sacrifice was indeed "once for all" (Heb. 9:26), and, like that sacrifice, our personal salvation happens just once. But I am speaking here of taking advantage of the removed veil through daily, passionate worship.

SAVIOR-SENSITIVE WORSHIP

Davidic worship reminds us that the veil is still removed. Worship for us is open! The tent curtains are up. We should not be afraid of open worship. To a degree, I can understand the seeker-sensitive mentality that in some church-growth models intends to create a comfort level for newcomers. Yet, we should also cultivate a Savior-sensitive worship model—one that seeks to create a climate for Jesus Himself to come, and to act! I believe it is possible to have both.

A worship mentor for many, Jack Hayford illustrated this important balance for several decades during his leadership as senior pastor at The Church On The Way in Van Nuys, California. My wife and I had the joy of attending Jack's church for more than a decade while Every Home for Christ was headquartered in the Los Angeles area in the 1980s.

We discovered quickly that The Church On The Way was a fellowship built on worship. Though we were deeply fed through the preaching of God's Word during those years, what we remember most is the open, sustained, focused worship in the services. During these days, something unique happened to my wife, and God used it to demonstrate to me the power of open praise. At the time, we lived in the Santa Clarita Valley, a good distance from The Church On The Way, which was located in the neighboring San Fernando Valley. We considered the drive well worth it for the worship and the teaching of the Word.

I mention the distance we traveled because it had some bearing on my wife's unusual experience. Dee had been to a hair salon close to our home and that evening shared something I thought was a bit odd. It concerned a conversation she had had with her beautician. At one point, her hairdresser had asked Dee about my occupation. Dee responded simply, "Oh, Dick is a Christian minister."

Not realizing that some ministers may not be pastors of congregations, the woman responded, "Oh, that's wonderful, Mrs. Eastman. What church does your husband serve as a minister?"

Because my wife was now paying the bill, and she was in a hurry to get to another appointment, she was hesitant to give the lady a lengthy explanation regarding the nature of our ministry. I was not, after all, a pastor of a church, but a leader of a parachurch ministry. So instead, Dee said simply, "Oh, we go to a church in the Valley called The Church On The Way."

Dee's hairdresser raised her head and with a look of both shock and joy said, "Oh, Mrs. Eastman, that's wonderful. I can't believe it. Oh, this is so exciting. I just can't believe it, Mrs. Eastman. What wonderful news!"

Dee was obviously startled by her response and commented, "I didn't know you attended our church."

"Oh, I don't go to any church, Mrs. Eastman," the lady explained. "In fact, I've never been to an actual church service in my life—only to funerals and weddings."

The woman could tell Dee was somewhat confused by her reaction. How could someone be so excited about a church she had never visited—especially someone who had never attended any church?

Dee's hairdresser quickly said, "I guess I should explain why I'm so excited about your church."

The woman then shared briefly about her bouts of discouragement and depression. On many days, she had wondered if she could make it. Then, just a few days earlier, another client began telling her about the change in her own life and how she had been healed of similar oppression. The transformation had begun when that client had attended a church in the San Fernando Valley of Los Angeles called The Church On The Way. It was there, the client explained, that she had found Christ as her personal Savior.

Dee's hairdresser's eyes filled with tears as she added, "Mrs. Eastman, the reason I'm so excited is this Sunday I plan to go to your church, and I just can't wait."

FAITH BY ANTICIPATION

Dee chuckled as she told me what had happened that day with her hairdresser. "Isn't it amazing," she said, "that someone can be so excited about going to church, even though she's never been there before?" *That's a different kind of faith,* I thought. *It's faith by anticipation!*

I am not sure I would even remember that conversation were it not for what happened the following Sunday.

We arrived for church at least 45 minutes prior to the third service that morning, hoping to get a seat in the main sanctuary (which at the time held about 700). Each Sunday had five identical services, but this still did not adequately handle the crowds. If you were merely on time (or, heaven forbid, slightly late), you would be ushered down a dark stairway into one of several auxiliary rooms in the basement where you could watch the worship and hear the morning message on a small-screen television. (This was more than two decades before large flat-screen monitors came on the scene.) I jokingly called it "ant worship" because Pastor Jack and the other pastors looked like ants.

Even if you did arrive in plenty of time, there would typically be people already standing in incredibly long lines that wrapped around the building and stretched down a side street or two, like young people queuing for a popular rock concert. Once in line, you still had to dig in, in a quasi-Christian military manner, to protect your position.

Suddenly, the doors would open and the jostling began as these normally nice worshipers struggled to move just a few places ahead in the line. I rejoiced merely because we "won the lottery" that day and made it safely into the main sanctuary. *No "ant worship" today*, I thought.

Suddenly two things happened simultaneously. While Pastor Jack headed toward the microphone to begin a worship chorus, Dee poked me forcefully to get my attention.

"Look," Dee said excitedly, "over there by the pillar." She was nodding her head as inconspicuously as possible toward one of several pillars scattered throughout the sanctuary.

"The lady in the yellow dress, just left of that pillar," Dee explained, "that's my hairdresser. She's here—in our service! I don't believe it!"

The opening phrases of the chorus were now being sung and, as was typical for worship at The Church On The Way, hands began to go up everywhere. It was a slow, worshipful chorus I still recall to this day: "In My Life, Lord, Be Glorified!"

As Dee nodded in the direction of her hairdresser, I remembered her telling me four days earlier that the woman had never gone to church anywhere. Naturally I wondered what her reaction would be.

So, as I worshiped, I peeked. What I saw next moves me to this day.

Because of the layout of the sanctuary, the row where Dee's hair-dresser stood was on an angle in front of us and to the right. This meant I could see her facial expressions clearly, at least from the side. Soon I could see them fully, because she turned her face right in my direction.

First, I saw her mouth drop wide open in astonishment. Her eyes were still wide open. She looked to the left, then to the right, and then up toward heaven. It was a jerky motion. Then, she shot up one hand and then the other. I had the sense that she was inwardly saying, *Well, if this is how they do it here, I'll do it this way, too.* (This all happened quickly—in a shorter amount of time, in fact, than it's taking me to tell the story.)

Her eyes were still wide open, and both of her hands were raised, as I watched two black parallel lines move visibly down from her eyes: Mascara was flowing freely with her tears. Gobs of it! She was weeping. Later I would learn that in those brief moments, not more than five minutes into the service, Dee's hairdresser had surrendered her life to Jesus. Worship had not frightened her away nor turned her off.

To Dee's beautician, open worship had been an open invitation to an open heaven—and she responded to that invitation by giving her heart to Christ. To me, this was a picture of the power of Davidic worship. Worship at David's tent was open, and David's kingdom was vastly multiplied as a result. Cultivating a climate of open worship, I believe, will help hasten the restoration of David's fallen tent (see Acts 15:16-18) and soften hearts for history's greatest harvest.

17

REFORM SEVEN

STRATEGIC WORSHIP

OPENING HEAVEN'S GATES

When Brother Lawrence, a radical seventeenth-century monk, was on his deathbed, he used the occasion to preach his lifelong worship message to fellow monks gathered about him:

> "I am not dying," Lawrence told them. "I'm just doing what I have been doing for the past 40 years, and doing what I expect to be doing for all eternity."
>
> "What is that?" a monk asked.
>
> Brother Lawrence answered, "I am worshiping the God I love!"[1]

Commenting on this passionate worshiper's dying words, A. W. Tozer said, "Worshiping God—that was primary for Brother Lawrence. He was also dying, but that was secondary."[2]

It is clear from even the most casual study of David's Tabernacle that the worship surrounding it was not an auxiliary function. It was absolutely the top priority. To David, worship was both primary and strategic. That familiar admonition on establishing priorities—"keep the main thing the main thing"—definitely applied to Davidic worship. In David's house, worship was the main thing! I've said it before and it is worth repeating—David was a full-time worshiper who had a part-time job as king!

This priority of Davidic worship is seen in such passages as 1 Chronicles 9:33, where we read, "The musicians, all prominent Levites, lived at the Temple. They were exempt from other responsibilities there since they were on duty at all hours" (*NLT*). David shared his own personal priority in worship when he voiced the passion of his life: "One thing I have desired of the LORD, that will I seek: that I may dwell in the house of the LORD all the days of my life, to behold the beauty of the LORD, and to inquire in His temple" (Ps. 27:4, *NKJV*).

Throughout these pages, I have suggested that a full restoring of all that we have seen related to David's ancient Tabernacle will sweep across the world in the last days, leading to history's greatest harvest (see Amos 9:11-15; Acts 15:16-18). If such is the case, we can expect intercessory worship to become the main thing in all we do as followers of Christ. Nothing could be more strategic in all of our planning. True, it may not be the only thing, but it will be the chief thing.

WORSHIPING WARRIORS

"It is no coincidence," Jack Hayford writes, "that Israel's greatest development in worship coincided with her broadest boundaries of government. David was the leader for both."[3] Hayford concludes, "There is no more insightful study in worship than the life and music of David. In worship he soars; with worship he wars."[4]

To David, worship was both primary and strategic. It was primary in that worship was the main thing; worship was central to all David and the people under his leadership did. But worship wasn't primary simply because David felt like making it so; it was primary because it was strategic.

In the simplest sense, "strategic" means that which counts the most. A hill taken in battle is said to be strategic if capturing that hill is critical to winning the battle. To David, worship was crucial to winning God's people's battles and, indeed, the entire war.

David was both a warrior and a worshiper. To David, worship provided supernatural ammunition against any enemy. He thought strategically. Hayford is right about David's worship strategy: "In worship he soars; with worship he wars."

Throughout the Davidic psalms we see how frequently spiritual warfare is woven together with themes of worship. One of David's psalms begins with the words, "I love you, O LORD, my strength. . . .

I call to the LORD, who is worthy of praise" (Ps. 18:1,3) and then transitions to this warfare theme:

> It is God who arms me with strength and makes my way perfect. He makes my feet like the feet of a deer; he enables me to stand on the heights. He trains my hands for battle; my arms can bend a bow of bronze. You give me your shield of victory, and your right hand sustains me; you stoop down to make me great. You broaden the path beneath me, so that my ankles do not turn (Ps. 18:32-36).

Elsewhere in Psalms we discover a similar "worship-warfare" theme. David sang, "Praise be to the LORD my Rock, who trains my hands for war, my fingers for battle" (Ps. 144:1). In an earlier psalm we read, "But you have raised a banner for those who honor you—a rallying point in the face of attack" (Ps. 60:4, *NLT*).

Especially familiar is David's declaration of praise: "May God arise, may his enemies be scattered; may his foes flee before him" (Ps. 68:1). This is a reference to God's glory cloud rising during Israel's journeys in the wilderness generations earlier and a reminder of how the cloud served as a symbol of God's presence as He went before His people into battle.

In all of these Davidic psalms, we see a clear relationship between strategic warfare and strategic worship—a relationship that many prayer practitioners of our day understand well. I have met few prayer leaders who have traveled to distant places throughout the world for prayer initiatives who did not recognize the strategic significance of intercessory worship. Most would never move into a sustained time of focused intercession without devoting considerable time to worship. These leaders understand the strategic importance of worship in our warfare. Joseph Garlington suggests, "If the music David played on a single instrument literally drove evil spirits away from King Saul [see 1 Sam. 16:23], then we need to wage Spirit-led warfare by worshiping God and playing on a hundred or a thousand instruments!"[5]

Further linking worship with warfare, Garlington asserts, "Anything God accomplishes in the earth is done through spiritual means using spiritual people.... The giving of tithes, offerings, and gifts are acts of war.... Praising God is an act of war.... Worshiping God is an act of war. . . . Prayer is an act of war. . . . Fasting is an act of war."[6]

We are indeed at war, and intercessory worship may well become our most strategic weapon. At stake in this war are multitudes of future believers, from every tribe, tongue, people and nation, who will someday worship God before His throne (see Rev. 7:9-10). We are at war for the harvest, and what the Church desperately needs more of today are worshiping warriors!

A Harvest Song

If "strategic" refers to that which counts the most, surely the souls of these vast multitudes fall into that category. Entire nations and people groups yet to be redeemed are at stake in this war.

We see this very harvest focus permeating the worship of David when he sets up his tent on that modest mountain in Jerusalem (which was more of a mound) that we call Mount Zion. It is amazing that at that celebration, David composed a Great Commission song 1,000 years before Christ gave His supreme commission! David's worship psalm was a harvest song.

Let's look again at the events surrounding the placing of the Ark in that modest tent when David moved it from Gibeon to Jerusalem. When the Ark was finally placed in the tent, David composed a song that in our various present translations includes but 30 verses of Scripture. It is remarkable that in this relatively brief song, David repeatedly links worship to impacting the entire world with a message of God's greatness and glory. Consider these Scriptures:

> That day David gave to Asaph and his fellow Levites this song of thanksgiving to the LORD: Give thanks to the LORD and proclaim his greatness. *Let the whole world know* what he has done. Sing to him; yes, sing his praises. *Tell everyone* about his miracles. . . . *Let the whole earth sing to the LORD!* Each day *proclaim the good news* that he saves. *Publish his glorious deeds among the nations. Tell everyone* about the amazing things he does. . . . *O nations of the world, recognize the LORD*, recognize that the LORD is glorious and strong. . . . *Let all the earth tremble* before him. *The world is firmly established* and cannot be shaken. Let the heavens be glad, and *let the earth rejoice! Tell all the nations*

that the LORD is King (1 Chron. 16:7-9,23-24,28,30-31, *NLT*, emphasis added).

In this brief song, there are at least 10 references to the nations, peoples, world or earth being impacted as the result of worship. Note the phrases "let the whole world know"; "tell everyone"; "let the whole earth sing"; "proclaim the good news"; "publish his glorious deeds among the nations"; "O nations . . . recognize the LORD"; "let all the earth tremble"; "the world is firmly established"; "let the earth rejoice"; and "tell all the nations that the LORD is King!" Can there be any question that David possessed a worship-vision for the world?

THE GREAT CONNECTION

It cannot be a mere coincidence that when David "pitched" his tent to house the Ark of God's presence, his song strategically focused on the entire world. There can be no mistaking the connection to the last-days restoration of the Tabernacle of David and God's ultimate harvest. Along with the Great Commission, we must recognize the "Great Connection"—that of intercessory worship to the great end-time in-gathering of the lost.

David was a man after God's own heart, and the heart of God clearly encompasses the whole world (see John 3:16; Mark 16:15). I believe David's song at the Tabernacle dedication was not his own song, but a song the Holy Spirit was singing through him. It is a song I am certain God wants to sing through each of us in a thousand different ways as He calls in His harvest.

The strategic tie of worship to the harvest is something John Piper addresses powerfully and beautifully in his book *Let the Nations Be Glad*. Piper especially helped me see the ministry of Every Home for Christ in a fresh light. I had always thought previously of EHC as a ministry primarily seeking to win souls through our home-to-home evangelism by systematically planting seeds of the gospel in all of these homes—and the Lord has been gracious to grant encouraging fruit over all these years.

Indeed, over EHC's 65-plus years of work, God has allowed the planting of over 3 billion printed salvation messages in homes in 227 countries. As of this writing, more than 101 million decision cards have been returned and followed up with Bible courses by trained Christian workers. That number is presently increasing by as many as one million each month!

But Piper helped me see that we are doing much more than just bringing souls into the Kingdom—not that this is in any way insignificant. Additionally, wonderfully, we are helping to mobilize redeemed worshipers, by the millions, who are being added to that awesome multitude of eternal worshipers that the apostle John tells us no man could number (see Rev. 7:9). What a glorious assignment!

John Piper also helped me see the Great Commission in a new light—the light of worship. This insight from Piper was especially helpful:

> God is pursuing with omnipotent passion a worldwide purpose of gathering joyful worshipers for himself from every tribe and tongue and people and nation. . . . Therefore, let us bring our affections into line with his, and, for the sake of his name, let us renounce the quest for worldly comforts and join his global purpose. If we do this, God's omnipotent commitment to his name will be over us like a banner, and we will not lose, in spite of many tribulations (Acts 9:16; Rom. 8:35-39).[7]

God Has a Plan

Because I believe God has called me, at least to some degree, to be a mission strategist, I have pondered the relevance of intercessory worship and David's Tabernacle being restored to fulfilling a particular ministry mandate—any mandate. Specifically, at Every Home for Christ our mandate is to participate with others in helping fulfill the Great Commission by seeing a presentation of the gospel taken to every home in the entire world. As stated earlier, most often two messages are given to most homes in a targeted area—one for adults and one for children.

It is estimated that as many as 2.7 billion people in the world may never have heard the name of Jesus even once, or, at best, have never received a clear presentation of the gospel. What would it take for our ministry to reach all of these lost people (living in some 500 to 600 million homes) in the space of a single decade?

As our global leadership team took a strategic look at this ambitious goal, we were repeatedly challenged by what seemed to be insurmountable obstacles. Consider, for example, the more than 100 million Muslim homes (500 million people) in the Arab Middle East, where restrictions seemingly stopped us dead in our tracks. This could have been cause to give up, were it not for similar circumstances faced in Soviet Russia prior to the 1990s. In that part of the world, things changed almost overnight, as I have described earlier. EHC has now visited more than 40 million households in Russia and the former Soviet Union, now known as the C.I.S. (Commonwealth of Independent States).

Besides government restrictions, there were other formidable obstacles as well. The cost of fulfilling our total mandate was daunting—approaching a billion dollars. We knew we could not do it alone, and we also realized that, although the Body of Christ already easily has the resources needed to accomplish the mission, much of what is presently being done is uncoordinated, often unnecessarily duplicated and frequently overtly sectarian.

So, we knew we had our work cut out for us. Obviously, we could not do it all, but we could do our part. Further, if all the critical parts came together in Christ, then all of us could, indeed, do it all!

In the midst of drafting our long-range plan, I was particularly encouraged by a promise from Isaiah that fell into one day's Bible-reading assignment. I read:

I have a plan for the whole earth, for my mighty power reaches throughout the world. The LORD Almighty has spoken—who can change his plans? When his hand moves, who can stop him? (Isa. 14:26-27, *NLT*).

God, indeed, has a plan, and it is a plan for the whole earth. We didn't have to come up with our own plan; we just had to tap into God's. It quickly became obvious to me that the restoration of David's Tabernacle was central to that plan. Of course, I readily realized that we couldn't restore David's Tabernacle (whatever that meant) by ourselves. Something of an unprecedented unity and spirit of cooperation would have to sweep across all spectrums of Christ's Body. *Still*, I wondered, *could intercessory worship somehow help make all this happen?*

A STRATEGIC OPPORTUNITY

Experts in the field of missions research helped me see the light on this issue. One of these was Dr. Todd Johnson, co-author with Dr. David Barrett of the highly regarded and definitive *World Christian Encyclopedia*. Johnson evaluated the progress of global missions in light of the then-approaching new millennium at a consultation in Colorado Springs in March 1999.

According to Dr. Johnson, more than 1,500 global plans, among both denominational and parachurch organizations, had surfaced in the previous two decades. Each of these plans focused on some aspect of completing the Great Commission in our lifetimes. Back in the early- to mid-1990s, many were embracing a goal of finishing the task by the year 2000. I even recall how several years before that deadline Dr. Bill Bright, founder of Campus Crusade for Christ, even gave me a watch that had a unique "countdown" on the dial to show how much time was left until the year 2000. This was a "big deal" for a "big task."

Sadly, as Johnson explained at that consultation, the vast majority of these 1,500 plans, though voicing a commitment to cooperation and partnership, were pretty much functioning independently. True, many had gathered for large consultations in the mid- to late-1990s to report on their activities, but when those consultations concluded, very little strategic partnering had actually occurred.

Dr. Johnson then shared several factors that he believed were essential to seeing the completion of the Great Commission in our time or any future generation. Included in his list were such factors as less duplication of ministry effort, increased "intentional" cooperation and planning, and a number of other ideas.

Presenting statistical data to back up his claims, Johnson predicted that unless God opened up a way to unite these independent plans in a far more focused manner, by the conclusion of the next decade there would still be the same number of unreached people groups as there currently were. The worse news was that those unreached groups would be even larger in population, with greater numbers yet to be evangelized. Keep in mind that this consultation took place in 1999. Here in our present day, we can say, sadly, that Todd Johnson was right.

Although Dr. Johnson's was understandably a negative assessment, I found my heart rejoicing in how God had been leading Every

Home for Christ to establish The Jericho Center, which at that time was soon to become a reality. I felt God would use this facility to help, if only modestly, in this cause of bringing ministries together, and to begin to reverse these trends. Our motto for the center is simply: "Where Christ's Body unites, walls fall!"

The center, now celebrating almost a decade of service, has been committed to hosting consultations of various potential participating entities wishing to be a part of strategic alliances for evangelism and discipleship. It also serves to saturate these plans in continuous worship and intercession. But what will it take for much greater cooperation and partnership to occur globally?

True, there is some measure of isolated partnering happening today, but could much more happen on a sweeping scale? If so, how? To me, the destinies of nations are at stake. I believe one key component could make the difference. That component is the subject of this entire book: intercessory worship.

A STRATEGIC COMPONENT

I believe intercessory worship could well be the difference between fulfilling and not fulfilling Christ's Great Commission to His Church.

For this reason, a foundational goal of The Jericho Center is to sustain a 24-hour covering of intercessory worship over the strategic consultations being hosted at the center, as well as the plans that will result from them. It is not known if such a strategy of on-site intercessory worship has ever been directly linked to an ongoing consultation process that seeks to develop such sweeping alliances for evangelism, discipleship and church planting. I believe this spirit of intercessory worship then needs to be taken to the darkest parts of our planet to lift a canopy of praise over these places as God's people intercede continuously for an open heaven above these nations so all can receive the knowledge of Jesus Christ.

Central to this desire for continuous praise and intercession is that biblical harp and bowl picture, found in Revelation 5:8-10 and highlighted in the first chapter of this book.

As stated earlier, the linking of these symbols to the ingathering of the harvest is immediately followed in the text by the corporate pronouncement directed to the Lamb of God Himself in the form of a new song: "You are worthy to take the scroll and to open its seals, because you were slain, and with your blood you purchased men for God from every tribe and language and people and nation" (v. 9).

Just how essential is worship combined with intercession to completing the Great Commission? Meditate again on these words of John Piper: "Missions exists because worship doesn't. . . . [Missions] is a temporary necessity. But worship abides forever. So worship is the fuel and the goal of missions."[8]

Further consider Eugene Peterson's unique paraphrase of Isaiah's lengthy prophecy as it nears its conclusion in chapter 66:

> I'm going to come and then gather everyone—all nations, all languages. They'll come and see my glory. I'll set up a station at the center. I'll send the survivors of judgment all over the world: Spain and Africa, Turkey and Greece, and the far-off islands that have never heard of me, who know nothing of what I've done nor who I am. I'll send them out as missionaries to preach my glory among the nations (Isa. 66:18-19, THE MESSAGE).

Personally, as I read this I see a vast army of a new order of missionaries (that some are labeling "intercessory missionaries") emerging in the immediate days ahead. These missionaries will declare God's glory and lift a canopy of praise throughout all nations. In practical terms, to see sustained intercessory worship reach into the darkest and most difficult-to-evangelize nations, ministries such as Every Home for Christ and Project Luke 18 in Kansas City are developing specific programs to equip these intercessory missionaries for this task.

Because we believe levels of intercession and worship must increase in order to confront the evil forces at work in these darkest regions, a new kind of missionary must be equipped and sent to these nations. These "intercessory missionaries" will have a primary responsibility of seeing continuous "worship-saturated prayer" rise in these places—particularly to cover national workers, missionaries and the Church in general as it reaches out to disciple the nations.

Working in conjunction with indigenous believers who will help take leadership in sustaining such prayer, teams of intercessory missionaries will establish centers of prayer and worship in these difficult regions and will labor to support the local church through prayer, encouragement and other practical avenues of support.

Note again the sentence in the Isaiah 66 passage cited above: "I'll set up a station at the center" (v. 19). Could it be that centers of sustained intercessory worship will become key to creating open heavens over these dark places so the work of evangelism and discipleship can accelerate significantly? Recently I told a friend, "I would like to see this happen just to see *what* happens!"

The overall objective of these training programs, therefore, is to train and send cross-cultural intercessory missionaries for up to two years (or longer) to establish such centers. They will partner with the indigenous church to see all local Christians discipled in their primary identity as worshipers of God, living unto the glory of God, and then carrying that identity into their neighborhoods and villages to gather in an even greater harvest of worshipers by winning multitudes to Jesus.

HEAVEN'S GATES

With all this in mind, return with me to the overall theme of part two of this book: worship reforms related to a last-days restoration of the Tabernacle of David. I fully agree with Mike Bickle's connection of intercessory worship to the fulfilling of the Great Commission. Bickle asks:

> What does the restoration of the Tabernacle of David mean to the Church today? I believe it means much more than incorporating the priestly worship and prayer practiced before the Davidic tabernacle. I believe it points the way for us to become a united, victorious apostolic Church that walks in mature love and reaches and reaps the great harvest in all the nations.[9]

Kevin Conner, whose in-depth study on the Tabernacle of David helped me immeasurably in developing these insights, also concurs. In his book *The Tabernacle of David*, Conner offers this concluding observation:

> Our study is completed. Under the outpouring of the Holy Spirit in the early Church on both Jew and Gentile, James, by a word of wisdom quoted the prophecy of Amos concerning the building of the Tabernacle of David. The whole purpose of this

was for the coming in of the Gentiles. The Gentiles were not to be placed under the Law, that is, in the Tabernacle of Moses under the Old Covenant. They were to come in on the ground of grace, that is, into the Tabernacle of David which was symbolic of the New Covenant. In this tabernacle, Jew and Gentile would become one in Christ on the ground of grace, apart from the works of the Law and ceremonials of the Law Covenant.[10]

Think of all this happening in our very lifetime. Could it be that much of what I have suggested in this chapter is truly possible?

Remember those consultations I spoke of earlier? One wonders what might happen if all these strategic consultations and their resulting alliances were bathed in both continuous worship (inviting God's supreme presence) and continuous intercession (entreating God's supernatural power). Might we not truly see the Great Commission completed?

Further imagine each God-saturated consultation having one primary objective: God's agenda for each organization or ministry as we corporately link together into one entity to honor Christ everywhere. Can you picture ministries and agencies of all sorts (and their leaders) laying their plans, egos and ambitions before the Lord to see His purposes fulfilled as His children truly unite?

I believe that one of the primary keys to this happening is intercessory worship. Will we recognize it and use it? Could what we have been suggesting in part two of this book provide just such a key? Is Christ's Body ready to open heaven's gates and release a global baptism of God's glory through an intercessory worship movement that restores the Tabernacle of David "so that the rest of humanity might find the Lord" (Acts 15:17, NLT)?

The scope of all this is obviously sweeping! Imagine "the rest of humanity" finding the Lord in these last days! Of course, for anything close to this to occur, we need to take the gospel to those who have never heard. I would suggest that this is entirely possible. Every Home for Christ's present decade-long goal, for example, is to work with Christ's Body globally to reach at least 500 million homes (families) with the good news of Christ's love. That's an average of some 50 million households per year. If the estimated global average of persons per home (between four and five) holds true, this means the gospel will be placed within reach of almost 2.5 billion people. At this writing, 142 million homes have been visited in just the past 24 months, meaning the goal is easily within reach.

Consider further the remarkable number of people responding to these outreaches. (Every Home for Christ includes a decision/response card with each gospel message given.) During the past 12 months alone, more than 13 million responses have been followed up with Bible courses as the result of these campaigns. *That's 13 million people expressing interest in knowing Christ in a single year.* Additionally, new churches are being planted in villages where there were previously no church fellowships. I referred to these as "Christ Groups" earlier. These new fellowships are encouraged to go into nearby villages and neighborhoods and reproduce themselves. In the most recent 12-month period, more than 22,000 new church fellowships were planted through these village campaigns.

Along with this, imagine other outreaches—such as Youth With A Mission (YWAM), Campus Crusade for Christ with its *Jesus* film strategy, various other denominational church-planting initiatives like the Southern Baptists and the Assemblies of God, and a host of others—all knit together in an atmosphere of joyful intercessory worship sustained by such ministries as the International House of Prayer and their hundreds of affiliates, the Jericho Center with their thousands of "Walls of Prayer" globally, and the 24/7 youth prayer movement out of the United Kingdom that now is operating in scores of nations. As we envision this united harvest work, we can begin to understand the joy that heaven must be experiencing among the peoples of the world. I believe joyful, exuberant Davidic worship will be central to all of this. There is little doubt that heaven must be ecstatic as more and more people are reached for Christ. Personally, I believe the angels are going nuts!

This is indeed an exciting time to be alive. It is a time to set our sights on finishing the task of world evangelization. It is a time to transform our families, cities and nations. But let's not miss our ultimate goal in the process. John Piper keeps it before us when he writes:

All of history is moving toward one great goal, the white-hot worship of God and his Son among all the peoples of the earth. Missions is not that goal. It is the means. And for that reason it is the second greatest human activity in the world.[11]

Let's not forget the first (worship), and we will surely succeed at the second (completion)! As we process these key worship realities and reforms and begin to embrace and apply Davidic worship personally and corporately, I see prophetic rivers of transformation beginning to flow into our neighborhoods and the nations. It's time to get our feet wet. Let's take the plunge.

PART THREE

RIVERS

18

Make Room for My Glory

RIVER ONE:
River of Intimacy—

The Prophetic Dimension of Intercessory Worship

For the tenth time, God whispered in my heart, *Make room for My glory*.

I knew it was the tenth time because I was counting. It was now past midnight, and I had little hope of sleep. I had no idea I would soon be introduced to the realm of prophetic response in worship. I was not into many "prophetic" concepts or ideas at that point in my life, and I doubt I had ever heard the term "prophetic worship" prior to this experience. I also realized that significant segments of the Body of Christ questioned some who emphasized prophetic ministry.

My journey into this dimension of worship had actually begun several months earlier, when I received the invitation to speak at a conference in Texas for a large gathering of university students. The conference planners expected more than 5,000 college-aged youth, representing almost every major university in America, as well as several overseas universities, to attend. I was surprised to be invited, especially when I saw the list of 10 other speakers—all of whom were well known. Most had radio or television ministries and were highly regarded conference speakers.

I was asked to lead several smaller prayer gatherings in the afternoons during the conference, as well as speak during three plenary sessions. A hotel ballroom had been reserved for this purpose. The organizers warned me in advance that the prayer sessions might only be attended by small numbers of participants, but that it was vital to provide a prayer covering over the conference. I was honored to accept the invitation.

WHISPERS IN THE NIGHT

For my plenary session presentations, I prepared three teachings with accompanying worksheets, each building on the previous lesson. The overall theme was "How to Be a Prayer Mobilizer." Lessons one and two were introductory to the third, which I felt was the most important lesson. Lesson three's worksheet included the "how to" portion of the teaching, a detail that I emphasize because of God's repeated whispers in the night: *Make room for My glory!*

I was excited about these messages because I felt students could use the information to mobilize others to pray when they returned to their campuses. I also realized I would have a captive audience because everyone was required to attend all three plenary meetings. I felt that as I built one lesson upon the other, these 5,000 student leaders would become better equipped to be mobilizers of prayer.

To spark interest, I intentionally distributed all three worksheets in the first session rather than handing out one lesson per session. I wanted to whet the students' appetites for further teaching by showing them the various outlines with many "fill-in" blank places in the notes.

Following the first lesson, I was encouraged by the increase in the number of students who attended the optional prayer meetings. From a handful the first day, attendance increased to 200 the second day. On the third day, the number increased even more.

The following morning would be my final plenary session, and I was to be the first of several speakers. That third night God would visit me in a most peculiar way. But before that, there was something unique He would show me that afternoon.

The prayer time was scheduled to last two hours. After a few introductory moments, we began to seek God. Then, about an hour into the gathering, I felt an impression to move from my kneeling position to lying prostrate before the Lord. I did not make any attempt to encourage others to do the same.

For almost an hour, I lay in that position. Soon I began to weep, and I could hear others weeping as well. A deep brokenness was settling in the room.

A WOMB OF GLORY

Finally I sat up and looked around—amazed. Every person was on his or her face in prayer without any direction from me. I felt the Lord speak: *This is a womb of My glory.* A womb, of course, is where life is conceived. It is from a womb that life is finally birthed into its fullness.

Another impression followed: *What you see here today I long to do for the entire group tomorrow. I desire to transform the entire convention center into a womb of My glory.*

I prayerfully thought, *That sounds nice, Lord, but how is it possible?*

This was one of those prayer questions to which an immediate answer was not necessarily expected. I even wondered if I was imagining all this. How could what happened so spontaneously with just a few hundred people happen in a highly structured plenary setting with thousands of people and many guest speakers, each with a burning message on his heart?

The more I thought about it, the more I concluded it was just wishful thinking. My mind kept coming back to my final message for that next morning. But first there would be that long, sleepless night and the repeated "still, small voice" of the Lord.

THE WHISPERS OF GOD

As Dee and I retired for the night, I am sure my wife sensed my restlessness. Yet, as is customary for Dee, she was sleeping deeply in seconds while I tossed and turned.

For me, sleep was not to be. I tried everything. I am sure I counted both sheep and blessings until I lost count of what I was counting. Finally I asked the Lord, "Why can't I sleep when I face such an important assignment?"

That's when I first heard God's whisper: *Make room for My glory!*

I responded, "God, is that You?"

I heard the words again: *Make room for My glory!*

"How, God? What do You mean?" I asked.

He answered with the same statement: *Make room for My glory!*

I inquired, "How can I make room for Your glory?" I really had no idea what God wanted me to do.

After hearing the same impression 10 times, I desperately said, "Okay, God! Whatever it means, I will do it!"

I still had no idea what God wanted me to do, but He seemed to honor my small step of faith. Suddenly He asked, *Have you ever heard finer Bible teaching than you've heard these past two days?*

I was not sure where this was going, but I said, "No, Lord, I can't remember being more inspired by teaching than at this gathering." It was, indeed, some of the best teaching I had ever heard. I was hoping mine was having as great an impact as the messages from the other speakers.

Have you ever experienced more zealous and joyful singing than among these college youth? the Lord asked.

I answered, "Never, Lord." Then I added, "These students radiate zeal!"

There's only one problem, He said firmly. *In all of this activity, no one has taken the time to make room for My glory. Through each of these days I have been longing to pour out My glory, but each time I am ready, someone interrupts with another message, song or announcement. Every moment has been packed with programming.*

A CALL TO DO NOTHING

Before I could ask God what all this meant for my final plenary session, He asked, *Would you make room for My glory during your last session in the morning? Are you willing to go to the lectern and do absolutely nothing? Will you stand there and simply trust Me to reveal My glory?*

I was stunned. What did He mean by "do absolutely nothing"? And what about my final integral lesson on becoming a prayer mobilizer? I had distributed three sets of worksheets. The third still had all those blank spaces for students to fill in the key aspects of the teaching. The students would be awaiting the climactic teaching, or so I thought.

Forgetting for a moment God's omniscience and foreknowledge, I said, "God, did You forget that my final session is the third of a three-part series? If I skip it, everyone will notice!"

Before I could say more, God asked again, *Will you make room for My glory?* He added, *All through this conference, I've been looking for someone in leadership who would set aside their plans to make room for My glory. Would you make room for My glory?*

It was now past 3 A.M., and although I was still uncertain as to what to do later that morning, I responded through tears, "Lord, whatever it takes, if You'll just give me courage, I will make room for Your glory."

LIQUID PRAYER

Before sunrise I quietly stepped into the shower; then I waited for my wife to awaken. I was dressed and sitting on the sofa when Dee finally showered and dressed. I asked her to sit beside me. I could not hold back the tears.

"Honey, what's wrong?" she asked.

"I didn't sleep at all last night," I answered. "God asked me to do something in my final session, and I'm not sure how to do it."

"What has He asked you to do?"

"Nothing!"

"What do you mean, 'nothing'?" she asked, confused.

"That's it—*nothing*!" I responded.

Perplexed, Dee asked, "How do you just do nothing?"

It sounded silly (even humorous), but I replied, "I have no idea. I've never just done 'nothing' before."

"But you can't just do nothing," Dee insisted.

"I know! But that's what God said. He wants me to set aside my third lesson and just go to the pulpit and wait for His glory."

My wife tried to pray for me, but each time she began to speak, she would simply begin weeping. Suddenly, Dee was sobbing. I decided I'd better jump in, or we wouldn't get any praying done before leaving for the auditorium. I began my own petitioning, and as I did, I felt God speak a final time: *I have heard all of Dee's tears today.*

As we left for the auditorium, I remembered Charles Spurgeon's unique definition of a believer's tears. Spurgeon labeled them "liquid prayer"![1]

A RIVER OF INTIMACY

Stepping to the lectern, I was both anxious and uncertain. *Here goes nothing*, I mused. My attempts at obedience that morning were further complicated by my introduction.

The emcee stressed how vital my final lesson would be. He proceeded to "fire up" the students, even sending ushers out into the aisles with extra worksheets in case some had forgotten theirs. I wanted to crawl into the proverbial hole and hide.

To my great relief, as I walked to the lectern, God gave me a simple directive. At least God's *nothing* would have a degree of specificity. I was to ask students to turn to Isaiah 6 and get on their knees facing forward. Then I was to ask all of them to pray verses 1 through 8 aloud—not in unison but aloud, each at his or her own pace. God wanted all present to identify with Isaiah's vision of his encounter with God Himself.

The *nothing* part of my assignment came after that. Indeed, nothing else would be required because God was clearly in charge. What happened in the next 20 minutes none present could forget. Students with Bibles in hand were kneeling face forward, as a cacophony of voices filled the convention center. Within moments, I understood what God intended to do.

Suddenly, without prompting, students began streaming into the aisles—getting on their faces. Brokenness spread across the auditorium.

Finally, my assigned hour was almost over. I turned to ask the emcee what to do, but he was prostrate under the piano, weeping. The worship team members were likewise scattered across the stage, each prostrate in prayer. Every delegate—all 5,000—was facedown before God. I had never seen anything like it.

The river of God's presence was clearly flowing. It was, paradoxically, a river of both travail and delight. More than that, it was a *river of intimacy*. I knew that something was being born in those moments. The delight came with the same intensity that usually follows childbirth. The promise of the day before had come true. The entire auditorium had become a womb of God's presence. Room had been made for God's glory, and when that crack in the dam appeared, God's fullness flowed. Many students remained on their faces well into the afternoon.

By day's end, extraordinary joy came. God had simply longed for these students to draw closer to Him—to allow the interruption of their plans and programs, and to seek Him alone. This experience showed me that all of His rivers of delight seem to begin with this *river of intimacy*. It is in this river that we come to understand *the prophetic dimension of intercessory worship*.

A CHANNEL OF WORSHIP

For a number of years, I have observed a growing recognition of prophetic ministry in the Body of Christ. More recently, I have noticed a similar openness to prophetic worship—something I will define shortly. I believe this is all related to what I have shared previously in this book about intercessory worship and particularly about the restoration of the

Tabernacle of David in the last days. Here I will simply say that not long after I began this unusual journey (with the 40-day worship fast mentioned at the outset), I began to envision rivers of passionate prophetic worship along with fervent, focused intercession flowing throughout the Church globally. The intercession was saturated in worship and became prophetic in nature.

As I shared in chapter 1, on the first day of what was to become my 40-day worship fast, God drew my attention to Psalm 37:4 and the familiar promise that He would give those who delight in Him the desires of their hearts. Of course, what I most desired then, and still do today, is that the entire world could experience the joy of knowing Jesus.

As I opened my Bible to Psalm 37:4 to read this beautiful promise once again, my eyes caught a glimpse of a phrase in the previous psalm, and I redirected my attention to read these verses: "All humanity finds shelter in the shadow of your wings. You feed them from the abundance of your own house, letting them drink from your rivers of delight" (Ps. 36:7-8, *NLT*).

In subsequent days the phrase "rivers of delight" filled my mind. What were these rivers? What did it mean to drink from them? How could we release these rivers into our everyday circumstances as well as the nations?

Several descriptions of life-giving rivers mentioned in Scripture immediately came to my mind. I reflected on how these rivers are associated with God's presence and His power to heal and restore. I felt God saying that He has numerous transforming "rivers of delight" that will someday flow through His people and into all the world. In those rivers, we will see the literal transformation of peoples and nations.

I soon envisioned an array of these prophetic, supernatural rivers being released through God's praying people. The channel that carried these rivers was prophetic intercessory worship. I was convinced that these rivers would flow out of the harp and bowl intercessory worship movement, which I have described earlier as being foundational to the restoration of the Tabernacle of David globally in the last days.

THE WINDS OF WORSHIP

It was not until 12 years after the Texas conference that I began to understand more fully the prophetic nature of those moments of making room for His glory and the relationship between that experience and a "last-days" movement of intercessory worship.

I also realized that because of the nature of such worship, it often becomes uniquely prophetic, a theme we will explore in these remaining chapters. We will see how rivers of God are being released, each representing a corresponding "prophetic dimension" of intercessory worship. These "rivers of delight" are indeed beckoning us to come and drink freely.

But first, what do we mean by "prophetic worship"?

Any study of prophetic intercessory worship must begin with a look at the word "prophecy" itself.

Both the Greek and Hebrew words for "prophecy" in the Bible mean "to speak before" or "to speak in front of."[2] In John's Revelation we find a phrase referring to Christ and the subject of prophecy: "For the testimony of Jesus is the spirit of prophecy" (Rev. 19:10). Jack Hayford explains:

> The entire Bible is a product of the Holy Spirit, who is not only "the Spirit of truth" (John 16:13), but also "the Spirit of prophecy" (Revelation 19:10). The verb "to prophesy" (derived from the Greek preposition *pro* and verb *pehmi*) means "to speak from before." The preposition "before" in this use may mean: (1) "in advance" and/or (2) "in front of." Thus to *prophesy* is a proper term to describe the proclamation of God's Word as it forecasts events. It may also describe the declaration of God's Word forthrightly, boldly, or confrontingly before a group of individuals—telling forth God's truth and will. So, in both respects, the Bible is prophetic: A Book that reveals God's will through His Word and His words, as well as a Book that reveals God's plan and predictions.[3]

When we speak of prophetic worship, we are speaking of prophecy as it is applied to and through our worship. Worship, in this sense, might be used by God to declare what may happen in the future or simply to deliver a message from His heart.

Interestingly, a message from God delivered through prophetic song might actually be delivered into the heavenlies before "principalities" and "rulers of the darkness" (Eph. 6:12, *NKJV*) to announce

God's intended will. Such worship thus becomes an act of spiritual warfare, even as the singers are exalting God. It becomes intercessory when the worship releases God's power into the circumstances of others, usually by first binding or restraining the invisible, dark powers.

PRAISING PROPHETICALLY

In David's day, prophetic praise or worship clearly was understood. Of this reality, Jack Hayford writes:

> After raising the Tabernacle in Jerusalem and anticipating the building of the Temple, David organized and provided for the support of music leaders and ministries to enhance Israel's worship (see 1 Chron. 25:2-7). Choirs and orchestras not only were prepared to sing and play skillfully, but they also were selected for their sensitivity to the spirit of prophecy.[4]

Notice the worship team David established around the Tabernacle: "David and the army commanders then appointed men from the families of Asaph, Heman, and Jeduthun to proclaim God's messages to the accompaniment of harps, lyres, and cymbals" (1 Chron. 25:1, NLT). To "proclaim God's messages" with musical accompaniment refers to prophetic worship.

Later in the passage we are given the names of six worship leaders "who prophesied, using the harp in thanking and praising the LORD" (1 Chron. 25:3). Then in verse 7, we are told that many other worshipers—all "trained and skilled in music for the LORD"—were similarly involved (including the leaders, this Davidic worship team had 288 members).

These worshipers were not only skilled, but they were also taught prophetic worship. Hayford adds:

> This description reveals a blend both of spontaneity to the Holy Spirit and preparedness for skilled musical presentation. Their prophesying involved more than setting existing Scripture to music. These musicians were to wait on the Lord for inspiration—living truth that would ignite worship and joy in the hearts of God's people.[5]

Suggesting that we need this same type of ministry in the Church today, Hayford queries:

> Moses longed for the day that all of God's people would prophesy (see Num. 11:29); shouldn't we also expect our choirs and instruments to minister with the gift of prophecy? Isn't it possible that the New Testament restoration of the Tabernacle of David may bring us to new dimensions of Holy Spirit-inspired praise and worship in song?[6]

I believe the answers to Hayford's questions are a resounding yes and that such prophetic worship is happening in the global harp and bowl intercessory worship movement. As I have documented earlier, this movement is already impacting the harvest of souls globally. The psalmist clearly observed the link between prophetic worship and the harvest. He sang, "All you have made will praise you, O LORD; your saints will extol you. They will tell of the glory of your kingdom and speak of your might, so that all men may know of your mighty acts and the glorious splendor of your kingdom" (Ps. 145:10-12).

DEEP AND WIDE: A WORD ABOUT RIVERS

What we're seeing today will, I believe, culminate as a glorious prophetic river of God's presence in all its fullness, to be released through our worship and channeled by our intercession. Consider the words of the psalmist: "There is a river whose streams make glad the city of God, the holy place where the Most High dwells. God is within her, she will not fall; God will help her at break of day" (Ps. 46:4-5).

The psalmist pictures a river with various streams that flow from God's dwelling place. God Himself is in the midst of the city and thus the river. Some would contend the river is God—the flow of His very presence by His Spirit—which is why I define our first river in this study as a *river of intimacy*. To get into the river is to get into God, and that is intimacy!

Ezekiel likewise described a life-giving river possessed of God's healing power (see Ezek. 47:1-12). When the prophet first steps in, the river's depth suddenly increases. It reaches the prophet's ankles and then rises to his knees. Next, the river's at his waist. Soon Ezekiel testifies, "The river was too deep to cross without swimming" (v. 5, *NLT*). The prophet continues, "Suddenly, to my surprise, many trees were now growing on both sides of the river!" (v. 7, *NLT*).

The prophet is envisioning a picture of life and health. He explains, "Everything that touches the water of this river will live. . . . Wherever this water flows, everything will live" (v. 9, *NLT*).

Generations later, the apostle John would receive his revelation and describe what some scholars contend is the same river of which Ezekiel spoke. John would write:

> Then the angel showed me the river of the water of life, as clear as crystal, flowing from the throne of God and of the Lamb down the middle of the great street of the city. On each side of the river stood the tree of life, bearing twelve crops of fruit, yielding its fruit every month. And the leaves of the tree are for the healing of the nations (Rev. 22:1-2).

If the river that flows from the throne of God is His very presence, then to step into it is to step into a *river of intimacy* with the Father. The deeper we swim in that river, the greater the intimacy.

In recent years, much has been spoken and written about authority in spiritual warfare. But as Alice Smith, a respected author on worship and intercession, wisely says, "Your authority in warfare will never exceed your intimacy in worship."[7]

The *river of intimacy* is the fountainhead where all the other rivers of God's transforming power begin. To stay in its flow, one needs to respond daily to God's admonition: *Make room for My glory*.

A Conch-Shell Encounter

River Two:
River of Sufficiency—
The Positional Dimension of Intercessory Worship

Tibet sits atop the world—a high place in more ways than one. Although Tibet is a land of mystery and intrigue, plagued by poverty and religious superstition, a trickle of a river of God's healing presence has begun flowing across this historically Buddhist land. It all began with a prophetic worship encounter at a sacred conch shell in Lhasa, Tibet.

The conch-shell encounter happened to my friend Mark Geppert and a team of worshiping intercessors who went with him to Tibet in August 1998. There, at the famed Jokhang Temple, the confrontation occurred.

Mark's unique experience introduces us to the *positional dimension of prophetic intercessory worship*. Simply stated, intercessory worship has the capacity to position God's people in a special place of prophetic authority. When that authority is exercised, something of the satanic influence of a city, region or entire nation begins to diminish. That is what I believe is happening in Tibet, the birthplace of the Dalai Lama and Tibetan Buddhism.

A Chinese Bird Dog

Mark took his team to Tibet to pray at the Potala Palace (the home of the Dalai Lama, who actually resides in exile in Dharamsala, India) and at the Jokhang Temple, the center of all of Tibetan Buddhism. They also hoped to distribute a large quantity of evangelistic literature, as they had on past journeys.

Mark and his team had developed a unique prayer strategy during previous visits to Tibet (and elsewhere in Asia). Several years earlier, Mark had met a Chinese brother, Hubert Chan, in Singapore, and together the two had developed this unusual way of working—especially in difficult places like Tibet. Mark would serve as a foreign distraction, while Hubert became, in Mark's words, "a Chinese bird dog."

This is how they worked: Because Mark is a white foreigner, the locals would closely watch him. Hubert, on the other hand, being Chinese, blends into the cultures of Asia. So, while Mark would wait outside a place like the Jokhang Temple, actually *hoping* to be noticed, Hubert would go inside and, as Mark explains, seek out the "strongman" of that particular place. Mark describes a "strongman" as a person who, through spiritual influences, controls or affects the population of a geographical region or seems to have unusual authority over an area. Mark's team has learned to spiritually discern who these individuals are.

Their strategy involves praying in person for that leader whenever possible (obviously with the person's permission) and even anointing him or her with oil. According to Mark, it has been amazing how often they have been granted such permission.

Mark is convinced that as team members take hold of a strongman's hands and pray, some sort of flow of the Holy Spirit begins. Although the strongman is not aware of all that is happening, Mark feels this prayer has the capacity to restrain demonic activity in the strongman, potentially breaking the power by which he or she influences that area. According to Mark, this is something they have seen happen with notable success in numerous places throughout Asia.

ENTERTAINING THE TROOPS

With this strategy in mind, Mark and Hubert and their team arrived outside Lhasa's Jokhang Temple on a mild summer day in August 1998. As usual, Mark "entertained the troops" (drawing attention from police authorities), while Hubert slipped into the temple to find the senior abbot—the man second in command to the exiled Dalai Lama.

Hubert found the abbot and told him their group had heard he was ill, which they had, and that a "fat holy man from the West" had come to bless him. The fat holy man, of course, was Mark Geppert, who readily admits he fits at least the first part of that description. The abbot was moved by Hubert's words and invited the team in.

It was a most significant moment. Almost immediately, the abbot agreed to receive the group between the conch shell—a venerated artifact embedded in the floor of the Jokhang Temple—and the Jowo Sakyamuni Buddha, the oldest and most revered Buddha statue in Tibet. The latter was brought there from China around AD 639 by King Songsten Gampo's Chinese wife, Princess Wencheng.

Regarding the conch shell, Mark explains that Buddhist devotees come from across Tibet and around the world to kneel before it. Many bow so that their foreheads touch the shell. Mark reports, "I've seen some Buddhist worshipers shake violently and their eyes actually roll into their heads while bowing before the shell. It's frightening."

The conch shell's significance in the Jokhang Temple, Mark tells me, comes from an ancient legend, of which there are many. According to this one, Princess Wencheng threw this very shell into what was then Lhasa's Lake Wothang and, suddenly, land rose up. She thus determined to build a temple for her treasured Buddha where the land had risen up.

In reference to the Jowo Sakyamuni Buddha, there is little doubt of the significance of this statue to Tibetan Buddhists. Depicting Buddha as a 12-year-old, this relic is believed to represent the beginnings of firmly established Buddhism in Tibet. Until the time of the statue's arrival, Buddhism had been rejected in Tibet, even though all other countries of the region had long embraced its tenets. Although it had resisted the religion previously, Tibet soon became the world's great Buddhist stronghold. Indeed, not long after Princess Wencheng brought the image of Jowo Sakyamuni to Tibet, King Gampo went so far as to pass a law making it illegal *not* to be a Buddhist in Tibet.[1]

Somehow this statue was (and continues to be!) a stronghold in and of itself. With its arrival in the seventh century, it brought the very throne of global Buddhism to Tibet. More than 1,300 years later, Mark's team stood before this famed Sakyamuni Buddha, just a few steps from the sacred conch shell, and prepared to engage in prophetic intercessory worship.

ANOINTING THE ABBOT

There is a 10-foot space between the embedded conch shell and the Buddha. Both are housed deep within the Jokhang Temple. It was into that small space that the abbot invited Mark's team. Through an interpreter, Mark asked if the abbot would permit them to anoint him with oil. The abbot agreed.

Mark then anointed the elderly Buddhist with oil and prayed. He recalls the exact words that began his prayer: "We take authority over all that pertains to you in the name of Jesus!" After adding a further blessing, asking God to touch the abbot's body, Mark gave him literature about Jesus in the Tibetan language. This probably was the first time the man was ever given a clear opportunity to know about Jesus.

The abbot was so touched by this act that he unlocked the large, 15-foot-wide chain grail (gate) covering the entry before the Buddha. He then ushered the entire team into the presence of Tibetan Buddhism's greatest treasure—the Jowo Sakyamuni Buddha.

Mark has no idea how many millions of people worldwide either worship directly or are influenced by demonic forces connected to this Buddha and conch shell. He believes these forces directly impact New Age and Tibetan Buddhism movements worldwide. Amazingly, Mark's team was allowed by the senior abbot of the Jokhang Temple to stand in this very place to exalt Christ. They experienced what I have come to call the *positional dimension* of intercessory worship. They had positioned themselves at the heart of the battle.

BUILDING A THRONE

According to Mark, the walkway around the five-foot-high Buddha was just wide enough for their team of 20 to make a complete circle. The abbot departed, leaving them alone in the small chapel for 30 minutes. The team of worshipers surrounded the Buddha and sang old hymns such as "There Is Power in the Blood" and "Oh, the Blood of Jesus." More as a prophetic directive than a song, they also sang Paul Kyle's inspiring chorus:

> Jesus, we enthrone You,
> We proclaim You are King.
> Standing here in the midst of us,

We raise You up with our praise.
And as we worship, build Your throne;
And as we worship, build Your throne;
And as we worship, build Your throne;
Come Lord Jesus and take Your place.[2]

As the team sang, they sensed a supernatural enthroning of God's presence within the chamber. They felt that what they were singing was actually happening. The team concluded by anointing the Sakyamuni Buddha itself with oil, even as they continued worshiping. Mark said the statue was dripping with oil.

They left the Jokhang Temple, and in less than 30 minutes distributed at least 2,000 messages about Jesus in the Tibetan language. Mark first asked a policeman if this would be permissible. Once the officer was assured that the literature did not mention the Dalai Lama (and especially that it did not contain his picture), they were allowed to freely distribute the literature. The policeman even offered to help hand out the booklets. (Chinese authorities that control Tibet consider the Dalai Lama a significant political threat. Even his picture is treated as contraband and is thus illegal.) Mark and the team were certain that their intercessory worship and their strategy of anointing a strongman, the abbot, were already taking effect.

That was only the beginning of this trickle of God's river of healing. Very soon the trickle would become a stream of God's blessing.

THE LANGUAGE OF TEARS

Two months later, Mark returned to Lhasa with yet another team. In addition to other sites, the team went to Tibet's famed Sera Monastery, one of the two significant Gelugpa monasteries in Lhasa. The Gelugpa order of Tibetan Buddhism is the main order associated with the Dalai Lama. (As with other religions, Christianity and Islam included, Buddhism has its branches or denominations.)

While the rest of the team went in different directions, Mark sat alone on a wooden bench, quietly worshiping Jesus in front of a large stone Buddha. Such quiet praying was not out of place in the Tibetan culture, in which meditation and reflection are the norm. Sitting near Mark was a monk reading his prayers. The monk was holding a tile inscribed with ancient Buddhist prayers written in Sanskrit. Mark began praying for the monk, asking God for an open door to share Christ with him. Mark's biggest challenge was the language barrier. He did not speak Tibetan, and he was sure the monk did not speak English.

Then Mark had an idea. He took a gospel message in Tibetan from his pocket and held it in front of him in the same manner the monk was holding his tile. Of course, Mark could not read a word of the tract, but he knew its message: It told how God had only one Son, Jesus, who came to live among men to sacrifice His life so that all who believed might have eternal life. This message would be totally foreign to a Tibetan Buddhist.

Mark's strategy paid off. Out of the corner of his eye, he could see the Buddhist worshiper gazing intently at his booklet. The monk was interested because he could see that it was in his language; and, as Mark explains, most Tibetan readers believe that anything written in their "high language" must be a message from God.

Noting the monk's interest, Mark offered him the booklet. Amazingly, the monk promptly replaced his tile with the tract and began reading it as prayerfully as he had been reading the tile just moments before. Suddenly the monk closed the tract and began weeping. Mark sensed what was happening. He realized the man had just read the part about praying the sinner's prayer. He was certain the monk had just prayed that prayer.

Now Mark was weeping too. He put his arms around the monk, who rested his face on Mark's shoulder. It was an unusual scene, almost certainly the only such encounter ever to happen in this monastery. For several minutes the two shared in the language of tears.

GROUNDWORK FOR A MIRACLE

The river of God's presence was, undoubtedly, beginning to flow—and it was about to be released in ways Mark could never have imagined. Those moments with the monk had been observed closely by a Chinese authority figure standing in the shadows. He had watched the white foreigner praying and had seen the monk meditating. He had noticed the exchange of the tract and the highly unusual display of emotions. Tibetans simply do not hug each other in public, let alone while sobbing.

As Mark regained his composure, he looked up to see a tall, well-dressed man approaching. He was not a Tibetan but a Han Chinese man. Mark's heart raced. He wondered if he was about to be expelled from the country.

God, however, had something else in mind. The intercessory worship team that anointed the abbot and the Buddha statue two months earlier had laid the groundwork for a miracle.

"Thank you for caring for that monk," the tall Chinese man said in English.

His gentleness surprised Mark, who had expected a rebuke, not a compliment.

Catching his breath, Mark responded, "Not at all." He was uncertain what to say next.

"May I know who you are?" the Chinese man asked in a friendly voice.

"Please do not be offended," Mark said, "but first, may I know who you are?"

Mark had learned discretion in times like these. Do not say too much until you know who is asking the questions and why.

The man presented his business card, which revealed that he was the public health director for all of Tibet. The man represented the government of China in Beijing.

Mark introduced himself as the leader of a small foundation in the United States, not explaining that his foundation's primary focus was prayer. He was surprised once more by the health director's next question.

"Would your foundation be interested in a health project for Tibet?"

By now, several of Mark's team members had gathered and were listening in. "Yes, we would," Mark responded on behalf of the group.

The health director asked, "What type of health project would you like to do in Tibet?"

Mark had no idea what to suggest, so he simply responded, "You are the director. Why don't you recommend a project, and we'll see if we can help?"

Mark hoped the proposed project would involve something within the realm of possibility for his small ministry, or perhaps it would be one that God could use to help his group serve as a catalyst for others.

The American missionary and the Chinese official agreed to meet again that evening at the team's hotel to discuss a specific project.

A River of Sufficiency

The meeting was held that night as planned. The health director came with representatives from the People's Regional Hospital of Tibet. In the brief hours between Mark's encounter with the health director and the evening meeting, the health director's team members had already formulated an idea they wanted to propose. They suggested that Mark's group consider joining them in a partnership to help identify and meet the needs of children with heart defects in Tibet. The project would be called The Survey and Treatment of Congenital Heart Disease Among Children in the Autonomous Region of Tibet.

The sweeping objective would include examining all school-aged children of Tibet, beginning in Lhasa, the region's capital, to determine the extent of congenital heart disease among Tibetan adolescents. (Apparently a major side effect of Tibet's unusually high altitude is damage to the hearts of young children.) The project would include providing education for health professionals, obtaining necessary equipment for the task and, ultimately, helping raise funds needed for corrective surgery for those who could not afford it (which would probably mean all who needed the surgery!).

Mark's foundation also was asked to participate in the general upgrading of the main hospital in Lhasa to help with the project. It was a huge assignment, but Mark reminded himself that we serve a big God! Mark was about to learn that one of God's rivers of delight is a *river of sufficiency*.

Bless Their Hearts!

Late that night, together with several Chinese leaders, Mark initialed the protocol for the project. Although the launching would be delayed for a year due to the bombing of the Chinese Embassy in Belgrade, Yugoslavia (during the war in the Balkans), the following year everything was approved. On January 26, 2000, Mark signed the final agreement. Six months after that, several trained medical teams saw their first young patients.

To date, Mark's teams have examined 17,000 children in all seven of Tibet's prefectures and the 74 counties comprising them. Thousands more are being examined annually. Thus far, 4 percent have abnormalities that require medical attention. No humanitarian or government entity had ever done anything like this until Mark's teams came along. As is typical with Mark, he developed a way in the examination process for the medical "intercessors" to lay hands on every child and consecrate each to Jesus! Every child is told the story of Jesus. "It's a way to bless their hearts in more ways than one," Mark says.

Obviously, there has been much warfare surrounding this project. Many intercessors have become involved in praying for this unique transformation strategy that could ultimately release God's river of healing—both spiritual and physical—to all of the children of Tibet.

Mark has established a 24-hour prayer covering to confront all the difficulties and obstacles head-on. These obstacles especially included the financial challenges. The $5 million budget over a four-year period initially seemed daunting for a ministry operating at the time on less than $100,000 annually. But Mark's faith has grown, and so have his supply lines. Recently a pediatric cardio catheterization lab and hospital wing was fully funded—much of the money came from Christians outside of Tibet, and the rest was provided by the Chinese government. This is the only such surgical unit for children in all of that part of Western China. The multi-million dollar wing and cardio lab is key in caring for children with heart defects from across Tibet who likely would have died by age 11 were it not for this specialized unit. Scores of children are being surgically treated annually. All of this began when a team of worshiping intercessors gathered around a stone Buddha and enthroned Christ!

Even more recently, another phenomenon has been occurring. When Mark's son, Matthew, who heads the "Touching Hearts" team, was last in Lhasa, 26 children were being prepped for surgeries scheduled over a two-day period. Matt arrived on the first of those days with a team of two intercessors who were to help him cover the procedures in prayer. As 14 children awaited surgery, the project coordinator, a woman named Gayle, rushed to Matt and explained they had encountered something unexpected. Matt's heart sank as he feared a serious problem. Had there been an equipment failure, or worse? But the coordinator quickly dispelled Matt's fears as she explained, "Seven of the 14 children no longer need the surgery. Their hearts have been completely healed since arriving at the hospital."

As Matt explained, "What made this so unusual is that doctors had diagnosed all seven of these children upon their arrivals and determined they each had a serious congenital heart defect." Matt then added, "The next day the same thing happened. Twelve children were slated for surgery, and Gayle came to me saying five of these showed no signs of the condition that was diagnosed only a day earlier. They, too, had been completely healed." God's *river of sufficiency* was flowing freely, and it's still flowing today. Mark and Matthew figure they are at least up to their ankles! Like Ezekiel, they'll be swimming soon.

Mark's conch-shell encounter at Tibet's sacred Sakyamuni Buddha indeed illustrates what I call the *positional dimension of prophetic intercessory worship*. Such worship, and its resulting intercession, leads us into the *river of God's sufficiency*.

A SUPERNATURAL REALITY

There's something beautifully symbolic in what is happening in Tibet, especially when it comes to the release of rivers. What is a geological reality in the physical realm could become a supernatural reality in the spiritual realm. Geologically, Tibet lies on a vast plateau as large as Western Europe, sandwiched between two Himalayan ridges five miles high. Geologists tell us that this plateau is the source of all the major rivers in South and East Asia including the Indus, Sutleg and Brahmaputra from the far western highlands of Tibet and the Mekong, Salween, Yangzi, Gyron, Yellow, Minjiang and Jialing from Tibet's eastern region.[3] All of these rivers flowing *below* begin from above in Tibet.

Supernaturally speaking, Tibet also has been the primary source of the flow of Tibetan Buddhism, as well as New Age occultism and mysticism, throughout the world. The Dalai Lama, for example, is one of the world's most worshiped and revered figures of our time. His influence is directly tied to Tibet.

Could it be that intercessory worship is beginning to change all this, starting at the very "roof of the world"—Tibet? Rivers that flow from Tibet clearly stream downward, impacting all that is below. This appears to be true both physically and spiritually. I believe a river of

God's presence has begun flowing across Tibet, and it, too, will soon flow downward. It could very well impact all that is within its path.

Have ministries like Every Home for Christ seen any impact since all this began in Tibet? Recently I examined the harvest results of our ministry in nations directly below Tibet—those to which those literal rivers flow from this roof of the world. Amazingly, since those worship encounters involving Mark's prayer teams, more than 50 million decisions and responses from our evangelism activities have been followed up with Bible courses for new believers *just in those very neighboring nations*. (That number represents half of all the decisions and responses followed up in our ministry's 65-year history, and it happened in only a decade in a region that once seemed impenetrable!)

I am not sure how many statues of Buddha have been anointed with oil and bathed in the sounds of Christ-centered intercessory worship, but I know of at least one—and it is at the top of the world. I believe a river of God's sufficiency has begun flowing throughout Tibet, and it already is sweeping into the valleys below. Fortunately this river is not reserved for only a few bold warriors who happen to travel to faraway places like Tibet to pray. This river of God's transforming power is flowing anywhere His people are willing to wait long enough in worship to freely drink. *Shall we gather at the river?*

20

AGATHA'S INTERCESSORS

RIVER THREE:
RIVER OF SUPREMACY—
THE PENETRATING DIMENSION OF INTERCESSORY WORSHIP

It was a sunny morning as the phone rang in our Hong Kong hotel room. There was little indication that a severe storm was heading our way as I looked out across beautiful Victoria Harbor. It was Sunday, September 26, 1999. I was to speak at two services that morning and then conclude a three-day conference on spiritual warfare that afternoon. More than 100 churches had sent delegates to the previous sessions.

The conference theme, Light the Window, had a particular emphasis on preparing intercessors for a month-long prayer focus for the 10/40 Window, slated for the following month, October. The "10/40 Window" is a term that was popularized in the 1990s through the AD2000 and Beyond Movement directed by Luis Bush, the originator of the term.

As you may recall, this geographic region is marked by the latitudinal boundaries of 10 degrees north of the equator to 40 degrees north, and it stretches from the west coast of Africa through the Middle East and on to the eastern border of China. The region is home to 97 percent of the world's least-evangelized nations. Yet it only has 8 percent of the world's missionary force laboring there. The 10/40 Window is also the headquarters (and birthplace) of most of the world's largest non-Christian religions: Islam, Hinduism and Buddhism. Of course, Judaism and Christianity likewise were born there.

Praying Through the Window

Every Home for Christ had been deeply involved in mobilizing prayer for this region since the term "10/40 Window" first became familiar. It was, in fact, at our EHC headquarters on June 13, 1992, that a handful of leaders met at the request of Luis Bush to discuss the feasibility of having an entire month of worldwide focused prayer concentrated on this region. Few realized as we met that morning that the largest focused prayer movement for the nations was being born during those several hours.

We met in our ministry's boardroom—adjacent to our prayer room, which was filled with intercessors from local churches. They had been invited to prayerfully cover what we believed was to be a strategic meeting. By noon the theme "Pray Through the Window" had emerged, and an ambitious goal had been set of mobilizing one million Christians globally to pray for these 10/40 Window nations (two nations per day) during October 1993. In that way, synchronized, focused prayer would touch all 62 nations during the 31 days of October. An idea also was born to send teams of intercessors into each of those 62 countries.

I had my doubts that 62 teams could be mobilized for such a task, and I was also skeptical that one million people could be enlisted to pray for this region for an entire month.

But to my surprise and delight, when all the groups, denominations, local churches and ministries reported their numbers, more than 20 million people had participated and an amazing 249 prayer journeys had been taken. The committee decided to sponsor a similar month-long focus every other year through the end of the decade.

October 1999, following our conference in Hong Kong, was to be the final month-long prayer focus of the decade for the 10/40 Window. For this final thrust, an even more ambitious goal had been set: mobilizing 50 million intercessors to pray for this region daily throughout the month. Because several million of these intercessors would be mobilized by radio across China's mainland (as well as among China's vast network of house churches), it seemed appropriate to have a special 10/40 Window focus meeting in Hong Kong.

The 800-seat auditorium had been filled for the first two days of sessions, with scores of interested intercessors turned away due to lack of space. It was clear that believers in Hong Kong recognized the significance of the need to focus prayer on China's mainland as well as other nearby Asian nations of the 10/40 Window.

ANTICIPATING CAM!

So as the phone rang that Sunday morning in Hong Kong, I was looking forward to the final session of the conference that afternoon. A day earlier, we had announced that this last session would be a special time for an intercessors' impartation—a time of laying on of hands for those interested, praying that God would impart to each a special anointing for more effective intercession. I particularly promised to pray specifically for all those who wanted to be involved in concentrated prayer the following month for the 10/40 Window. My hope was that numerous teams of intercessors from Hong Kong would journey to the mainland for prayer during that month, joining others who would be coming from around the world. Our committee had set a goal of 3,000 prayer journeys throughout the region, including mainland China. For this reason I felt that the final session was especially critical.

The phone call appeared to change all that. The caller was Agatha Chan, the conference coordinator. Tropical Storm "Cam," which we had heard about several days earlier, had been heading for Taiwan (far to the south) but had changed directions and was now moving directly toward Hong Kong. The storm had become a full-blown typhoon, already reaching a Signal 8, only two degrees below the highest level for typhoons (what we call hurricanes) in the region. Agatha explained that when a warning reached a Signal 8, all public transportation had to be shut down and all public facilities closed. This meant there could be no church services held that morning, and the final session of the conference would need to be canceled.

But Agatha was not about to give up. True, a Signal 8 storm was heading our way, and no storm of this magnitude had ever changed directions again when so close to land, but Agatha decided to bring together a small group of intercessors to pray anyway.

We had known for several days that there was a possibility of bad weather that weekend. But because the typhoon had been heading toward Taiwan, it caused us little immediate concern. Now all that had changed. Cam was coming!

Interestingly, the storm's turn toward us may well have had something to do with the prayers of the participants on the first day of our conference. A few weeks earlier, Taiwan had suffered a devastating earthquake. So when intercessors in Hong Kong heard that Typhoon Cam was heading toward the area in Taiwan where massive relief efforts were underway, Agatha suggested they ask God to change the direction of the typhoon. They took her words to heart—and what they asked for happened. Apparently, though, no one had thought to pray that if Cam did change direction, it would not head our way.

Praying and Praising Strategically

Cam was closing in, and Hong Kong was closing down—except for Agatha's intercessors. Though there was no public transportation, a small team still showed up at Agatha's office by midmorning. Many had walked to the place of prayer. The wind had picked up noticeably, and dark clouds gathered on the horizon. Hotel staff members had come to our room and affixed huge strips of tape to the windows facing Victoria Harbor. If the windows broke, the tape would help keep pieces of glass from flying haphazardly. This was not terribly encouraging, so we headed down to the lobby 16 floors below.

Meanwhile, Agatha's team had assembled at her office. Soon their worship and warfare began. The small group decided to pray through the seven steps for strategic prayer that I had taught the previous afternoon. These seven steps came from one of my earlier books, *The Jericho Hour*. I had begun the session by defining strategic-level prayer, highlighting the fact that "strategic" suggests that which counts the most. Strategic-level prayer, I explained, is prayer at a level that really counts. It is prayer of truly eternal consequences.

To illustrate the point, I suggested that there's a big difference between praying for relief from a toothache and praying for the salvation of an unreached people group. The latter is clearly more strategic (unless, of course, it's *your* toothache!).

I proceeded to list seven primary characteristics of strategic praying, including a key word to expand each aspect and a core attribute (or quality of spirit) highlighted by a particular characteristic. The list included:

1. AUTHORITATIVE PRAYING

First, I suggested that strategic-level prayer is *authoritative*, expanding the definition with the key word "confident." Authoritative praying, I explained, embodies a *spirit of audacity*. Such praying believes and claims the promise of Jesus: "I have given you authority to trample on snakes and scorpions and to overcome all the power of the enemy; nothing will harm you" (Luke 10:19).

2. COMBATIVE PRAYING

Second, I emphasized that strategic-level prayer is *combative*. My key word for this point was "aggressive." Combative praying requires a *spirit of militancy*. I reminded participants that Scripture is filled with military symbolism. I cited Joshua 5:14-15; 2 Corinthians 10:4-5; Ephesians 6:10-18; 1 Timothy 6:12; and 2 Timothy 2:3-4. I explained that the very phrase "Lord of hosts," which appears 273 times in the Old Testament, refers to the leader of a "heavenly army." Even in Exodus, God is described as "a man of war" (Exod. 15:3, *KJV*). Combative praying, I suggested, is to put some "fight" into our intercession.

3. INTENSIVE PRAYING

Third, I emphasized that strategic-level prayer is *intensive*. This, I told the group, is summarized by the word "fervent." Such praying expresses a *spirit of determination*. James describes it this way: "The effectual fervent prayer of a righteous man availeth much" (Jas. 5:16, *KJV*). *The Amplified Bible* translates this verse: "The earnest (heartfelt, continued) prayer of a righteous man makes tremendous power available [dynamic in its working]." I noted that the English word "intense," meaning "existing in an extreme degree," comes from the Latin *intensus*, meaning "stretched tight."[1] There are occasions, I suggested, when "uptight" prayers are in order.

4. CONFRONTATIONAL PRAYING

I next highlighted that strategic-level prayer is *confrontational*, suggesting the key word "boldness." Confrontational praying, I explained, manifests itself in a *spirit of tenacity*. Perhaps this is what Jesus pictured when He told His disciples they could command mountains to be moved (see Mark 11:22-23). I added that the first three characteristics on the list—authoritative, combative and intensive prayer—combine to produce the boldness needed for confrontational praying. Such praying becomes boldly tenacious or, as a colleague of mine once personally described it: *praying with a passionate tenacity and a touch of insanity.*

5. COMPREHENSIVE PRAYING

Fifth, I suggested that strategic-level prayer is *comprehensive*. This is summarized by the key word "focused." If our intercession is to be comprehensive, it must have a clear focus. Such praying, I added, requires a *spirit of totality*. This means we should fully (i.e., comprehensively) address a particular issue in prayer. Jesus said, " 'And all things, whatsoever ye shall ask in prayer, believing, ye shall receive' " (Matt. 21:22, *KJV*). The *New International Version* translates this verse: " 'If you believe, you will receive whatever you ask for in prayer.' " "Whatsoever" or "whatever" is a sweeping expression that involves totality in our praying.

6. CREATIVE PRAYING

Next, I described strategic-level prayer as being *creative*, emphasizing the key word "faith." This kind of praying, I suggested, involves a *spirit of vision*. We allow God to use our imaginations to help us pray creatively. Creative praying stretches our faith. Paul said, God "quickeneth the dead, and calleth those things which be not as though they were" (Rom. 4:17, *KJV*). The author of Hebrews explains, "Now faith is being sure of what we hope for and certain of what we do not see" (Heb. 11:1). Such faith, I once heard someone suggest, is to reach into nowhere, grab hold of nothing and hang on until it becomes something!

7. DECISIVE PRAYING

Seventh, and last on my list that day, I explained that strategic-level prayer is *decisive*. In a word, decisive prayer is "conclusive" (my key word for this point). This kind of praying, I told the group, represents a *spirit of finality*. I cited Revelation 12:7-12 as a biblical basis for this characteristic. Here we see a conclusive victory in the heavenlies where Satan is dethroned by angelic forces. But those forces only win the victory because God's saints on earth employ their weapons of "the blood of the Lamb" and "the word of their testimony" (Rev. 12:11). This could only happen, I suggested, through decisive prayer.

Confronting Cam

Although it is always encouraging, as a teacher, to see your students apply your teaching, I was surprised to learn how specifically Agatha led her small prayer band through the seven characteristics that stormy Sunday morning. Step by step, methodically and carefully, they prayed and praised their way through each aspect.

Agatha later told me they began by praying *authoritatively*, just as I had suggested in my presentation. They confidently prayed through the various Scriptures I had given for the point and added others that came to their minds. They prayed with a *spirit of audacity*, an expression they had to translate into its Cantonese equivalent (Cantonese being the dialect in which they prayed that morning). According to Agatha, they spoke with authority into the physical atmosphere over Hong Kong.

Then their prayer became *combative*, the second characteristic on the list. They were aggressive as they sought to pray with a *spirit of militancy*. To the team, this was combat—real warfare—and they saw themselves as a small army strategizing for a victory.

Agatha's intercessors then looked at characteristic three and asked God to give them a *spirit of determination*. They sought the Lord with intensity. They were reminded of the promise I had shared from James 5:16 that "effectual fervent prayer" (*KJV*) of righteous people produces results. Soon they were praying fervently, with a determined intensity. They sensed that something was happening in the heavenlies. Little did they realize all that was actually happening in that moment. Just a few miles away, at Hong Kong's weather observatory, meteorologists began to see strange behavior being exhibited by Typhoon Cam.

Back in Agatha's "war room," intercessors kept praying. Now their praying became *confrontational*. They looked at my description of a *spirit of tenacity* and searched for a Cantonese equivalent. Soon they were praying with tenacity, confronting Satan for attempting to disrupt the conference. To them, Typhoon Cam was the mountain, and they were commanding it to be removed!

Cam was already in trouble. But Agatha's intercessors were not finished yet. Item five on the list was *comprehensive* prayer. So they asked the Holy Spirit to help them focus their prayers with a *spirit of totality*. In the moments that followed, they listened and prayed (and prayed and listened) as they pressed in to seek God even more comprehensively regarding Cam and the conference.

SPLITTING THE 8

Then they came to characteristic six on the list, *creative prayer*. Initially uncertain as to how to apply this, a member of the group remembered Paul's declaration that God "quickeneth the dead, and calleth those things which be not as though they were" (Rom. 4:17, *KJV*). Faith began to build within the small team. They sought God for a mental picture of how they were to pray.

Suddenly, one of the intercessors saw in her mind a gigantic "8"—the number that represented the level of the approaching storm. She knew that if somehow the Signal 8 could be lowered to a Signal 3, transportation could resume. In the natural, this seemed impossible.

Then, quite unexpectedly, the intercessor pictured a gigantic hand slicing the huge 8 in half. The left half of the 8 fell to the ground. Only a 3 remained standing! She told the group what she had seen, and soon they were moving their hands up and down, symbolically splitting the 8.

The team knew this was a prophetic picture of impending victory. Cam would become a level 3 typhoon. Quickly they moved to the last item on the list: *decisive* prayer. They prayed with a *spirit of finality*, praising God for the coming miracle. In actuality, that miracle was happening in those very moments.

At our hotel, Dee and I had moved back to our room on the sixteenth floor. We wondered when this dreadful storm would hit. However, there was no sign of it. The harbor was completely calm. But because it was now after 2:00 P.M., I was convinced the conference would be canceled no matter what the weather conditions were at that point. It was just too late for all the attendees to gather, even if the storm fizzled totally.

Then the phone rang. It was Agatha. Someone was coming immediately to take us to the meeting. Amazingly, at 2:10 P.M. Cam had completely disappeared. The storm didn't just move—it totally disappeared! In minutes (not hours), Cam had been lowered from a Signal 8 to a Signal 3. In actual fact, the 8 had symbolically been cut in half as that intercessor had envisioned. It had become a 3, which was but a breeze compared to a full-blown typhoon.

As we headed to the final session, I wondered how many people would attend since public transportation had only resumed some 45 minutes earlier. I soon learned that participants had been watching the weather carefully, and the moment the Signal 3 was announced, they headed for the conference. I was amazed. Every seat was taken.

Worship began promptly at 3:00 P.M. At 3:20, Agatha came to the microphone to announce that the Hong Kong Weather Observatory had just issued a bulletin. Typhoon Cam had completely dissipated. It was gone! Agatha later explained that a storm of this magnitude is usually followed by days of heavy rain. But following Cam's "disappearance," there wasn't even a sprinkle. Even the Signal 3 announced at 2:10 P.M. lasted only about one hour and 10 minutes. Then all signals were lowered to normal. According to Agatha, this was unprecedented!

BUILDING A NEW WALL FOR CHINA

In that final session, I was able to pray personally for several hundred intercessors. It was obvious God had something significant planned for this meeting that almost didn't happen. As Agatha's intercessors prayed earlier that day, *a river of God's supremacy* began to flow in Hong Kong. There is little doubt that their praying was prophetic. If prophecy is "to speak before" or "to declare in front of," the intercessory worship of that stormy morning surely was prophetic. It declared God's power "in front of" as well as "before" Typhoon Cam.

The manner in which Agatha's team prophetically penetrated a storm many miles away reminded me of prophets, like Ezekiel and Elijah in ancient times, who prophesied against mountains, valleys, high places and even idols. In the case of Agatha's intercessors, they prophesied against a storm—and they did it through intercessory worship.

Significantly, that September 1999 spiritual warfare conference in Hong Kong gave birth to a Harp and Bowl Intercessory Worship Conference on Easter weekend the following year. (This was the year that began with my 40-day worship fast.) The 2000 conference was the first gathering for Hong Kong Christians at which the Harp and Bowl model of intercessory worship was formally introduced. As a result of that conference, believers from more than 150 churches began helping sustain numerous 24-hour-a-day "Walls of Prayer" in every district of Hong Kong. A Wall of Prayer is built when all 168 hours of a week are covered with prayer in a given area. Six complete walls were formed in the 24 months following the conference.

This prayer vision is now rapidly spreading from Hong Kong into all of mainland China. Phil Bennett, a pastor of prayer from North Carolina who went with me to Hong Kong to introduce the idea for establishing these Walls of Prayer, had a vision on his flight prior to the training. He saw the Great Wall of China become a Great Wall of Prayer—filled with intercessors standing shoulder-to-shoulder and stretching across all the provinces of China. Little could Phil have known that less than a decade later we would receive reliable reports that more than 2,500 such prayer walls had been launched throughout China as the result of those visionary seeds planted at our conference. Put in perspective, if 2,500 Walls of Prayer were faithfully maintained for all 168 hours each week, this would represent 420,000 hours of prayer rising to God's throne throughout mainland China *each week*! One key Chinese leader in this growing movement told me personally that their ministry has set a goal for the coming decade to establish 10,000 such 24/7 prayer ministries all across the mainland.

There was certainly a penetrating dimension to the prophetic intercessory worship of that small band of Hong Kong warriors in September 1999. I believe they released *a river of God's supremacy* that will ultimately flow out to all of that region of the world and beyond. They also may have given birth to a prayer movement for China that is unparalleled in history. A great wall, indeed, is rising.

21

THE DARK SIDE OF BALI

RIVER FOUR
RIVER OF DISCOVERY—
THE PERCEPTIVE DIMENSION OF INTERCESSORY WORSHIP

As one seasoned traveler said, "From the air, Bali rises fresh and green from the Indian Ocean, a verdant, glistening butterfly against a backdrop of gray."[1] The island is indeed one of the most beautiful places on earth.

Bali is an island of southern Indonesia, just east of Java, and one of an estimated 17,000 islands in the Indonesian chain (about 3,000 of which are inhabited). Some 210 million people, mostly Muslim, live in this vast archipelago scattered across 741,052 square miles of the Indian and Pacific Oceans. With its towering mountains, tropical climate and fertile soil, Bali stands out in beauty above the other islands. Just 90 miles long by 60 miles at its widest point, and not much more than one mile at its narrowest, Bali has become known as "the Jewel of the East."

But there is a dark side to Bali. It is like so many places on our planet that are rich in culture, awe inspiring in its geography and wonderfully inviting to tourists looking for an exotic place to visit for a week or two. Most people have no idea of the power of darkness controlling these regions and the impact of that spiritual darkness as it reaches out to other areas—sometimes, as we saw in the case of Tibet, touching the entire world.

PROPHETIC PERCEPTION

A friend and prayer strategist, John Robb, chairman of the International Prayer Connection, believes this is the case with Bali, where he once traveled with a prayer team of 10 seasoned intercessors from five nations.

They met at Besakih, Bali, with a larger group of 70 Balinese believers and other Christians from neighboring Indonesian islands. Additionally, thousands of other intercessors around the world were supporting the initiative through their prayers. These intercessors included believers involved with 40 global prayer networks plus thousands of praying Christians from Dr. Yonggi Cho's massive congregation at Yoido Full Gospel Church in Seoul, South Korea. Even 340 churches in Sri Lanka agreed to cover this strategic initiative in prayer.

John and his team learned numerous interesting lessons from their Bali prayer initiative that help us define *the perceptive dimension of intercessory worship* and introduce what I believe to be God's *river of discovery*. At the heart of this dimension is an understanding of what George Otis Jr. refers to as "informed intercession," a concept we will examine shortly.

The prophetic, by its very nature, is perceptive. To "perceive" is "to apprehend or observe especially through sight or with the mind." To perceive also means "to understand, discern, comprehend or grasp." "Perception," as a noun, is "the intuitive recognition of a truth or reality." "Intuition" is "immediate insight or understanding without conscious reasoning."[2]

When you add to these concepts the supernatural dimension of the Holy Spirit's providing these insights, the result is prophetic perception that releases this *river of discovery*. To me, the best channel for the flow of this prophetic river is intercessory worship. Worship enthrones God, thus releasing His power for ready application, while intercession focuses or applies that power to specific needs. The discovery part is the manner in which God reveals exactly how to pray in specific situations.

Such dependence on the Holy Spirit is not to suggest the intercessor is merely a passive player in such praying—someone who waits for the Spirit's prompting to intercede for a certain situation and only then gets involved by praying. It seems those who flow best in this river of prophetic discovery are those who do their homework in prayer, which brings us back to the phrase George Otis Jr. uses: "informed intercession."

The expression defines itself: It is the gleaning of accurate information leading to appropriate intercession. Armies devote considerable time and resources to gathering accurate intelligence, so they will know how to wage war effectively. We, too, need to do our homework for prayer by gathering as much information as possible regarding the focus of our intercession. Then when the prophetic element is added to what our homework has produced, incredible prayer possibilities await us. The power of such praying is further amplified when our prayers are saturated with fervent worship. Still, we must do our homework. Preparation for worship-saturated prayer often leads to unusual prophetic perception in prayer.

A BALI PRAYER PRIMER

John Robb understood the importance of informed intercession as he prepared to lead the Bali prayer initiative. For several months prior to the journey, John researched all he could about this exotic place—its history, culture and religious beliefs, including the status of Christianity in the island. In a sense, he compiled his own Bali "prayer primer."

According to John, he was specifically searching for two things: (1) What is the identity of any specific "strongman" over the island? and (2) How does this "strongman" maintain his control?

Bali, John explains, is known as *Pulau Dewata*, the "island of the gods." There are many gods, demons and ancestral spirits worshiped in Bali. But John wondered if there was one specific entity or force that seemed to rise above all the others—one that would fall into the category of a "strongman" like Jesus described in Mark 3:27. If this force could be identified, John felt his team of intercessors could focus prayers on restraining (binding) the influence of this entity and thus "carry off his possessions" (Mark 3:27), which in this case were the souls of the Balinese.

John also wondered how this strongman maintained his control, because, as John explained to me, that control is the essence of the demonic. The goal of principalities and powers (see Eph. 6:10-12) is to control and dominate human beings and their institutions. We saw something of this reality when we looked at Mark Geppert's conch-shell encounter in Tibet.

What John learned in his research was that Bali is the lone Hindu outpost amid the thousands of islands that make up the largely Muslim Indonesian archipelago. Before Hinduism came to Bali, ancient Indonesians on this small island worshiped what they termed "great native gods" consisting of the sun, mountains and the sea. Additionally, they invoked the souls of their ancestors, who, they believed, descended to dwell on large stones that had been erected for these departed souls. Even today, many Balinese believe their gods live upon the mountains as well as in rocks, trees, wind, birds, streams and lakes. They believe Bali literally *belongs* to the gods and that all human beings are but transitory tenants. The gods are the true landowners.

It was in the context of this powerfully demonic climate that the even stronger satanic forces of Buddhism and Hinduism came to Java and Bali in the fifth century. Hinduism eventually gained the upper hand in gleaning the devotion of ancient Balinese sun worshipers, and soon they were worshiping Shiva, the Hindu god of destruction, and Surya, the Hindu sun god. These two gods merged into one for the Balinese and are now particularly identified with Bali's highest mountain, Mount Agung, another obvious demonic high place. Shiva/ Surya, according to Balinese tradition, represents divinity, which permeates everything. Balinese believe they combine to become the totality of all the forces they call god. As you can see, John learned many things that would help his team pray meaningfully.

Balinese Hindus further believe their existence is a continuous cycle of life, death and rebirth until one reaches the state of *moksha*— when the body becomes one with the universe. Obedience to various rituals at different times in a person's life supposedly ensures that the person is progressing properly toward this desired and ultimate goal.[3]

Central to these beliefs is their particular worship of Shiva, believed by the Balinese to be the spirit of their very first ancestor. It was Shiva, they say, who made Brahma (another Hindu god), and Brahma who made the world. This leads them to believe that all human beings are descendants of Shiva.

These details led John Robb to conclude that the strongman of Bali is Shiva/Surya, which really is a human name for some specific demonic principality or authority in the heavenlies (see Eph. 6:10-12). This power, John was convinced, had a firm grip on the people of Bali. So John felt he had identified his Mark 3:27 "strongman" even as he continued his research to learn more about how these powers control the Balinese. God clearly was preparing to equip a small cadre of "informed intercessors" for this Bali prayer initiative.

A FORMIDABLE FORCE

Soon 10 international ministry leaders from five nations joined the 70 indigenous Indonesian spiritual warriors to form a formidable force of informed intercessors to begin the prayer initiative.

When the combined team first met, it quickly became clear that the prayers of those thousands of supporting intercessors from around the world mentioned earlier were taking effect. John Robb reported, "We could feel their prayers as the Spirit of God moved powerfully among us, giving prophetic words and visions about the destiny of the Balinese people and church, and producing times of deep identificational repentance for the woundedness and idolatry of this people."[4]

Identificational repentance, to which John Robb referred, is that aspect of intercession in which those praying identify with members of a people or culture, usually from the past, who had sinned deeply but never repented (Daniel, Isaiah, Nehemiah and others in Scripture serve as examples of those who prayed in this way). Identificational repentance is to repent on behalf of others' past failures and the entry those failures may have provided to allow demonic powers to infiltrate a land or culture.

Such repentance happened at the Bali initiative. Early on in the praying, Indonesian intercessors repented, particularly for idolatry. They also repented for the multitude of covenants made by Balinese Hindu worshipers with false gods like Shiva and Surya.

During these initial prayers, one especially noteworthy prophetic insight came from the late Kjell Sjoberg, one of the pioneers of the spiritual warfare movement in Europe. Sjoberg specifically spoke of the power of the shed blood of Jesus to bring healing to Bali and the absolute necessity of reconciliation in Christ's Body in Bali in order for this to happen. Sjoberg explained,

> God created Bali with a purpose to reveal His own personality and purpose. Satan wants to block God's voice in creation. He has done this most effectively in Bali since the whole island has been sanctified to demon gods. . . . Spiritual strongholds are no problem for a united church. Therefore the groundwork before spiritual warfare that can be effective always involves reconciliation in the Body of Christ. . . .

The deeper we go in repentance, the higher we go in spiritual warfare.[5]

This prophetic statement led to significant repentance. Participants identified with many sins of their various cultures and peoples. For example, a man from Java (a main island of Indonesia) repented of the way his people had mistreated the people of Bali. Then, an Indonesian with Dutch blood asked for forgiveness for the massacres of Balinese, generations before, by Dutch colonialists.

THE FALL OF ANCIENT COVENANTS

This spirit of repentance soon was taken beyond the walls of the prayer meeting in Besakih and into the surrounding community. Almost 50 of the intercessors participated in a quiet, low-profile prayer walk that included a visit to Bali's main Hindu shrine where several of the Balinese leaders, acting on behalf of their people, prayerfully broke the covenants the ancient inhabitants of Bali had made with Shiva/Surya. There was considerable weeping, repentance and intercession, even though it was done in public. Clearly God was moving, and the brokenness of these Balinese believers seemed to be breaking a stronghold in the heavenlies.

Soon, four smaller teams, each led by a local Balinese Christian, were dispatched to various additional locations, including major temples and places of historic massacres and bloodshed.

John Robb joined a team that journeyed to the southernmost temple in Bali, Uluwatu. Outside that temple, they prayerfully sought God to break the powers of darkness over it, including its obvious occultist link to other shrines and temples throughout Bali. Not long after their prayers at Uluwatu, this temple was struck by lightning and burned. The fire caused over $100,000 worth of damage—a huge sum to the people of Bali. A local newspaper lamented, "Why did our god allow this to happen to his temple?"

Amazingly, falling logs struck two other temples, both of which had been visited by prayer teams. A short time later, the government of Bali destroyed yet another major temple that had been prayed over, in this case for developmental purposes. Additionally, since this prayer initiative, the mother temple of all of Bali's temples—the one in Besakih where those initial prayers of repentance occurred—has been closed to all outside visitors. No explanation for the closure has been given.

At the end of the Bali initiative, everyone involved in the prayer thrust sensed a noticeable change in the spiritual atmosphere over the island. This was especially true of local leaders. They said they could feel the oppression lifting.

The following morning, a minor earthquake shook Bali as an almost symbolic gesture that God had begun to shake the island with His presence. The earthquake reminded John of two prayer pictures that intercessors had seen before the initiative began. One saw a dark blanket being rolled back off the island as God's light began to shine over it. Another had seen a mushroom cloud of darkness being lifted from the island.

In the months immediately following the initiative, there were specific signs of spiritual renewal among nominal Christians in Bali. Churches reported a growth in the number of healing and deliverance meetings, something desperately needed in this dark island. There was also a noticeable increase in responsiveness to the gospel by unbelievers. In one particularly resistant region, an area where one of the intercessory teams had gone for prayer, a local pastor baptized 15 new believers—a true miracle for this dark area.

In another place, where pastors united to begin a monthly prayer meeting, an especially strange phenomenon occurred. When the Indonesian government began to build a 400-foot statue honoring the Hindu god, Vishnu, the local pastors made it a target of their prayers. A short time later, the statue's head mysteriously caught fire and was destroyed. Such phenomena have often preceded increased openness to the gospel. For Bali, all of this could well represent the beginnings of a spiritual breakthrough.

Noteworthy in this account is how it all began with John Robb's team flowing in God's *river of discovery*. In it they experienced what I refer to here as "the perceptive dimension of intercessory worship." They saw into the invisible and discerned strategies for effective intercession. Intercessory worship was not a popular expression when this Bali prayer initiative was launched, but such worship-saturated prayer was certainly what the team engaged in. The light of Christ has begun to shine more brightly in Bali as a result!

Grandma's Surprise

River Five:
River of Liberty—

The Personal Dimension of Intercessory Worship

I call her Grandma Anna. No one knows her real name for certain. I chose this pseudonym because this Asian grandmother reminds me of the elderly prophetess, Anna, of Luke 2:36-37. My Anna was a 90-year-old convert from the least-evangelized Isaan people group in northern Thailand. Her people, about 17 million who speak the Lao/Isaan language, are classified as "least evangelized" because less than 5 percent of their population has been converted.

One day, as Anna sat quietly on her straw mat listening to the leader of her small Bible-study group, she had a strange urge. It was a surprise that would stun the group. The 90-year-old saint soon would step into God's prophetic *river of liberty* and, in so doing, open the heavens for a remarkable release of God's presence among her people. Anna's act introduces us to the *personal dimension of intercessory worship* and reveals how our individual worship can have unusual prophetic implications. (More about Grandma Anna's surprise in a moment.)

Keeping It Personal

All that might be said about the various dimensions of intercessory worship mentioned on these pages, and how they might impact those around us as well as distant nations, has relatively little significance if the principles cannot be applied personally. To King David, worship was always personal. He said, "One thing I ask of the LORD, this is what I seek: that I may dwell in the house of the LORD all the days of my life, to gaze upon the beauty of the LORD and to seek him in his temple" (Ps. 27:4).

Notice the expressions "I ask," "I seek" and "that I may dwell." Knowing God and worshiping Him was David's supreme passion. And it was personal.

Years ago, while reading through the Psalms, I was fascinated by the repeated requests for personal blessings. I counted at least 50 occasions on which David and other psalmists used expressions such as "lead me," "strengthen me," "guide me," "heal me," "revive me," and so forth. Psalm 143, for example, has some 15 such appeals. This suggests that even as we develop prayer of an intercessory nature (which focuses on others), there is nothing wrong with seeking personal blessing.

David especially understood that God's presence was the greatest of all personal blessings. Another of his psalms says, "O God, you are my God; I earnestly search for you. My soul thirsts for you; my whole body longs for you. . . . I have seen you in your sanctuary. . . . How I praise you! I will honor you. . . . You satisfy me. . . . I will praise you with songs of joy" (Ps. 63:1-5, *NLT*).

Notice the expressions "I earnestly search," "my soul thirsts for you," "my whole body longs for you," "I will honor you," "You satisfy me" and "I will praise you." There are 12 personal references to being blessed in just these five verses. Although David led worship corporately, he also kept it personal.

Also consider Paul's challenge to make worship both corporate and personal: "Be filled with the Spirit. Speak to one another with psalms, hymns and spiritual songs. Sing and make music in your heart to the Lord" (Eph. 5:18-19).

On the one hand, Paul says, "Speak to one another with psalms, hymns and spiritual songs," which is corporate worship. But then he says, "*Sing and make music in your heart to the Lord*" (emphasis added), which involves a personal dimension of worship. It also suggests a measure of spontaneity. We are to "make music" in our individual hearts and sing these songs to the Lord. Sometimes this spontaneous worship can become prophetic, which brings us back to Grandma Anna.

REVERENT DETERMINATION

I was first introduced to Grandma Anna by Paul DeNeui, who wrote about indigenous worship in an article featured in *Missions Frontiers* magazine. DeNeui described an experience of missionaries Jim and Joan Gustafson who had gone to Thailand in 1971. Their mission was to minister among the nearly 20 million "least-evangelized" people of northern Thailand.[1]

According to the Gustafsons, the primary forms most Thai Christians have adopted to express their worship are Western imports. Thus, the average unconverted Thai, when viewing typical church worship, would say Christianity is a foreigner's religion.

Because the Gustafsons particularly wanted to evangelize the Isaan people of northern Thailand, and do so in an Isaan cultural context of music and dance, they began praying about how to accomplish this. Central to such worship would be the use of the Isaan *kaen* (bamboo panpipes) along with their traditional dance. But this had its challenges. When Christianity had first come to northern Thailand, converts were taught to worship only in the Central Thai language and in a Western way. In fact, many Thai Christians still associate the use of the *kaen* and Isaan dance with worship of animistic spirits. Amazingly, in earlier days, even teaching people to worship in their own local language (in this case, Lao/Isaan) was considered radical.

Then a breakthrough came. It happened with Grandma's surprise. During one of the local language Bible studies, as a small group of students sat in a circle on straw mats listening intently, Grandma Anna slowly stood up, unannounced. With a look of reverent determination she moved to the center of the circle. In an instant, Anna was dancing freely in the traditional Isaan fashion. The thin arms of this frail 90-year-old woman were waving gracefully as her fingers moved expressively.

In deliberate steps, Anna silently swayed in worship. There was no music. Onlookers were stunned. Most in the group believed the use of traditional Thai worship was satanic. No Isaan Christian had ever danced like this in worship. They were aghast.

Finally, one shouted, "Grandma, sit down! What do you think you're doing?"

Without a pause, Anna declared, "You don't tell your old grandma to sit down. I'm 90 years old, and I'm just thanking the Lord."

No Need for New Mouths

Anna's dance was pure and personal. But even more, it was prophetic. Something broke in the heavenlies over northern Thailand that night. The missionaries reported that everything changed in their worship following Grandma's surprise. Isaan dance soon became a part of their worship, and indigenous Isaan music quickly followed. Now the *kaen* panpipes were sending melodies of praise heavenward. These panpipes, once used to worship satanic spirits, had become instruments of praise to Jesus. One Isaan worshiper, defending the use of the *kaen*, queried, "Why can't we use the *kaen* to praise God? We used our same mouth to worship the spirits before. Does this mean we need to get a new mouth to praise God now?" There was, indeed, no need for new mouths!

Before long, Isaan believers developed their own hymnody (indigenous songs). One recent Isaan chorus focuses on Jesus, the Word:

> From the Heavenly City the Word came down.
> He was born right here where we live.
> We Isaan people have new happiness now.
> He loves us and that will not change! . . .
> The Lord Jesus Christ, the Victor over death,
> Is born in our cultural forms.
> Listen to the sounds of the flute and the drum.
> All Isaan rejoices in Him![2]

Grandma Anna's act of worship, initially a personal desire to honor the Lord, had prophetic implications. Through her dance, Anna stepped into a *river of liberty* and released something of the flow of that river among her people. Soon, far more Isaan people were able to receive the gospel in their cultural context. Those who found Christ were then able to worship the Lord in the liberty of that same indigenous context.

Taking a Few Steps

How does one *step* into this *river of liberty*? The answer, I believe, begins with that lone word: "step." Grandma Anna's prophetic act began with a single step. It took her toward the center of the circle during that Bible study. It became a step into God's *river of liberty*.

Recently God has been dealing with the leadership of Every Home for Christ about His taking us "a new way" toward accomplishing our goal of mobilizing Christ's Body globally to reach every home in the world with a presentation of the gospel. Although the goal may sound impossibly ambitious, in EHC's 65-year history, campaigns already have occurred in 210 nations where more than 3 billion printed gospel messages have been planted. As stated earlier, the ministry has been encouraged by more than 101 million follow-up decision cards and responses as of this writing (and that number has been increasing by as many as a million a month) and by the planting of more than 175,000 New Testament fellowships, called Christ Groups.

Even though we have seen these gratifying results, the task ahead—reaching every home among remote people groups and in highly restricted areas such as Middle Eastern Islamic nations and the nations of Central and Far East Asia—is daunting. New ideas with new strategies are necessary to accomplish this objective. Something prophetic is required.

In this context, I thought about a familiar Old Testament lesson about Joshua leading God's people across the Jordan River and into their land of promise (see Josh. 3:1-17). Although it was a corporate crossing, it became personal to everyone who journeyed.

For three days the Israelites had camped at the Jordan before their crossing. Interestingly, in the same way that Israel miraculously fled Egypt with the parting of the Red Sea, they would now enter the Promised Land with the parting of the Jordan River. But first there were critical requirements. Joshua sent his leaders throughout the camp with this directive:

When you see the Levitical priests carrying the Ark of the Covenant of the LORD your God, follow them. Since you have never traveled this way before, they will guide you. Stay about a half mile behind them, keeping a clear distance between you and the Ark. Make sure you don't come any closer (Josh. 3:3-4, NLT).

Joshua added this especially vital assignment: "Purify yourselves, for tomorrow the LORD will do great wonders among you" (v. 5, NLT).

God was clearly taking His people a new way. Joshua had said, "You have never traveled this way before" (v. 4, *NLT*)!

The final phase in the process of moving in this new way was reduced simply to stepping out. God told Joshua, "Give these instructions to the priests who are carrying the Ark of the Covenant: 'When you reach the banks of the Jordan River, take a few steps into the river and stop'" (Josh. 3:8, *NLT*).

Everything remarkable accomplished in our walk *with* Jesus begins by taking a few steps in Him. Then we must willingly wait for Him to act. Consider Joshua's dilemma. His priests were being asked to step into the Jordan at the worst time of the year to attempt such a crossing. According to Scripture, "Now it was the harvest season, and the Jordan was overflowing its banks" (Josh. 3:15, *NLT*).

Still, the priests obeyed, and the Bible records: "As soon as the feet of the priests who were carrying the Ark touched the water at the river's edge, the water began piling up. . . . Then all the people crossed over" (Josh. 3:15-16, *NLT*).

Although the Jordan soon became a dry riverbed, it was still the Israelites' *river of liberty*. They were being released into God's promise for them. Though we talk of "Israel" crossing the Jordan in a corporate sense, each Israelite obviously had to cross it individually. Each one had to exercise the faith to take those first few steps and begin his or her personal encounter with the *river of liberty*. In the years that followed, each would be able to say, "I was there that day!"

A WALK IN THE RIVER

I remember such a day, when Pastor Jack Hayford stepped into the *river of liberty* and led 40,000 pastors and other leaders with him. It happened at the Promise Keepers Clergy Conference in Atlanta's Georgia Dome in February 1996.

Jack was assigned the topic "guarding your heart as a man of worship." Early in his message, Hayford said, "Ultimately everything about my ministry, about my family, about my congregation—everything about my life boils down to my private worship-walk with God."[3] Hayford suggested that even though these thousands of pastors had gathered in an obviously corporate setting, he hoped that God would somehow insulate each one in his own "booth of private worship" before God's throne.

Jack's message dealt primarily with King David, who authored more worship passages in Scripture than any other person and is best remembered by his biblical label: a man after God's own heart (see 1 Sam. 13:14; Acts 13:22).

Hayford particularly drew attention to the fact that David's main priority as Israel's king was to bring the Ark of the Covenant, God's dwelling place, back to Jerusalem. The Ark had been held in captivity for years, and David desired to bring it home.

When he did, as Hayford emphasized, David did not build an elaborate temple for the Ark, but he erected a simple tent, a place called the Tabernacle of David (which we spoke of at length in part two of this book). David did this, Hayford suggested, because the king wanted the presence of God to be where he could access it personally and regularly. When the Ark finally arrived at this tent, David was overwhelmed with joy and danced wildly before God.

A Hop and Step

Jack Hayford's lesson that day was poignant—but the real message came in the last few minutes, when he spoke about a trip he had taken several years earlier to a nation he did not name. Believers there had an unusual worship tradition that troubled him. Jack explained that as these worshipers would sing bright, cheerful choruses, they would do "something like this—a little hop and step," he said, while giving a quick demonstration.

Jack had seen various worship styles over the years as he traveled, and he certainly understood that some cultures, like many in Africa and the Pacific, customarily include dancing as a part of their worship traditions. But this bothered him. He was in a more conservative, Western culture. He even spoke to some of the Christian leaders there—graciously, but expressing his dismay. He thought he was giving them a point of wisdom. But, as Jack recounted, "They kindly tolerated my remarks, and didn't rebuke me, but they didn't change their worship either."

When Jack returned home, several of his staff members asked about the trip. Some especially wondered about how believers worshiped there. So, in a staff meeting, Hayford gave them a brief demonstration, hopping and stepping with a quick kick or two. He even

added a smirk, as if to suggest, "Can you believe sane Christians actually do something like this during Sunday morning worship?"

Jack thought little about this "staff dance lesson" until three
months later, during a personal time of worship. It had been a deeply
moving time, and Jack found himself saying, "Jesus, I love You so
much, I praise You, Lord—I love You more than words can express!"

God's presence filled the room. Suddenly Jack heard God's unmistakable voice: *Will you dance for Me?* (Hearing this, of course, reminded me of my dancing before the Lord in those woods near
Washington, as I described in chapter 7.)

DANCING WITH DELIGHT

Jack was stunned. "Everything within me wanted to scream, 'You've
got to be kidding!'" he told the 40,000 clergymen. He added, "Never
in the world would I do that. I don't do that stuff!"

Yet Jack knew it was an invitation from the Lord Himself. Jack
continued, "The option was mine. While I knew I wouldn't lose my
salvation or my ministry if I didn't do it, I knew I would lose something of my availability to be intimate with God if I didn't dance."

Jack admitted, "For a second I thought, *I know what I'll tell the Lord.
I'll tell Him I don't know any dance steps.*"

But the Holy Spirit was one jump ahead and said, *You showed all
your staff what you saw in that other country. So you know at least one!*

In that private moment, Jack began to weep. He saw himself not
as a pastor of a large, respected congregation but as a two-year-old
wearing a diaper and lacking any dance coordination.

Now these many years later, he was recounting this occasion before 40,000 fellow pastors.

What happened next was not unlike Grandma's surprise during
that Bible study in northern Thailand. A *river of liberty* had begun to
flow in the Georgia Dome, and Jack Hayford was leading the way
into it.

Continuing his testimony, Jack explained, "That day in worship
I saw that little diaper-clad baby as myself, dancing with delight. And
I suddenly felt the shame of my reserve, my pride."

Jack then tearfully told the pastors' gathering, "In that moment,
alone, I started to dance, just like this . . ." and suddenly this

respected leader was more than demonstrating; he was worshiping. Jack Hayford was dancing before the Lord—and in front of 40,000 Christian leaders.

The Georgia Dome exploded into a chorus of weeping and worship. The weeping was not that of sorrow but of a personal longing for the same liberty that Jack demonstrated.

All of this happened in less than a minute or two, but that *river of liberty* flowed freely for the remainder of the conference. Five years later, a well-known pastor from a conservative tradition told me those moments were the most liberating of his entire ministry. Like 40,000 others that day, including myself, Jack Hayford had discovered the *personal dimension of intercessory worship* by stepping into God's *river of liberty*. It is a river of God's delight ready to carry us a new way to a new day in Him. The river is waiting. The main channel is intercessory worship. Just take a few steps!

A Fragrant Flame

RIVER SIX:
River of Humility—

The Purifying Dimension of Intercessory Worship

I tossed a match into our fireplace and watched the dry kindling ignite beneath the split oak logs. What would happen that morning in our living room would release an aroma of worship into the heavenlies unlike any I could recall.

That day, many things would come together in my mind about the nature of God, what most gives Him delight, and the relationship between humility and healing.

Part three of this book has been about prophetic rivers. I have suggested that the flow of such worship ultimately will bring healing to the nations. It will be instrumental in releasing these rivers of God's presence, which will bring healing to all levels of society. At the heart of this healing will be a spirit of humility.

A Purifying Dimension

Naturally a river whose source is the heart of God will contain something of the very heart of God in its waters. Further, if that river is to carry healing to the nations, it will flow through God's people into a dying world. God has chosen no other means.

The river God showed me before our fireplace that day was a *river of humility*, and it introduces us to the *purifying dimension of intercessory worship*.

It may seem strange to link humility with the healing of nations, but there is a biblical case to be made. God is a holy, yet humble, God. We know God is holy—perfect and complete in every way. The biblical expressions for "holiness" suggest that which is "above weakness and imperfection." [1]

Holiness in reference to God connotes separation from all that is human or earthly. God neither needs nor requires anything—or anybody—to sustain Him; He is complete in the unity of His Trinity. He is above all that is human.

Yet God created humanity in a remarkable act of humility. He did it so that we might someday know Him and all His splendor. In creating humankind, God literally gave away a part of Himself.

Now think of the incarnation—God chose to become a man, in Christ, to live and die among other human beings.

John makes it clear that from the very beginning, Christ, as the Word, existed as One *with* God. We read, "In the beginning was the Word, and the Word was with God, and the Word was God" (John 1:1). The "incarnation," a theological expression describing God coming "in Christ" to live in the world, is described in John's declaration: "The Word became flesh and made his dwelling among us" (v. 14).

The apostle Paul likewise highlighted the quality of humility in reference to Christ:

> Who, being in very nature God . . . made himself nothing, taking the very nature of a servant, being made in human likeness. And being found in appearance as a man, he humbled himself and became obedient to death—even death on a cross! (Phil. 2:6-8).

The river of God's healing power begins in Christ, and Christ is the embodiment of humility.

HUMILITY AND HEALING

The link between humility and healing is seen in God's directive to Solomon, often quoted in the context of revival: "Then if my people who are called by my name will humble themselves and pray and seek my face and turn from their wicked ways, I will hear from heaven and will forgive their sins and heal their land" (2 Chron. 7:14, *NLT*).

The first necessity of this conditional promise is humility. All else flows from that first quality. The final promise is that God will "hear from heaven" and "heal their land." Healing the land begins with the humbling of the saints—God's people. What starts with humility ends with healing.

Few people Dee and I have met carry the burden of 2 Chronicles 7:14 more faithfully than our friend Nancy Leigh DeMoss. Nancy, a gifted speaker and writer, has for years served in a key leadership position with Life Action Ministries and hosts a daily radio program called *Revive Our Hearts*, aired on more than 300 stations.

Dee and I first became acquainted with Nancy through her challenging teaching on "The Heart that God Revives," which includes a checklist to help believers evaluate their hearts before God. Nancy presented this teaching to 5,000 Campus Crusade for Christ field staff in Fort Collins, Colorado, in 1995, and the result was many hours of public repentance. We sent this teaching to leaders in more than 100 nations who are associated with Every Home for Christ.

Sensing a unique touch on her life, I began praying for Nancy daily. I asked if she had any personal things we might pray about, and she began sending us her prayer letters and itineraries.

In one letter, Nancy requested prayer for two specific personal issues. One was for spiritual discernment and the other for protection against pride. Nancy referred to a file of letters of commendation to her from leaders—a file that was getting "quite fat." She explained that although she appreciated the letters, she did not want them to become a catalyst for pride in her life.

Sitting in my prayer closet, I presented Nancy's letter to the Lord. I dismissed her concern about pride because, of all the people Dee and I had met in leadership, Nancy seemed least concerned about herself. Still, I prayed.

I concentrated a portion of my prayer that day on Nancy's specific request for spiritual discernment. Suddenly, I felt compelled to write to Nancy, even while still in prayer. I grabbed a tablet and began writing.

A Symbolic Suggestion

I scribbled a letter, including a quotation I had heard once about hearing God's voice. When I finished, I remembered the file of letters Nancy had mentioned, so I added a postscript. But I felt awkward about it, so I decided to ask Dee if she thought it appropriate.

The postscript suggested that if Nancy had a fireplace, she might want to do something symbolic with some of the letters in her file. Because the Bible tells us that all of our works will someday be tested by fire, I suggested that she might consider burning a few of those letters to give herself a sense of release. I realized as I wrote it that it was an odd suggestion.

Dee read the postscript and suggested that if I felt God truly had put this on my heart, I should say it. My letter was sent the next day with the postscript included.

Several months later, a Revive Our Hearts conference was scheduled in our city. Nancy Leigh and Henry Blackaby were to speak. I wrote to Nancy and invited her to our home for dinner, or at least for a time of prayer. Before Nancy could respond, Dee and I left for Australia. We would arrive back home only a few days before the conference began.

While in Australia, I phoned my secretary, Debbie Lord, to check in. Debbie told me, "Nancy wrote and said she would be delighted to come to your home for prayer, but she had a strange question. She asked if you have a fireplace." Debbie was confused about the request for a fireplace (no one had ever asked a question like that before), but I knew immediately what Nancy meant.

I told Debbie I would explain it all when we returned and asked her to let Nancy know we did indeed have a fireplace.

An Isaac Moment

The flames grew brighter in our fireplace that chilly March morning as Nancy sat in our living room, clutching her file of letters. With her was a longtime personal intercessor whom Nancy wanted to join her during this personal moment.

I had not really talked to Nancy except briefly, to confirm this time together in our home. I did not mention the letters then, because I knew what was on Nancy's mind when she asked if we had a fireplace. Now here we were, and it was an awkward moment. I found myself mentally looking for a good "biblical" way out for Nancy, hoping she would not have to do this after all.

Then Abraham's willingness to sacrifice his son Isaac came to mind. "You know, Nancy," I suggested, "it's possible that what's happening today may be one of those Isaac moments."

I recounted the familiar story from Genesis 22. God asks Abraham to sacrifice his beloved son. Only at the last moment, as Isaac was placed on an altar stacked with wood and Abraham's hand clutched the sacrificial blade, did the angel of the Lord shout, "Do not hurt the boy in any way, for now I know that you truly fear God" (Gen. 22:12, *NLT*). In that moment, God provided a ram to take Isaac's place.

"Nancy," I advised, "God may have brought you to this point to say, 'Now I know what's in your heart, and you don't need to sacrifice these letters.' "

I quickly added, "Or maybe God wants you to do what I suggested in my letter—sacrifice two or three of these letters as a symbol of your desire to allow nothing to stand between you and God's best."

An Aroma of Praise

I could tell by the look on Nancy's face that she wasn't buying it. *This would be a great time to get out of God's way,* I thought.

Then Nancy spoke. "No, Dick," she said softly. "It has to be all of them, and it has to be today." So after a prayer of release, Nancy stepped toward our fireplace and knelt.

One by one, she tossed each letter into the flames. To my amazement, I even saw one of the letters I had written two years earlier tossed into the flames. It must have been the letter in which I told Nancy how her teaching on keeping our hearts pure had so impacted my life and ministry.

Nancy's sacrificial act of worship was pure and prophetic. I believe the smoke of that fire birthed a fragrant aroma of praise that rose to God's very throne. I was reminded of the psalmist's prayer:

> We went through fire and flood. But you brought us to a place of great abundance. . . . That is why I am sacrificing burnt offerings to you—the best of my rams as a pleasing aroma (Ps. 66:12,15, *NLT*).

In the following months, a fresh anointing came upon Nancy. Each CD of her teaching or page from one of her books seemed to speak the very heart of God. Nancy had plunged into God's *river of humility*—and she had plunged in all the way. Her experience introduces us to what I call the *purifying dimension of intercessory worship*.

A Strange Apprehension

I did not realize at the time how deeply that fireplace encounter had impacted my life. If a prophetic word is to "speak before" a person or group in delivering a special message from the Lord, then a prophetic act would be to "act before" a person or group in such a way that a message or directive from God is delivered. Nancy's act of humility spoke a word from God's heart profoundly into mine, and I pray it has the same effect on yours!

By the fall of that year, our executive ministry team had started to draft our *Completing the Commission* plan. The plan, as you may recall from chapter 17, included forming strategic alliances to mobilize Christ's Body to launch and sustain systematic, home-by-home evangelism and discipleship campaigns in every nation on earth in our generation.

By late fall I had decided to set aside December 1998 exclusively for prayer. I knew our senior executive team would understand and even join me for some of the days. As I did during the first time I set aside such a month for prayer, which was December 1987, I committed to spend the hours I would normally spend at my desk or in other meetings in prayer.

There was, however, one glitch: Many months earlier, Dee and I had committed to conduct a Change the World School of Prayer in Singapore the first week of December. I decided that since much planning had gone into local preparations and because this seminar only involved a couple of evenings and a Saturday morning, I could still spend all the rest of the days of that week and month in prayer, thus honoring my commitment.

As the month approached, I became apprehensive. It was as if God had something significant He wanted me to focus on, but it escaped me. Suddenly, it was the night before we were to fly to Singapore, and Dee and I were packing. I was in the kitchen when I saw a brown, padded envelope from that day's mail. It was a package from Nancy Leigh.

In the package was a small book by Andrew Murray titled *Humility*. I knew the author well. In fact, our *Change the World School of Prayer*, which God has used to train many thousands of believers globally, got its name from Andrew Murray's classic book *With Christ in the School of Prayer*.

On the inside cover, Nancy had written a note suggesting the book might be a blessing to me at that season in my life. *Take this with you on your trip,* I instructed myself silently. I soon discovered that this decision would transform the whole month.

A Garden Encounter

We arrived in Singapore at midnight on Sunday, November 29, and spent the next day adjusting to the time change. On Tuesday, December 1, I would begin my month of prayer. I decided to go to the beautiful botanical gardens of Singapore to spend my first full day in prayer.

Preparing to leave the hotel room, I saw Andrew Murray's book on the hotel coffee table and decided to take it with me. Soon I was sitting on an old wooden bench under a huge banyan tree where I had sat in prayerful worship on several previous trips to Singapore.

As I worshiped quietly, I realized these were the first moments of an entire month committed to seeking the Lord—specifically regarding our emerging *Completing the Commission* ministry plan. But I felt something was missing.

I grabbed Andrew Murray's little book. For several seconds I gazed at the title—*Humility*. I wondered how this book and its theme might relate to reaching the nations for Jesus. I whispered, "Lord, does this have something to do with my month of prayer?"

An Infallible Touchstone

For some reason, I opened the book not to the beginning but to the last two pages, where I found a brief epilogue by the author. It was titled simply, "A Prayer for Humility." Sensing it did in fact have something to do with my month of prayer, I read:

> I will here give you an infallible touchstone. . . . It is this: retire from the world and all conversation, only for one month; neither write, nor read, nor debate anything with yourself; stop all the former workings of your heart and mind: and, with all the strength of your heart, stand all this month, as continually as you can, in the following form of prayer to God. Offer it frequently on your knees; but whether sitting, walking, or standing, be always inwardly longing, and earnestly praying this one prayer to God: "That of His great goodness He would make known to you, and take from your heart, every kind and form and degree of Pride, whether it be from evil spirits, or your own corrupt nature; and that He would awaken in you the deepest depth and truth of that Humility, which can make you capable of His light and Holy Spirit."[2]

In that moment, I knew I had found my prayer-theme for the month. Here I was, on the first day of a month committed to prayer, asking God if He had a special focus for the month—and I opened to a page in a book written a hundred years earlier suggesting the reader set aside a month to pray over one focus—*humility*. God had my attention, and He was ready to point me in the direction of His *river of humility*.

So rich were the insights on humility from Andrew Murray's pen that since those memorable moments I have catalogued several specific focuses to help us soak in this transforming river of God's delight.

THE *ESSENCE* OF HUMILITY

First, there is the *essence* of humility. Essence refers to the fundamental nature or inherent characteristics of an idea or person. It really represents the core or heart of something highly valued. Of course, the very heart of humility is God Himself. Andrew Murray wrote, "The Christian life has suffered loss, because believers have not been distinctly guided to see that nothing is more natural and beautiful and blessed than to be nothing, so that God may be all."[3] Later Murray expressed, "Humility is simply the sense of entire nothingness, which comes when we see how truly God is all, and in which we make way for God to be all."[4]

THE *EXCELLENCE* OF HUMILITY

Second, there is the *excellence* of humility. Excellence concerns the best there is, suggesting superiority or preeminence. Andrew Murray believed excellence in Christ is measured by one's humility. He declared, "The life God bestows is imparted not once for all, but each moment continuously, by the unceasing operation of His mighty power. Humility, the place of entire dependence on God, is, from the very nature of things, the first duty and the highest virtue of man. It is the root of every virtue."[5] Murray added, "Humility is one of the chief and highest of graces. It is one of the most difficult to attain, and one to which our first and greatest efforts ought to be directed."[6]

THE *EXAMPLE* OF HUMILITY

Third, there is the *Example* of humility. I intentionally capitalize the letter *E* in "Example" because I refer not to an abstract quality but to a Person. That Person is Christ. *Jesus is the embodiment of humility*. Andrew Murray summarized, "Christ is the humility of God embodied in human nature."[7]

Murray was convinced that everything Christ did to bring redemption to humanity was because of His humility. Note this statement from the author:

It is of inconceivable importance that we should have a correct understanding of who Christ is. We should properly comprehend what really constitutes Him, the Christ, and especially of what may be counted as His chief characteristic—the root and essence of all His character as our Redeemer. There can be only one answer: it is His humility. What is the incarnation but His heavenly humility, His emptying Himself and becoming man? What is His life on earth but humility, His taking the form of a servant? And what is His atonement but humility? "He humbled himself and became obedient unto death."[8]

THE *EFFECT* OF HUMILITY

Fourth, there is the *effect* of humility. Andrew Murray was convinced that all spiritual fruit originated from the soil of humility. He wrote:

Humility is the only soil in which the graces root; the lack of humility is the sufficient explanation of every defect and failure. Humility is not so much a grace or virtue along with others; it is the root of all, because it alone assumes the right attitude before God and allows Him as God to do all.[9]

THE *EVIDENCE* OF HUMILITY

Finally, there is the *evidence* of humility. "Evidence" is the proof or validity of a thing that may be in question. When Andrew Murray wrote his book on humility, an emphasis on holiness was sweeping the globe. Murray was troubled by the potential for pride that easily found entrance to those who were convinced they had attained holiness. He preached, "Let all teachers of holiness, whether in the pulpit or on the platform, and all seekers after holiness, whether in the closet or in the convention, take warning. There is no pride so dangerous, none so subtle and insidious, as the pride of holiness."[10]

Andrew Murray pointed to Christ as our supreme example of both holiness and humility: "Jesus the holy One is the humble One. The holiest will always be the humblest. There is none holy but God. We have as much of holiness as we have of God."[11]

THE AROMA LINGERS

The aroma from our fireplace that March morning lingers in my memory. There was something purifying about the flow of God's presence that day. It was a river of delight, and the delight was in the joy God experiences when His children humble themselves before Him—and others.

That day I realized that those whose ministries and strategies will most impact the world for Jesus are those who most humble themselves before God. I knew Every Home for Christ had to pursue our challenging ministry plan from a foundation of humility if we were to succeed. The alliances and partnerships needed to complete the Great Commission necessitate a unity that will only come through a new level of humility.

Andrew Murray was right in his assumption: Humility is the infallible touchstone that will make all this possible. Intercessory worship plays such a critical role in this humility because, as the late Paul E. Billheimer said so persuasively, "Here is one of the greatest values of praise: It decentralizes self. The worship and praise of God demands a shift of center from self to God."[12]

Nothing I know of has a greater capacity to unite Christ's Body in purity and humility than a passionate movement of intercessory worship. As this unity through humility emerges, I believe it will release a flow of prophetic purity that will "speak before" the whole world, declaring the transforming power of Christ's love. What a glorious river to swim in!

24

Adam's Song

River Seven:
River of Destiny—

The Possessive Dimension of Intercessory Worship

I'm not sure I always recognize when an action in prayer (or worship) is prophetic. Nor am I sure it needs to be recognized as such at the time. Sometimes it may be months or even years before we realize that such an act was, indeed, of a prophetic nature.

That's what I believe happened the day Dee and I prayed and sang over Garrett and Carol Lee in the prayer room at Every Home for Christ.

A few days earlier, our first grandchild, Jack, had been born. Jack was a great joy, and our EHC staff rejoiced with us. Yet for Garrett and Carol, our joy quickly became a sad reminder of their personal loss. Just days after Jack's birth, Carol had a miscarriage. With it came the fear often associated with a first-baby miscarriage—the fear that maybe one will never have children. Dee and I could see that the Lees were heartbroken.

Garrett and Carol were both on our staff, so it was easy for me as president to invite them to my office and suggest that Dee and I would like to pray with them. Tears came to Carol's eyes the moment I mentioned it.

Moments later, we were sitting in our ministry prayer room—a small chapel where we have little flags of all the nations positioned in the molding around the room. This creates an atmosphere that reminds us we are always "praying among the nations."

That day, prayer for Garrett and Carol would be particularly personal. Only much later (months, in fact) would these flags have special meaning in the miracle that would follow.

MEMORIES OF A SONG

As we sat in the prayer room, I looked at Garrett and Carol without a clue as to what to pray. My mind was blank. Dee rescued me by saying that we wanted them to know how much we loved them, and that life sometimes surprises us with difficult challenges. Nothing about these challenges, she continued, ever changes the character of God. (At the time we did not know it, but just a few years later we would learn this truth all too well when our little Jack, who gave us such joy, would be taken to heaven suddenly as a five-year-old.)

As Dee spoke, I had the sudden memory of a song. It was not a song I had sung; rather, it was a song I had heard about someone else singing. The song had been sung years earlier to an audience of one, in a church Dee and I had been attending at the time. The soloist was a little eight-year-old girl named Aimee. The audience was our pastor at the time, Jack Hayford. Jack recounts this experience in his inspiring book, *Worship His Majesty*.[1]

Little Aimee had grabbed Jack's coattail one Sunday morning as Pastor headed down a hall between services. She asked happily, "Pastor Jack, wanna hear my song?"

Jack could not resist Aimee's innocence. Even though he was in a hurry, he waited as the child sang her made-up song. It was over in moments, and Pastor assured her it was a great song. Aimee's tune brought back memories for Pastor Jack—memories that, all these years later, I was now recalling based on what I had read in his book.

Aimee's melody reminded Jack of a message he had spoken some nine years earlier at The Church On The Way in Van Nuys, California, where he pastored at the time. His sermon was titled "The Conceiving and Bearing of Life." It was based on the opening verses of Isaiah 54.

Jack especially highlighted the first words of the passage—"Sing, O barren woman, you who never bore a child"—emphasizing the irony of a prophet in that culture telling a "despairing reject of society" (which in that era a barren woman was) to sing. It seemed foolish to suggest such a thing, at least in ancient Israel. As Hayford explains:

> In ancient Israel, nothing prompted song less than the barren condition of a woman. A woman without children was disenfranchised, discredited, suspect of spiritual unworthiness and potentially subject to divorce—all on the grounds of

her biological incapability for childbearing. Into this depressing situation of personal hopelessness, the prophet commands the woman to sing and, incredibly, directs her to start preparing a nursery for there are babies (plural) coming![2]

Jack then read the heart of the passage. It is a passage most preachers use to support a new building project or some expansion of ministry. In reality, it speaks of a barren woman having so many babies that her husband needs to build a bigger place to house them. Jack read, "Enlarge the place of your tent. . . . For you shall expand to the right and to the left, and your descendants will inherit the nations. . . . You will forget the shame of your youth. . . . For your Maker is your husband, the LORD of hosts is His name" (Isa. 54:2-5, *NKJV*).

BARRENNESS IN THE BLEAK SPOTS

Jack explained that his message that morning had not been a lesson on having children in the physical sense, but on overcoming barrenness in the bleak spots of our Christian walks. Worship, Jack suggested, was a key to bring victory when circumstances appeared hopelessly unfruitful.

Jack suddenly paused. He was midway through his sermon and sensed the Holy Spirit's prompting. He explained:

> My message [this morning] has specifically *not* had to do with natural childbearing. . . . Still, the Holy Spirit is impressing upon me that there is a couple here this morning who has longed for a child, who has been told they cannot have one and whom the Lord wants to know He is present to speak to your need in a personal way this morning.[3]

What Pastor Jack said next, I believe, was prophetic, and introduces us to the *possessive dimension of intercessory worship*—a dimension that releases us into God's *river of destiny* for our lives.

Jack spoke to anyone who felt this "word" was specifically for them: "Begin to fill your house with song, and as you do, the life-giving power of that song will establish a new atmosphere and make way for the conception which you have desired."[4]

Jack did not ask anyone present to indicate that this was their need. He merely spoke what he felt God was impressing on his heart at that moment.

About a year later, Mike and Cheri, a couple in the congregation, were chatting with Pastor Hayford about the dedication of their first child that following Sunday. The Church On The Way had a congregation of thousands, and Jack could not recall ever having had a conversation with this couple previously. He recalls, "After brief opening exchanges, Mike came to the point. 'Pastor Jack, we wanted to talk with you for a few minutes because of this Sunday's dedication of our baby. There's something about it we felt you would want to know.' "[5]

Mike then recounted the pastor's sermon on bearing life a year earlier, and particularly, the prophetic word he gave about someone in the crowd who longed to have a child and had been unable.

"That word you spoke, Pastor," Mike explained, "the one about a couple who desperately wanted a child—that was us."

Mike told how he and Cheri went home that day and began filling their house with spiritual songs. He and his wife would walk hand-in-hand into each room and sing spontaneous praises and worship to the Lord. They now were certain that this new, precious baby girl to be dedicated the following week was the result of God responding to their spiritual songs.

Mike and Cheri had named their daughter Aimee; eight years later, this same little girl would sing her special song to Pastor Jack as he walked down a church hall after a service, triggering this amazing memory. Now Jack's memory had become mine, as Dee and I prepared to pray that morning over Garrett and Carol Lee. *I knew in that moment that I had to sing.*

A SONG OF PROMISE

By the time Dee had shared her feelings, which only took a few minutes, I sensed even more that Carol felt "barren." I again recalled Isaiah's prophecy: "Sing, O barren woman" (Isa. 54:1). I quickly turned to the passage and read it to Garrett and Carol. I told them I felt I was to sing a song of fruitfulness over Carol.

Before we stepped into the prayer room, a psalm had come to my mind—one I sensed was particularly appropriate for this couple.

However, I had not thought of singing it until that specific moment. It's Psalm 20—a psalm of hope and encouragement. I asked them to bear with me as I attempted to sing the words of the psalm, spontaneously, as my prayer. They knew I was not a soloist and graciously tolerated what happened next.

Singing a psalm spontaneously in front of other people was not something I was comfortable doing. To that point in my several decades of ministry, in fact, I had only done something like this once before. You may recall from chapter 10 the story of how I sang two psalms over my new friend Bill just before he opened my understanding to the significance of an end-time restoration of the Tabernacle of David (see Acts 15:16-17).

So, in the presence of Garrett and Carol, and my wife, I began to sing, one verse at a time, through Psalm 20. Like little Aimee's song, it was a made-up melody from my heart, and certainly nothing special. I sang, "May the LORD answer you when you are in distress; may the name of the God of Jacob protect you. May he send you help from the sanctuary and grant you support from Zion" (Ps. 20:1-2).

I continued, "May he give you the desire of your heart and make all your plans succeed. We will shout for joy when you are victorious and will lift up our banners in the name of our God. May the LORD grant all your requests" (vv. 4-5).

I sang each verse slowly, and in my heart faith began to build. Verse 7 was especially encouraging: "Some trust in chariots and some in horses, but we trust in the name of the LORD our God."

As I finished my song, faith filled my heart. It felt like the faith of 1 Corinthians 12:9—the kind that comes as a supernatural gift.

"Carol," I suggested, "what I just sang contains a promise—not just a promise from God but a promise to you from us—that when God gives you your heart's desire, we will return to this very place waving banners and shouting joyfully over your victory. We'll even invite the whole staff to join us."

I looked at a calendar as we left the prayer room. It was November 2, 1998.

A FLAG FOR ADAM

In a few weeks (early December), we heard that Carol was again pregnant. Nine months after that, little Adam Lee was born. On September

9, 1999, just three days after his birth, Garrett and Carol brought the tiny infant to the office. We called everyone together, and for the first time I told them about the song and promise I had sung over Garrett and Carol barely 10 months earlier.

Knowing that Garrett and Carol were bringing baby Adam to the office that morning, and remembering the promise I had made of coming back to that very prayer room—waving banners—I asked my secretary, Debbie Lord, if she would locate some banners for us to wave. Debbie phoned a few nearby churches that she knew displayed worship banners, but could not reach anyone in time to get permission to borrow even a few.

Then Debbie got an idea: "What about waving the flags that we have in the prayer room?" she asked me. "Flags are banners, aren't they?"

Because all the flags in our prayer room are on pencil-sized sticks placed in the molding around the room, they could easily be removed. So, we had our banners.

I told the staff the whole story, including my promise that when Garrett and Carol experienced their miracle, Dee and I would return, inviting the staff to join us, waving banners and shouting for joy. I invited all who wished to join us.

In moments, the room was packed. Garrett was cradling Adam, sitting beside Carol in the center of the room. The rest were standing. Everyone, including Garrett and Carol, had a flag of a nation. We indeed had our banners. Although most on our staff would not be accustomed to a worship tradition of loud shouting, I told them I wanted to fulfill this promise of Psalm 20 as literally and expressively as I had pictured it all those months earlier, when first singing Adam's song. Understandably, I wondered how the staff would respond.

No one held back. The staff shouted and waved their flags joyously. Then, even baby Adam, just three days old, joined in. He reached out with his tiny hand and grabbed his father's flag. Though having no idea what he was doing, infant Adam began waving his flag happily back and forth.

We had, indeed, returned to our little sanctuary where God first gave us Adam's song. God had even provided the needed banners. To complete the picture, the shouts of joy came easily.

A GOOD PLACE

Although some might see all this as cute, and even curious, but still coincidental, I will always believe that Adam was conceived of a song and that something of his destiny was possessed in those prophetic shouts 10 months later. There is, indeed, a possessive dimension to prophetic intercessory worship, which I believe that song and those subsequent shouts (with banners) involved.

Pursuing our destiny in Christ is a continuing process of possessing God's best for our lives. Destiny is defined as "something to which a person or thing is destined."[6] Destiny, of course, is related to the word "destination." Merriam-Webster provides the following as its first definition for destination: "The purpose for which something is destined."[7]

Soon after Adam's birth, as Every Home for Christ was building its international ministry headquarters, The Jericho Center, I returned again to that unusual vision of the patriarch Jacob, when the heavens were opened and he saw a stairway touching the heavens (see Gen. 28:11-22). It was during that powerfully prophetic encounter that Jacob would discover his destiny.

I was understandably drawn to this passage because of a longing to see our new ministry center embody something of Jacob's words: "What an awesome place this is! It is none other than the house of God—the gateway to heaven!" (v. 17, *NLT*).

The story was quite familiar to me, as it likely is to you as well, but this time, as I reread the description of Jacob's encounter, I noticed a phrase in the text of the *New Living Translation* that I had overlooked on previous readings. The passage says, "Meanwhile, Jacob left Beersheba and traveled toward Haran. At sundown he arrived at *a good place* to set up camp and stopped there for the night. Jacob found a stone for a pillow and lay down to sleep" (vv. 10-11, *NLT*, emphasis added).

My eyes fixed on the phrase "a good place." No matter the challenges we face in our Christian walks, God can turn any tough place into a good place. For Jacob, even sleeping on a stone as he journeyed toward Haran became a good place. It was a good place because God was there.

It was here that the patriarch experienced a supernatural power encounter as he slept on that rock. He saw into the supernatural. The text tells us, "As he slept, he dreamed of a stairway that reached from earth to heaven. And he saw the angels of God going up and down on it" (v. 12, *NLT*).

This is one of the more remarkable visions in all of Scripture. Jacob was witnessing the flow of divine activity between heaven and earth. This experience would shape and prepare Jacob for the rest of his pilgrimage.

We, too, need to experience God's power if we are to reach our potential in Him. As we flow in the river of God's destiny for our lives, powerful encounters await us. We will need them from time to time. Pray much for God's power. Paul said, "For the kingdom of God is not a matter of talk but of power" (1 Cor. 4:20).

It certainly didn't take long for the patriarch to realize this was no ordinary pause on the journey to his destiny. We read, "Then Jacob woke up and said, 'Surely the LORD is in this place, and I wasn't even aware of it'" (Gen. 28:16, *NLT*). Trembling with fear, Jacob added, "What an awesome place this is! It is none other than the house of God—the gateway to heaven!" (v. 17, *NLT*).

It was then that Jacob took the stone he had slept on the previous night and stood it up as a memorial pillar. After pouring oil over it, he declared, "This memorial pillar will become a place for worshiping God" (v. 22, *NLT*). Amazingly, what began as a "stone pillow" had become a "praise pillar." There is no better place to pause from time to time in our journey to God's destiny than the place of praise. Praise, to me, is the "possessive tense" of pursuing our destiny. *To praise is to prevail!* That's why I believe this whole matter of intercessory worship is so important as we pursue our destinies, both individually and corporately, in Jesus.

A DREAM OF DESTINY

My wife, Dee, has an uncle, Francis Jones, who served for many years as a missionary to Kenya, East Africa. Francis grew up on a farm in northern Wisconsin and learned to "rough it" by sleeping among farm animals in a drafty barn during many cold Wisconsin winters. Francis did not think twice of using the corner of a hay bale for a pillow. He figured that farming was his destiny, just like it was his dad's.

But God touched the heart of Francis when he was 18 years old. Soon he was on his way to Bible college. That was in 1952. Francis ultimately became a missionary to Kenya and, during his years of tenure, became a respected professor at the East African School of Theology in Nairobi.

Although Francis loved to teach students at the seminary, he especially enjoyed those occasions on which he could travel into the bush to help evangelize the lost or disciple new believers—especially those of the Massai tribe. The Massai are famous for their striking dress (they are most often arrayed in red) and their commitment to maintaining their indigenous culture.

Francis did not mind those assignments away from the city—even when they meant sleeping on mud floors in huts made with cow dung. Sleeping in a barn with a hay bale for a pillow had prepared him. Indeed, those nights in the African bush brought back fond memories.

One day, Francis traveled into the bush in Kenya's Narok district to teach a Massai discipleship class. About 70 people attended the three day-long sessions. They sat under the shade of an old African thorn tree, some squatting in Massai fashion the entire time. For hours, Francis opened God's Word and taught about Jesus.

As he taught, Francis noticed something peculiar. Off to the side, in the shadows of another tree, stood a Massai elder listening intently to all Francis said. Later, the missionary would learn that the man was more than 100 years old.

Though not a part of the class, the old man took in every word. He came all three days. Francis could not help but notice. As the missionary concluded his teaching on that final afternoon, he observed the old man coming toward him.

"Perhaps you wonder why I've stood by the tree listening to you for three days," the old man said.

Francis could understand and speak the man's language, and he acknowledged that he had indeed observed the elder. The old man spoke again.

"Many years ago, when I was very young, I had a dream. A white man came from a great distance and brought me truth about how to know God."

The old man carefully studied Francis's features and added, "Your face is the face I saw in my dream."

That hot African afternoon, the elderly Massai accepted Christ as his Savior. There was no mistaking his joy.

Francis realized that if the old warrior had seen his face in a dream while the man was yet young, perhaps as a teenager or even a child, the missionary would not yet have been born. He was reminded of God's message to Jeremiah: "Before I formed you in the womb I knew you, before you were born I set you apart; I appointed you as a prophet to the nations" (Jer. 1:5).

Based on the old Massai's recollection of witnessing the completion of Africa's East-West Railway as a youth, which Francis later learned happened in 1899, the man was probably 105 years old at the time of his conversion. He lived another nine years before he went to be with Jesus.

When young Francis Jones was sleeping among those cows in that drafty Wisconsin barn, he never could have imagined that someone in Africa had already seen his face in a dream—three decades earlier. All Francis had to do to fulfill his divine destiny was to step into this river of God's delight and go with the flow.

You may not presently see or even conceive the ultimate destiny God has planned for your life, but the river of His presence will take you there. It is God's river of your destiny. Plunge in. Swim deep. Drink freely. It is one of God's glorious rivers of delight, and intercessory worship will help you take the plunge.

Perhaps someone has even seen your face in a dream. Don't miss that divine appointment. Your destiny is waiting. *It's a good place!*

For the LORD your God is bringing you into a good land of flowing streams and pools of water, with springs that gush forth in the valleys and hills.

DEUTERONOMY 8:7, *NLT*

APPENDIX A

Cultivating Your "Harp and Bowl"

Use these steps daily (with the guide on the following page) to apply these intercessory worship realities. You can "sing it" (the harp) and "pray it" (the bowl). Compile your own list of Scriptures to sing or declare in prayer for each of the seven focuses. (The Scripture references in the guide will help you get started.)

Reality	Principle	Application
1. Intercessory Worship **ENTHRONES GOD**	Worship provides a place for God to dwell on earth in all His fullness.	Declare in song (worship) and prayer (intercession) that God dwells in every situation.
2. Intercessory Worship **ENCOUNTERS GOD**	Worship provides an opportunity to encounter God in all His fullness, first hand.	Declare in song and prayer your desire to meet with God—then be still and wait in His presence.
3. Intercessory Worship **ENLARGES GOD**	Worship provides an atmosphere to expand and increase our knowledge and understanding of God in all His fullness.	Declare in song and prayer God's greatness in comparison to every attack of the enemy.
4. Intercessory Worship **ENJOYS GOD**	Worship provides a place of entry into the delights and pleasures of God's presence.	Declare in song and prayer your delight and joy in God for who He is and what He has done.
5. Intercessory Worship **ENLISTS GOD**	Worship provides our primary means to mobilize and release the resources of God into the needs of people and nations.	Declare in song and prayer that God's power is being released into your needs and the nations.
6. Intercessory Worship **EXCITES GOD**	Worship provides a place for God to dwell on earth in all His fullness.	Declare in song and prayer your desire to excite the Lord through your worship and obedience.
7. Intercessory Worship **EXALTS GOD**	Worship provides a place for God to dwell on earth in all His fullness.	Declare in song and prayer that God is exalted over every need, opportunity and nation on earth.

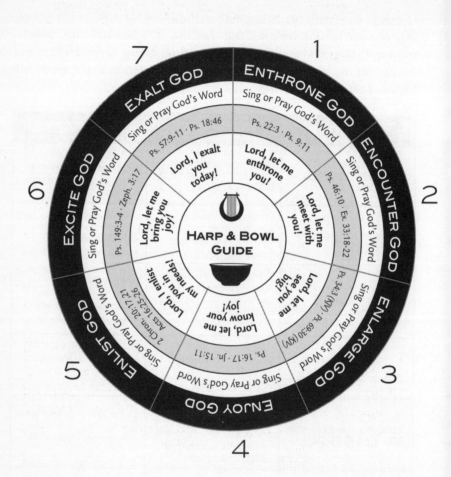

7 — EXALT GOD — Sing or Pray God's Word — Ps. 57:9-11 · Ps. 18:46 — Lord, I exalt you today!

1 — ENTHRONE GOD — Sing or Pray God's Word — Ps. 22:3 · Ps. 9:11 — Lord, let me enthrone you!

2 — ENCOUNTER GOD — Sing or Pray God's Word — Ps. 46:10 · Ex. 33:18-22 — Lord, let me meet with you!

3 — ENLARGE GOD — Sing or Pray God's Word — Ps. 34:3 (KJV) · Ps. 69:30 (KJV) — Lord, let me see you big!

4 — ENJOY GOD — Sing or Pray God's Word — Ps. 16:11 · Jn. 15:11 — Lord, let me know your joy!

5 — ENLIST GOD — Sing or Pray God's Word — 2 Chron. 20:17 · Acts 16:25-26 — Lord, I enlist you in my needs!

6 — EXCITE GOD — Sing or Pray God's Word — Ps. 149:3-4 · Zeph. 3:17 — Lord, let me bring you joy!

HARP & BOWL GUIDE

APPENDIX B

INTERCESSORY WORSHIP

A HARP AND BOWL PRACTICUM

A "practicum" is a course designed to give students practical applications of previously studied theory. Some of what has been shared about intercessory worship in the foregoing pages might appear to readers as theory. We've cited what David did in ancient times and suggested that a restoration of this model will be used of God in remarkable ways in the last days to bring about a glorious harvest of multitudes finding Christ as Savior. But in a practical sense, how do we do it? We will answer that question in this appendix.

Keep in mind that what follows primarily involves corporate intercessory worship, although ideas may be gleaned from these thoughts that might enhance personal prayer and worship. A good deal of the practical insights shared in this appendix were provided by Murray Hiebert, one of the founding worship leaders of the International House of Prayer in Kansas City, who now directs the overall prayer ministry at Every Home for Christ. After you have read the following, I invite you to visit our website (www.ehc.org) to view a brief training session, titled "Intercessory Worship: A Practical Workshop," that demonstrates what is shared in this appendix.

At Every Home for Christ, we sincerely believe that history's greatest harvest is soon to be gathered in. We also believe the Church, with many diverse models and streams, is about to unite as never before, saturated in a Harp and Bowl intercessory worship expression. Intercession, saturated in worship, will create a climate for the most productive, united evangelism advances in history!

Therefore, at the heart of our work in Every Home for Christ, we have established a day-and-night prayer room at our international headquarters, The Jericho Center. We refer to this room as *TheWall*, and in it we are establishing "live" 24/7 worship and prayer focusing on all the nations of the world. Indeed, as a part of this expression, we imported 50 tons of Jerusalem stone from Israel to build an actual prayer wall (patterned after the Western Wall in Jerusalem) that houses numerous prayer grottos for individuals and small groups to use day and night. Prior to presenting a brief "practicum" on intercessory worship, I offer several primary passages of Scripture that serve to build a biblical case for cultivating just such an intercessory worship strategy.

INTERCESSORY WORSHIP: A BIBLICAL BASIS

The following is a sampling of numerous passages of Scripture that may help you better understand and communicate aspects of intercessory worship for a prayer group or an emerging 24/7 prayer ministry:

> And when [the Lamb] had taken [the scroll], the four living creatures and the twenty-four elders fell down before the Lamb. Each one had a harp and they were holding golden bowls full of incense, which are the prayers of the saints. And they sang a new song: "You are worthy to take the scroll and to open its seals, because you were slain, and with your blood you purchased men for God from every tribe and language and people and nation" (Rev. 5:8-9).

> Sing to the LORD a new song, his praise from the ends of the earth, you who go down to the sea, and all that is in it, you islands, and all who live in them. Let the desert and its towns raise their voices; let the settlements where Kedar lives rejoice. Let the people of Sela sing for joy; let them shout from the mountaintops. Let them give glory to the LORD and proclaim his praise in the islands. The LORD will march out like a mighty man, like a warrior he will stir up his zeal; with a shout he will raise the battle cry and will triumph over his enemies (Isa. 42:10-13).

> "For from the east to the west my name will be great among the nations. Incense and pure offerings will be offered in my

name everywhere, for my name will be great among the nations," says the LORD who rules over all (Mal. 1:11, *NET*).

I'm going to come and then gather everyone—all nations, all languages. They'll come and see my glory. I'll set up a station at the center. I'll send the survivors of judgment all over the world: Spain and Africa, Turkey and Greece, and the far-off islands that have never heard of me, who know nothing of what I've done nor who I am. I'll send them out as missionaries to preach my glory among the nations (Isa. 66:18-19, *THE MESSAGE*).

"My name will be great among the nations, from the rising to the setting of the sun. In every place incense and pure offerings will be brought to my name, because my name will be great among the nations," says the LORD Almighty (Mal. 1:11).

After these things I looked, and behold, a great multitude which no one could number, of all nations, tribes, peoples, and tongues, standing before the throne and before the Lamb, clothed with white robes, with palm branches in their hands, and crying out with a loud voice, saying, "Salvation belongs to our God who sits on the throne, and to the Lamb!" (Rev. 7:9-10, *NKJV*).

O Jerusalem, I have posted watchmen on your walls; they will pray to the LORD day and night for the fulfillment of his promises. Take no rest, all you who pray. Give the LORD no rest until he makes Jerusalem the object of praise throughout the earth (Isa. 62:6-7, *NLT*).

Meanwhile, the fire on the altar must be kept burning; it must never go out. Each morning the priest will add fresh wood to the fire and arrange the daily whole burnt offering on it. He must then burn the fat of the peace offerings on top of this daily whole burnt offering. Remember, the fire must be kept burning on the altar at all times. It must never go out (Lev. 6:12-13, *NLT*).

So [David] left Asaph and his relatives there before the ark of the covenant of the LORD to minister before the ark continually, as every day's work required (1 Chron. 16:37, *NASB*).

And then there were the musicians, all heads of Levite families. They had permanent living quarters in The Temple; because they were on twenty-four-hour duty, they were exempt from all other duties (1 Chron. 9:33, *THE MESSAGE*).

I will bring [people of all nations] to my holy mountain of Jerusalem and will fill them with joy in my house of prayer. I will accept their burnt offerings and sacrifices, because my Temple will be called a house of prayer for all nations (Isa. 56:7, *NLT*).

Then another Angel, carrying a gold censer, came and stood at the Altar. He was given a great quantity of incense so that he could offer up the prayers of all the holy people of God on the Golden Altar before the Throne. Smoke billowed up from the incense-laced prayers of the holy ones, rose before God from the hand of the Angel. Then the Angel filled the censer with fire from the Altar and heaved it to earth. It set off thunders, voices, lightnings, and an earthquake. The Seven Angels with the trumpets got ready to blow them. . . . The seventh Angel trumpeted. A crescendo of voices in Heaven sang out, The kingdom of the world is now the Kingdom of our God and his Messiah! He will rule forever and ever! (Rev. 8:3-6; 11:15, *THE MESSAGE*).

THE HARP AND BOWL MODEL: LEADING A SESSION OF INTERCESSORY WORSHIP

In Isaiah 42 the prophet foretells the coming of a climactic day, preceding Christ's return, when people from all over the globe will worship the King of the Ages with "a new song" (Isa. 42:10). While more familiar Scriptures such as Matthew 24:14 promise that "this gospel of the kingdom will be preached to the whole world as a testimony to all nations" before the end will come, prophecies such as this one found in Isaiah shed light on the outcome of the spread of the gospel. The result of the gospel going forth will be a global chorus of singers declaring the glory of God from every corner of the globe—"from the ends of the earth . . . down to the sea . . . [the] islands and all who live in them . . . the desert and its towns . . . from the mountaintops. Let them give glory to the LORD and proclaim his praise in the islands" (Isa. 42:10-12).

In a subsequent prophecy of Isaiah, we read that God will bring peoples to His holy mountain and make them joyful in His "house of prayer" (Isa. 56:7). God desires to release enjoyable prayer into the Church because such joyful praying is vital if intercession is to be sustainable! The model that *TheWall* Prayer Room utilizes (sometimes referred to as the Harp and Bowl Model) simply combines prayer and worship with creativity and spontaneity to create a structure in which prayer and worship can go on continually. A two-hour prayer meeting that happens only once a week in a church or other setting does not necessarily require a specific model to sustain it. However, a two-hour prayer meeting that happens 12 times in the same day, and then continues into the next day and the next, and so on, requires a structure and atmosphere that can be sustained even while allowing for significant spontaneity.

A key to enjoyable prayer (which we have repeatedly defined in this book as "worship-saturated prayer") is the combination of prayerful (and often prophetic) declarations from the Word and anointed worship that can be both traditional and spontaneous. King David was the first to combine the beauty of God with music and intercession through the antiphonal singing of the Word. Antiphonal refers to "occurring or responding in turns or alternating."

Additionally, we see a prophetic dimension to such worship. Scripture relates, "David, together with the commanders of the army, set apart some of the sons of Asaph, Heman and Jeduthun for the ministry of prophesying, accompanied by harps, lyres and cymbals" (1 Chron. 25:1). David, indeed, brought together in one setting the doctrine of God's beauty, desire for God, prophetic music and antiphonal singing, as well as day-and-night prayer.

We see this model of antiphonal worship continuing long after David's era and even into Nehemiah's day. Note this rendering of Nehemiah 12:24 in *The Amplified Bible*: "And the chiefs of the Levites . . .

with their brethren opposite them" were appointed "to praise and to give thanks, as David, God's man, commanded, [one] watch [singing] in response to [the men in the opposite] watch." We see something similar when the Temple was being rebuilt in Ezra's day. As the foundation was being set in place, the worshipers "sang responsively, praising and giving thanks to the Lord, saying, For He is good, for His mercy and loving-kindness endure forever toward Israel" (Ezra 3:11, *AMP*).

In a practical sense, at the Jericho Center our corporate intercessory worship is made up of two-hour prayer sessions that involve the following:

CORPORATE WORSHIP SONGS

The worship team for a particular two-hour session (or set) begins with several familiar worship songs that direct hearts to focus on the beauty of God and His Son, Jesus. (We strongly urge our team leaders to feature songs that honor and exalt Christ rather than songs merely about our being blessed.)

SPONTANEOUS SINGING

The worship team then leads the room into a time of spontaneous singing of Scripture and other individually "made-up" songs that blend together (see 1 Cor. 14:15; Col. 3:16). This comes naturally as a group experiences it.

DEVELOPING A BIBLICAL PASSAGE

The worship leader or prayer leader then prays or sings a passage of Scripture. If he or she decides to sing the passage, it is done spontaneously rather than using a known chorus. This, of course, requires both creativity and courage. It may also involve pre-planning on the part of the leader, who may practice certain key passages he or she intends to use in an assigned two-hour session. On the other hand, the leader may ask for someone (or several persons) in the meeting to stand and read as well as pray a particular passage. Or, the leader may have assigned some in advance to pray specific passages. This allows participants to give some thought to praying over a passage and provides more order to the overall intercessory worship session. (All of this is what might be described as "ordered spontaneity."

There is order, but there is also room for spontaneous participation.) Of course, with mature intercessors, simply inviting people to come and pray the Word usually needs little further direction. They will readily respond.

BACKGROUND MUSIC

Meanwhile, if a keyboard or guitar is being used, the background music should continue as passages are read and turned by the readers into prayers. This is commonly referred to as "praying the Word." In this case it is being done corporately (that is, in front of a group) and then turned into song. The worship team or leader will generally sing phrases of the passage, rather than the one who reads and prays the passage. The apostolic prayers of Paul (e.g., Eph. 1:17-18; 3:16-22) or some of the great prayers of the Psalms (e.g., Ps. 96:1-4,8-12 and Ps. 67:1-7) are ideal. Leaders will want to begin compiling numerous passages that can be used in these settings to add variety to an on-going intercessory worship plan. (In the example that follows, we will use Ephesians 1:17-19 as our selected passage.) As becomes obvious, some pre-planning is required. Key to this model is the centrality of God's Word. As the Holy Spirit illuminates our hearts by the Word, the prayer meeting is unified around the yearnings of God's heart. This is usually accomplished in five parts:

1. Pray or sing through a biblical passage. For example, in Ephesians 1:17-19 we read: "I keep asking that the God of our Lord Jesus Christ, the glorious Father, may give you the Spirit of wisdom and revelation, so that you may know him better. I pray also that the eyes of your heart may be enlightened in order that you may know the hope to which he has called you, the riches of his glorious inheritance in the saints, and his incomparably great power for us who believe." This passage could serve as a main focus to begin a season of intercessory worship and could be applied in various ways to situations where God's wisdom is particularly needed (e.g., for local church leadership; for a new undertaking or vision; for local or national government; or for leaders of a missions ministry or denomination, to name just a few).

2. Isolate one or more phrases from the biblical sentence that the singers can then develop. After the leader or reader prays through the passage, begin selecting phrases that can become brief focuses or themes for song. For example, these six phrases stand out in the Ephesians passage just cited:

- "that . . . God . . . may give [us/them] the Spirit of wisdom and revelation"
- "that [we/they] may know him better"
- "that the eyes of [our/their] heart[s] may be enlightened"
- "in order that [we/they] may know the hope to which he has called [us/them]"
- "that [we/they] may know . . . the riches of his glorious inheritance in the saints"
- "that [we/they] may know . . . his incomparably great power for [us/those] who believe"

Notice that if the passage applies to those present, or if those present are related to those who are being prayed for (such as our church, our ministry, and so forth), the words "we," "us" and "our" would be appropriate. If, however, we are praying for others, like local or national governmental leaders, the words "they," "them," "their" and "those" would be used.

3. Develop these themes through antiphonal (alternating) singing with short phrases to build on a specifically isolated phrase. For example, the worship leader may begin to sing the phrase "Give us the spirit of wisdom and revelation" several times, and may then nod to others on the worship team to invite them to begin to repeat the phrase in song. If there are no others on a team, the worship leader would just keep singing until others in the meeting enter in. This will come naturally for those who participate for any extended time in such an intercessory worship session.

4. Spontaneous choruses are then established for all to sing. This means that people will simply join in, realizing that

they, too, can sing these phrases. This simple process provides a communication tool that is repeated a number of times throughout a two-hour prayer meeting. It easily provides any team or individual a model that is transferrable, sustainable and reproducible.

5. Another aspect of a session that can add variety and greater participation is what some refer to as "rapid-fire" prayers. Periodically during a session, participants may be encouraged to come to a microphone (or in smaller groups just to stand where they are) and pray brief prayers, usually 15 to 30 seconds in length, focusing on whatever the direction of the prayer meeting may be at that time. Usually the leader will announce this focus and invite intercessors to join in. Still another aspect of a session that might add variety is to form small groups for prayer, again focusing on a theme introduced by the leader. During all these breaks from intercessory singing, music (keyboard, guitar or other instruments) should continue if possible.

A VIRTUAL PRAYER ROOM

You don't have to live in Colorado Springs to join *TheWall* Prayer Room! We invite you to join us by committing to pray for at least one designated hour during the week (or each day). When you register on our website (www.ehc.org), we'll provide you with daily, specific focuses from our workers in scores of nations across the globe, so that you can partner with them through your prayers of intercession. Imagine thousands of people praying in a focused way in agreement with you at that very hour for a specific need or opportunity in some distant region of our world. Visit www.ehc.org to enroll.

Endnotes

Chapter One

1. Edward Reese, *The Life and Ministry of David Livingstone* (Glenwood, IL: Fundamental Publishers, 1975), p. 5.
2. I do not believe this vision suggests that every person in every village and home on earth will someday be saved. However, I take great encouragement from passages of Scripture, such as Isaiah 11:9 and Habakkuk 2:14, that prophesy that the earth will be "filled" with the knowledge and glory of the Lord "as the waters cover the sea." The *New Living Translation*'s rendering of Isaiah 11:9 is especially inspiring: "as the waters fill the sea, so the earth will be filled with people who know the Lord."
3. Don Melvin, "Under African Skies," *Minneapolis Star Tribune*, January 15, 2000, p. B5.
4. "Intercessory worship" is an expression that I first heard through the ministry of Mike Bickle, founder of the International House of Prayer, Kansas City, Kansas.
5. John Piper, *Let the Nations Be Glad!* (Grand Rapids, MI: Baker Book House, 1993), p. 11.
6. Jack W. Hayford, *Worship His Majesty* (Waco, TX: Word Books, 1987), p. 191.
7. A. W. Tozer, *That Incredible Christian* (Camp Hill, PA: Christian Publications, 1964), p. 46.
8. A. W. Tozer, *Whatever Happened to Worship?* (Camp Hill, PA: Christian Publications, 1985), p. 86.

Chapter Two

1. Joseph Garlington, *Worship: The Pattern of Things in Heaven* (Shippensburg, PA: Destiny Image Publishers, 1997), p. 1.
2. Jack W. Hayford, *Worship His Majesty* (Ventura, CA: Regal, 2000), p. 158.
3. Every Home for Christ is a worldwide ministry of house-to-house evangelism that has been working actively since 1946 with more than 500 mission agencies and denominations to place printed messages of the gospel (one for adults and one for children) in every home in the world. Since its inception, EHC, with over 4,000 full-time supported staff (as of this writing) plus an average of 30,000 monthly volunteer workers, has distributed over 3 billion gospel messages worldwide, resulting in more than 101 million followed-up decisions and responses. Where there are no churches for new believers, New Testament fellowships (house churches) are established. To date, more than 175,000 such fellowships, called Christ Groups, have been formed. Where largely illiterate people groups exist, EHC distributes gospel records and audiotapes and uses other means to reach non-readers. In a recent 12-month period, 13,400,284 people received follow-up materials or were personally visited by EHC workers in response to these home-to-home contacts. In that same 12-month period, an average of 58 house fellowships of new believers (baby churches) were formed "daily" (approximately 22,000 in a single year).
4. A quote from George Barna's research given in a cassette teaching by Robert Stearns, *The Tabernacle of David* (Clarence, NY: Kairos Publications, 2000), tape #2.

Chapter Three

1. A. W. Tozer, *Whatever Happened to Worship?* (Camp Hill, PA: Christian Publications, 1985), p. 62.
2. Ibid., p. 88.
3. Ibid., p. 31.
4. Ibid., p. 30.
5. A. W. Tozer, *The Quotable Tozer I* (Camp Hill, PA: Christian Publications, 1984), p. 89.
6. Ibid., p. 99.

7. Francis of Assisi, *The Writings of Francis of Assisi*, trans. Benen Fahy, O.F.M. (Chicago: Franciscan Herald Press, 1976), p. 8.

8. A quotation often attributed to Francis of Assisi. Although the source is unconfirmed, the sentiment is well within the spirit of the way Francis of Assisi conducted his life.

Chapter Four

1. John Piper, *Let the Nations Be Glad!* (Grand Rapids, MI: Baker Book House, 1993), p. 40.

2. Max Lucado, *Just Like Jesus* (Dallas: Word Publishing), p. 82.

3. A. W. Tozer, *The Quotable Tozer II*, comp. Harry Verploegh (Camp Hill, PA: Christian Publications, 1997), p. 202.

4. A. W. Tozer, *Whatever Happened to Worship?* (Camp Hill, PA: Christian Publications, 1985), p. 44.

5. Joseph Garlington, *Worship: The Pattern of Things in Heaven* (Shippensburg, PA: Destiny Image Publishers, 1997), p. 109.

6. Bruce Watson, "Science Makes a Better Lighthouse Lens," *Smithsonian* (August 1999). http://www.smithsonianmag.com/science-nature/object_aug99.html.

Chapter Five

1. Gordon Morse, *My Moloka'i* (Volcano, HI: My Island Publishing, 1990), p. 17.

2. Madame Guyon, *An Autobiography* (Chicago: Moody Press, n.d.), p. 67.

3. Ibid., p. 94.

4. Francis of Assisi, *The Writings of Francis of Assisi*, trans. Benen Fahy, O.F.M. (Chicago: Franciscan Herald Press, 1976), p. 52.

5. Ibid.

6. Brother Lawrence, *The Practice of the Presence of God* (Old Tappan, NJ: Spire Books, Fleming H. Revell Co., 1958), p. 45.

7. A. W. Tozer, *Whatever Happened to Worship?* (Camp Hill, PA: Christian Publications, 1985), p. 30.

8. Mike Bickle, "The Tabernacle of David," *Pray!* vol. 19 (July/August 2000), p. 19.

9. Ibid.

10. Ibid., p. 18.

11. Ibid.

12. Saint Augustine, *Patrologia Latina*, quoted in Dick Eastman, *A Celebration of Praise* (Grand Rapids, MI: Baker Book House, 1984), p. 9.

Chapter Six

1. A. W. Tozer, *Whatever Happened to Worship?* (Camp Hill, PA: Christian Publications, 1985), p. 18.

2. Ibid., p. 86.

3. "Fire Destroys a Famed Buddhist Shrine in Bhutan," *International Herald Tribune*, April 23, 1998, p. 4.

4. Dexter Filkins of the *LA Times*, quoted in the *Denver Post*, February 15, 1999, section A, p. 14.

5. Ibid., emphasis added.

Chapter Seven

1. A. W. Tozer, *Whatever Happened to Worship?* (Camp Hill, PA: Christian Publications, 1985), p. 61.

2. John Piper, *Let the Nations be Glad!* (Grand Rapids, MI: Baker Book House, 1993), p. 15.

3. Ibid., p. 16.

4. Ibid., p. 21.

5. Ibid., p. 12.

6. Tozer, *Whatever Happened to Worship?*, p. 18.

Chapter Eight

1. John Piper, *Let the Nations Be Glad* (Grand Rapids, MI: Baker Book House, 1993), p. 11.
2. Ibid., p. 40.
3. Mike Bickle, "The Tabernacle of David," *Pray!* vol. 19 (July/August 2000), p. 21.
4. Joseph Garlington, *Worship: The Pattern of Things in Heaven* (Shippensburg, PA: Destiny Image Publishers, 1997), p. 129.

Chapter Nine

1. The name has been changed because the worshiper wished to remain anonymous.
2. Joseph Garlington, *Worship: The Pattern of Things in Heaven* (Shippensburg, PA: Destiny Image Publishers, 1997), p. 1.

Chapter Ten

1. Kevin J. Conner, *The Tabernacle of David* (Portland, OR: CIM Bible Publishing, KJC Publications, 1976), p. 79.
2. Ibid., p. 80.
3. Philip Yancey, *Reaching for the Invisible God* (Grand Rapids, MI: Zondervan Publishing House, 2000), p. 192.
4. James Strong, *The Exhaustive Concordance of the Bible*, "A Concise Dictionary of the Words in the Hebrew Bible" (Nashville, TN: Abingdon, 1894), s.v. "sookah."
5. Ibid., s.v. "skene."
6. Conner, *The Tabernacle of David*, p. 11.
7. Ibid., p. 12.
8. Ibid., p. 17.
9. Ibid., p. 28.
10. Ibid.
11. Ibid., p. 21.
12. Ibid., p. 81.
13. Robert Stearns, *The Tabernacle of David*, audiotapes of lectures (Clarence, NY: Kairos Publications, 2000).
14. Dr. Edward W. Li, *Science and Faith* (Singapore: Every Home Crusade Co., Ltd.), p. 24. For more information regarding this book, contact Every Home for Christ at Singapore: Every Home Crusade Co., Ltd., No. 8, Lorong 27-A, Geylong Road #02-04, Gulin Building 388106 or by e-mail at ehcspore@singnet.com.sg.
15. Ibid., p. 25.

Chapter Eleven

1. *Vine's Expository Dictionary of Old Testament Words* (San Jose, CA: Bible Explorer Epiphany Software, 1999), s.v. "tamiyd."
2. A. W. Tozer, *Whatever Happened to Worship?* (Camp Hill, PA: Christian Publications, 1985), p. 24.
3. Ibid.
4. Leslie K. Tarr, "The Prayer Meeting that Lasted 100 Years," *Decision Magazine* (May 1977), p. 14.
5. Ibid.
6. Ibid.
7. Ibid.

Chapter Twelve

1. Aristotle, *Nicomachean Ethics*, circa 350 bc.
2. James Strong, *The Exhaustive Concordance of the Bible*, "A Concise Dictionary of the Words in the Hebrew Bible" (Nashville, TN: Abingdon, 1894), s.v. *kabowd*.
3. Ibid., s.v. *hadar*.

4. Ibid., s.v. *howd*.

5. *Webster's New World Dictionary*, 3rd ed., s.v. "unique."

6. Ibid., s.v. "diversity."

Chapter Thirteen

1. Evangeline Booth, quoted in Kevin J. Conner, *The Tabernacle of David* (Portland, OR: CIM Bible Publishing, KJC Publications, 1976), p. 181.

2. Jack W. Hayford, *Worship His Majesty* (Waco, TX: Word Books, 1987), p. 163.

3. Joseph Garlington, *Worship: The Pattern of Things in Heaven* (Shippensburg, PA: Destiny Image Publishers, 1997), p. 140.

4. Sharon Begley, "Music on the Mind," *Newsweek* (July 24, 2000), p. 50.

5. Ibid., p. 51.

6. Ibid.

7. Ibid.

8. Brother Lawrence, *The Practice of the Presence of God* (Old Tappan, NJ: Spire Books, Fleming H. Revell Co., 1958), p. 45.

Chapter Fourteen

1. *American Heritage Dictionary of the English Language*, 4th ed., s.v. "extravagant."

2. Tommy Tenney, *God's Favorite House* (Shippensburg, PA: Destiny Image Publishers, 1999), p. 34.

3. Tommy Tenney suggests this. He writes: "When David made his second attempt to bring the Ark to Jerusalem, he carefully followed God's instructions. In fact, every six paces they would sacrifice an ox." Tommy Tenney, *God's Favorite House* (Shippensburg, PA: Destiny Image Publishers, 1999), p. 34.

Chapter Fifteen

1. A. W. Tozer, *Whatever Happened to Worship?* (Camp Hill, PA: Christian Publications, 1985), p. 14.

2. Ibid., p. 43.

3. Jack W. Hayford, *Worship His Majesty* (Waco, TX: Word Books, 1987), p. 148.

4. Ibid., p. 149.

5. James Strong, *The Exhaustive Concordance of the Bible*, "A Concise Dictionary of the Words in the Hebrew Bible" (Nashville, TN: Abingdon, 1894), s.v. *machowl*.

6. Ibid., s.v. *karar*.

7. Ibid., s.v. *raqad*.

8. Ibid., s.v. *agalliao*.

9. Tozer, *Whatever Happened to Worship?*, p. 82.

10. Ibid., p. 84.

Chapter Sixteen

1. Mike Bickle, "The Tabernacle of David," *Pray!* vol. 19 (July/August 2000), p. 19.

2. Ibid.

3. Ibid.

Chapter Seventeen

1. A. W. Tozer, *Whatever Happened to Worship?* (Camp Hill, PA: Christian Publications, 1985), p. 56.

2. Ibid.

3. Jack Hayford, *Worship His Majesty* (Waco, TX: Word Books, 1987), p. 129.

4. Ibid., p. 130.

5. Joseph Garlington, *Worship: The Pattern of Things in Heaven* (Shippensburg, PA: Destiny Image Publishers, 1997), p. 59.

6. Ibid., p. 79.

7. John Piper, *Let the Nations Be Glad!* (Grand Rapids, MI: Baker Book House, 1993), p. 40.

8. Ibid., p. 1.

9. Mike Bickle, "The Tabernacle of David," *Pray!* vol. 19 (July/August 2000), p. 22.

10. Kevin J. Conner, *The Tabernacle of David* (Portland, OR: City Bible Publishing, KJC Publications, 1976), p. 253.

11. Piper, *Let the Nations Be Glad!*, p. 15.

Chapter Eighteen

1. Charles H. Spurgeon, *Twelve Sermons on Prayer* (Grand Rapids, MI: Baker Book House, 1971), p. 14.

2. Jack W. Hayford, ed., *Spirit-Filled Life Bible* (Nashville, TN: Thomas Nelson, Inc., 1991), p. 1424.

3. Ibid.

4. Jack W. Hayford, *Worship His Majesty* (Ventura, CA: Regal, 2000), p. 163.

5. Ibid., p. 164.

6. Ibid.

7. Alice Smith, conversation with her husband, Eddie, Washington, DC, February 7, 2002.

Chapter Nineteen

1. *Tibet* (Hawthorn, Victoria, Australia: Lonely Planet Publications, 2000), p. 13.

2. Paul Kyle, "Jesus We Enthrone You," copyright 1980, by Kingsway's Thankyou Music. All rights reserved. Used by permission.

3. *Fodor's Nepal, Tibet and Bhutan* (New York: Random House, 2000), p. 123.

Chapter Twenty

1. *Merriam-Webster's Collegiate Dictionary*, 10th ed., s.v. "intense."

Chapter Twenty-one

1. *Fodor's Bali and Lombok* (New York: Random House, 2000), p. 2.

2. *Merriam-Webster's Collegiate Dictionary*, 10th ed., s.v. "perceive," "perception," "intuition."

3. *Knopf Guide: Bali*, 3rd ed. (New York: Alfred A. Knopf, 1996), p. 52.

4. John Robb, conversation with author, 1996.

5. Ibid.

Chapter Twenty-two

1. Paul DeNeui, "What Happened When Grandma Danced," *Missions Frontiers* (June 2001), pp. 18-19.

2. Ibid., p. 19.

3. Jack Hayford, "Guarding Your Heart as a Man of Worship" (teaching presented at the Promise Keepers Clergy Conference, Georgia Dome, Atlanta, GA, February 14, 1996).

Chapter Twenty-three

1. *Theological Word Book of the Old Testament*, Bible Explorer (San Jose, CA: Epiphany Software, 1999).

2. Andrew Murray, *Humility* (New Kensington, PA: Whitaker House, 1982), p. 105.

3. Ibid., p. 6.

4. Ibid., p. 12.

5. Ibid., p. 10.

6. Ibid., p. 37.

7. Ibid., p. 18.

8. Ibid.

9. Ibid., p. 12.

10. Ibid., p. 56.

11. Ibid., p. 54.
12. Paul E. Billheimer, *Destined for the Throne* (Fort Washington, PA: Christian Literature Crusade, 1975), p. 118.

Chapter Twenty-four

1. Jack W. Hayford, *Worship His Majesty* (Ventura, CA: Regal, 2000), pp. 161-162.
2. Ibid., pp. 182-183.
3. Ibid., p. 185.
4. Ibid.
5. Ibid.
6. *Merriam-Webster's Collegiate Dictionary*, 10th ed., s.v. "destiny."
7. Ibid., s.v. "destination."

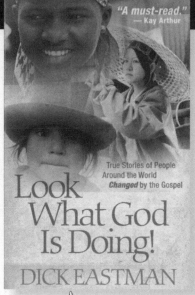

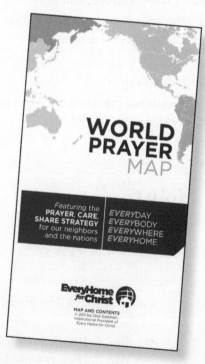

Every Home for Christ's Vision

Every Home for Christ exists to serve the Church
to reach every home on earth with the Gospel.

Every Home for Christ's
Three Unalterable Convictions

1. The Great Commission must be taken literally.
"All the world" and "every creature." *(Mark 16:15)*

2. Without unity, finishing the task of world evangelization
is impossible. *(John 17:21-23)*

3. Prayer, alone, will remove every obstacle that
stands in the way of fulfilling the
Great Commission. *(Mark 11:22-23)*

EHC's History at a Glance

The ministry of Every Home for Christ
began in Canada in 1946.

The first Every Home Campaign (EHC) involving systematic
home-by-home evangelism began in Japan in 1953.

There have been campaigns in 208 nations,
with complete coverages in 101 nations.

More than 3 billion gospel booklets and
face-to-face contacts have been made. To date more than
101 million decision cards and responses
have been followed-up.

Decisions/responses are followed-up with Bible
lessons. Where there are no churches, Christ Group
fellowships are planted. To date, more than 175,000
Christ Groups have been formed.

In a recent 12-month period EHC workers visited
an average of 200,000 families every day, with an average of
39,000 decisions/responses received daily.

More than 30,000 workers worldwide are involved
with EHC in any given month, of which
80 percent are volunteers.

Every Home for Christ Internships

Every Home for Christ internships exist to see this generation filled with the knowledge of God and the knowledge of His will, fully equipped as intercessors, worship leaders, singers, musicians, and messengers, for the growing movement of worship, prayer and missions throughout the nations of the earth.

Interns will also engage in works of mercy. As an expression of our intercession we will GO to the poor, sick, widow and orphan, as well as engage with community evangelism efforts. An optional international trip will focus on building the Global House of Prayer through the training and encouragement of the local church.

EHC Internships call a generation to abandon earthly dreams and pursue the dream on God's heart. This season of consecration will focus on a passionate pursuit of God through worship, prayer, and missions, resulting in lives consumed with the House of God (Psalm 132:4, 5).

For more information on Every Home for Christ internships, please contact:

thewall@ehc.org | 1-800-423-5054
www.wallsofprayer.com
Every Home for Christ | 640 Chapel Hills Dr.
Colorado Springs, CO | 80920